Jay Rayner is an award-winning journalist, writer and broadcaster. He has been reviewing restaurants for the *Observer* since the late '90s and in 2006 was named critic of the year in the British Press Awards.

Praise for Jay Rayner and THE MAN WHO ATE THE WORLD:

'a warm and affecting writer' *Telegraph*

'Rayner is agreeable company and a good writer' *Review (Observer)*

'Funny and engaging, it's an entertaining and informative look at global gastronomy' *BBC Good Food Magazine*

'sharp and often funny' *Foodies Magazine*

'definitely worth sinking your teeth into' *Food & Travel*

'a witty world tour of gastronomic culture' *Scotland on Sunday*

The Man
Who Ate The World

In Search of the Perfect Dinner

Jay Rayner

headline
review

First published in 2008
by HEADLINE REVIEW
An imprint of HEADLINE PUBLISHING GROUP

First published in paperback in 2009
by HEADLINE REVIEW
An imprint of HEADLINE PUBLISHING GROUP

1

Cataloguing in Publication Data is available from the British Library

ISBN 978 0 7553 1635 9

Typeset in Sabon by Avon DataSet Ltd,
Bidford on Avon, Warwickshire

Printed and bound in Great Britain by
Clays Ltd, St Ives plc

Headline's policy is to use papers that are natural, renewable and
recyclable products and made from wood grown in sustainable forests.
The logging and manufacturing processes are expected to conform to the
environmental regulations of the country of origin.

HEADLINE PUBLISHING GROUP
An Hachette UK Company
338 Euston Road
London NW1 3BH

www.headline.co.uk
www.hachette.co.uk

For Daniel, a small boy with a big appetite.

Contents

Warning!

Reading this book will make you hungry. Hunger can seriously affect your ability to concentrate and, after a few pages, you will be incapable of appreciating either the grace or the subtleties of my writing. You will also become confused by the twists in the narrative. As a result, you may fail to grasp my justifications for some of the dodgier episodes, particularly the Paris thing. I need you at the top of your game when we finally get to the Paris thing. It is therefore in my interest to give you some tips on how to read this book.

Do not attempt to read it after dinner. You might think that, being sated, you will not succumb to hunger. This is true, but you will succumb, instead, to drowsiness, and that is worse than hunger. Unless, of course, you are the type of person who does not eat a dinner substantial enough to engender drowsiness, in which case you are not greedy enough to be reading this book. Put it down. You won't enjoy it.

Better to read it between mealtimes with snacks at your

side. Salted nuts are a good idea, but not shell-on pistachios. Even if you get into a good rhythm, expertly picking the kernels from their shells, you will still be partially distracted, and that serves nobody. You would be wise to leave them in the cupboard for time spent in front of the television, unless they are Turkish pistachios. Turkish pistachios are the best in the world and deserve to be eaten whenever the opportunity arises. If you have some Turkish pistachios, leave this book until later and eat them first.

Fruit is a good idea, though not all of it. A banana is both satisfying and easy to eat while reading. An orange is not. Naturally, being a person of taste, you will choose a quality orange, a seriously juicy one, which will make your hands sticky, and that can only hinder your enjoyment. I want you to have a good time during your reading of this book, and juice-slicked hands will surely only get in the way of the perfect experience.

The best option is to read it over a meal by yourself in a small restaurant, the kind that doesn't have too much glassware on the table. Some people are wary of eating alone in restaurants, for fear that others will think them a complete loser. Don't worry too much about this. At times you may find yourself laughing out loud at what you have just read. Other diners will immediately decide that you are not a loser, just a little mad. They will stop staring at you after that. If nothing funny has happened in the book by about halfway through your main course, you may want to laugh out loud anyway, while staring at your plate. This is always a good strategy when eating by yourself. If it's available, be sure to order Armagnac. This has nothing to do with a successful reading of the book. People just don't drink enough

Warning!

Armagnac in restaurants these days and those that serve it ought to be encouraged.

I will understand if you choose to ignore my advice, for many people have. I am aware I don't have all the answers. Still, I hope you won't blame me if, after a few pages, you find yourself feeling ravenous and irritable and desperate. This is something my time as a restaurant critic has taught me: I can only be a guide, not a leader. I can point people in the direction of a good place to eat. I can tell them which are the best dishes on the menu and which are not. But I can't do the ordering for them, however much I might wish to.

You have been warned.

I Want Proper Dinner

I was eleven years old the first time I ate alone in a restaurant. It was the dining room of a wooden-framed hotel in an unglamorous Swiss village close to the Italian border, and I wasn't even meant to be there. I was staying down the road at another hotel, with a group from my school on a skiing trip, and had to pass it every day, as I trudged back from the slopes, bruised and humiliated. The place where we were staying was an unlovely, grey, modern block that smelled of mothballs. This hotel was built from heavily carved and darkly varnished timbers, and looked like a stately galleon afloat on the oceans of that winter's snows. By the front door, under glass, was a menu written in an expansive italic font. Most of it made no sense to me. It was in two languages and I understood neither of them. There was one word I did recognise, a word no restaurant ever bothered to translate because the original French did the job: escargots.

I had first eaten snails in garlic butter at home in north-west London, where my mother prepared them from a do-it-

5

yourself pack sold in the local supermarket. They came in a transparent plastic tube. At the bottom was a can of the naked snails, which looked like big, fat commas when they were pulled from the brine and laid out to dry; stacked above them in the tube were the creamy-coloured shells, patterned with swirls of brown and grey. Laboriously my mother poked the snails into the shells. She back-filled them with garlic and parsley butter, and then grilled them. They were cooked often in our house in the 1970s, mostly as dinner-party food, when the kids were not there, but sometimes we got to eat them too, and I loved the hot, salty, garlicky melted butter and the dark, rubbery prey that bathed in it.

Now I was in Switzerland and, having been surprised to discover that skiing was not a sport for an overweight boy with weak ankles and fallen arches, I was horribly homesick. With the twisted logic of the eleven-year-old, I concluded that eating something French would make me feel better about not being in Britain.

That evening, after we had been served dinner at our hotel – a grey soup of some kind, some greyer meat and vegetables – I slipped away in search of Technicolor. I cannot imagine what the staff made of the prepubescent English boy sitting alone in the almost deserted dining room, round belly to the table's edge, humming to himself as he set to work, expertly, with the spring-loaded escargot tongs, a spiked prong and an arsenal of fresh, crisp bread. I know I was happy. The snails came on their own ornate iron stand, complete with inbuilt meths burner, and as the flame guttered underneath, the generous slick of butter from the shells became so hot in each dimple I could fry my bread in it. This I did until all the bread and all the butter were gone. I paid and left, absolutely clear in my mind as to how I would be spending my evenings on this trip from now on.

I returned the next day, and the day after that (once with a friend), until on the fourth night the waiter didn't even bother to bring me the menu; he just presented me with the snails.

I had emptied all the shells and was busy frying my bread when I noticed wisps of smoke lifting from the plate. I liked my bread really crisp and on this evening had turned the flame up as high as it could go without, for a moment, thinking there might be consequences. Within seconds of the smoke appearing, the butter ignited, producing an impressive cone of flame at least a foot high, which burned enthusiastically on the ponds of dairy fat.

I must have sat rigid with terror, because I have no memory of the waiter advancing upon me, only that he was suddenly at my side. This was a dangerous moment. The only thing that wasn't immediately inflammable in that restaurant was the cutlery, and the inferno on the table in front of me posed a real threat. The waiter didn't flinch. He opened the window next to me, letting in a sudden burst of frigid night air, picked up the burner from the base and heaved it out into the snow. He wiped his hands on his apron, closed the window and we agreed it was time he brought me the bill. My adventure was over.

Walking back to my own hotel that night I was disappointed, because I knew I couldn't return. Nevertheless I was comforted by the knowledge that my family would be impressed by what had happened. It wouldn't have mattered to them if, in that one week, I had developed into a world-champion downhill skier. It would have made no difference if I had broken the slope record. They would have been pleased for me if I was pleased with myself; however, as far as my parents were concerned, any eleven-year-old kid could learn to ski. But ordering snails in a restaurant! All by himself! That was a different matter entirely.

This is how it had always been in my family. My parents were both children of the Depression, knew what it was to go without and were not about to revisit the experience, either on themselves or their kids, so ours was a house of plenty. I always said that culturally I was only a Jew by food, and it's true that there was no room at the Rayner house for ritual or faith. The Jewish God was far too picky an eater to be given space at our table. Forego sausages and bacon? Reject shellfish and cheeseburgers, all in the name of mumbo-jumbo? Don't be ridiculous.

Yet there was, I think, something fundamentally Jewish about our way with food: the noisiness of the dinner table, the stomach-aching generosity, the deep comfort we sought from it. Food was what we did. Long before anybody had thought to initiate a debate on the importance of allowing small children into restaurants, my parents were taking all three of us out to eat on a regular basis: to Stone's Chop House near Piccadilly Circus; a grand old Italian called Giovanni's on the Charing Cross Road; and the great Chinese places in Chinatown or along Queensway, near Hyde Park, where the chefs stood in the window hand-pulling noodles. By the time he was four my brother was so good with chopsticks the waiters often assumed he had been raised in Hong Kong, and I had developed a taste for chicken with cashew nuts in yellow bean sauce, and for deep-fried seaweed scattered with golden crumbs of dried scallop –

dishes that were rarely found outside of Chinatown back then, let alone outside of London.

Unsurprisingly the story my parents most like to tell about me involves a rebellion at the kitchen table. It was a hot summer's evening in 1973, I was six years old and for dinner my mother had decided to serve salad and a slab of mahogany-brown smoked mackerel, with a brutal cure and slimy skin. I hated smoked mackerel and said so. My mother told me that if I didn't like it I should leave the table, so I did.

A quarter of an hour later, when I hadn't sloped back to my chair and my plate, they came looking for me. I was nowhere to be found and my parents became worried until, looking out of the window, they spotted me on the pavement in front of the house. I had known exactly how to respond to this challenge of theirs. After all, it was a time in Britain of great industrial strife and protest. Pictures of it were on the television news every evening. Taking my lead from those images, I had gone upstairs and found a piece of the card round which my father's shirts were folded when they came back from the laundry. To that I had taped a ruler. I had then scrawled a message on the card and was now to be found picketing the house with the placard held high, bearing the legend 'I want proper dinner.'

My parents laughed. As I recall, they also congratulated me on my initiative, though they still insisted that I come back inside to the kitchen table from which I had fled and eat what I had been given. I did as I was told.

Despite its repetition, I like this story. It's the sort of story that should lie in the history of someone who later became a restaurant critic. Yet it was precisely because of my family's interest in food that it didn't for a moment occur to me that it might be possible to earn a living from going out to eat. Sitting round a well-laid table was such a part of life, of being, that it couldn't possibly be a job. Look, Mum! They're paying me to breathe!

Instead I became a different type of journalist. I wrote about murderers and politicians. I covered war-crimes trials and pursued terrorists. I interviewed movie directors, worked abroad occasionally for the foreign pages and once interviewed a high-class hooker about the business of prostitution while sitting in a bath with her. I still wanted proper dinner but, for the moment, I had to pay for it myself.

All that changed in 1999 when the editor of the *Observer*'s magazine supplement suggested quietly that I might like to try my hand at the restaurant column. The editor of the newspaper resisted the appointment. He wanted me to carry on pursuing terrorists and sitting in baths with cocaine-snorting hookers, but I wasn't giving up that easily. This was too great an opportunity, not least because Britain's restaurants were undergoing a period of revolution and renewal unlike any other. It was on my watch that both Heston Blumenthal of the Fat Duck and Gordon Ramsay would achieve their third Michelin stars. With his high-end French cooking Ramsay displayed a mastery of crisp neo-classical technique; Blumenthal experimented with snail porridge and smoky-bacon ice cream, and showed it was possible to innovate and startle without losing sight of the imperative of deliciousness. Together, they inspired a new generation of talented chefs. Gastropubs spread around the country and, while it remained (and remains) possible to starve across huge swathes of Britain for want of a good meal, there was no doubt the map was being redrawn. It was a very good time to be patrolling the waterfront.

I wasn't satisfied, though. A part of me – the large, greedy part – was constantly pursued by the fear that, for all the good food I was getting to experience, somewhere out there was a great meal, the ultimate meal, and that I was missing out on it. My day job was to travel the country eating in restaurants. At night, in my time off, I would go online and read about restaurants elsewhere in the world that I couldn't reach.

I would spend hours on websites like egullet.com, where obsessives with deep pockets write long accounts of the meals they have eaten, complete with photographs. There were, it seemed, a lot of people out there who loved photographing their dinner. More worrying was the fact that I liked looking at them. I wanted to know what the tasting menu was like at Hôtel Le Bristol in Paris or Charlie Trotter's in Chicago or Tetsuya's in Sydney.

I became an avid reader of food blogs written by people with ripe and exotic names. There was Steve Plotnicki, a multi-millionaire New Yorker with a wheat intolerance and a habit of taking with him to restaurants hugely expensive bottles of wine from his own cellar, even when he was visiting a cheap kebab joint. There was Pim Techamuanvivit, a Thai woman now living in San Francisco whose blog, Chez Pim, had become a cult because of its mix of intricate recipes from the streets of Bangkok and its detailed accounts of dinners in the three-star gastronomic temples of Paris. There was Simon Majumdar, a half-Welsh, half-Bengali London-based publisher whose slogan was 'Carbs are death' and who liked to write long eulogies in praise of the pig.

The Man Who Ate The World

The more I read, the more it became clear to me that in these, the early years of the twenty-first century something fundamental was changing in the world of high-end restaurants. Once, their spiritual home had been Paris. There were good restaurants elsewhere, of course, but if you were looking for a whole city that expressed its self-confidence through the life at its most expensive tables, the French capital was where you had to go. Nowhere else came even close. The end of the Cold War had changed all that. A new, international moneyed class had arisen, not just in Europe or America, but in Russia and China, the Middle East and Japan; this new tribe had developed a taste for symbols of their affluence that were less tangible than the yacht or the top-of-the-range Mercedes. They needed lifestyle too. They wanted experiences, and that meant hotels and health clubs and, yes, restaurants. Paris was still important – nothing was going to change that – but many other cities were important for restaurants now as well. Gastronomy had gone global.

I read about the new big-ticket restaurants that were opening around the world, and felt guilty about my interest in them. Most other food writers I know claim to despise this sort of thing. For them, what matters is authenticity and, as far as they are concerned, that is never to be found at a table laid with heavy white linen and sparkling glassware: it is all contrivance and artifice. For them, the real thing is up on the hill, far from the last metalled road. It is in the farmhouse or down by the stream where the salmon leap. It is on the table of the local peasants whose family have tilled the land for generations and who feel the pulse of the teat in the palm of the hand.

I have long been suspicious of all this. It is not that I

despise simplicity. It is appetite that drives me, and I can just as easily satisfy that in a tapas joint that has done nothing more than slice the ham as I can in a Michelin-starred restaurant. Even so, there is something about the cult of authenticity that bothers me. It venerates lifestyles lived in poverty for being in some way more genuine than those lived in comfort with silly modern conveniences like, say, clean drinking water and electricity. It feels like a middle-class fetish.

Then again, I may just be making excuses for the fact that I love and always have loved the unique glamour and expectation produced by arriving at a restaurant of ambition. As a food writer, I know I am meant to be in touch with my inner snaggle-toothed peasant; as a restaurant critic, I have long suspected I am actually in touch with my inner pearly-toothed plutocrat. The more I learned about the world's new restaurants, the more my inner plutocrat wanted to get out there and experience them.

In November 2005 the Michelin organisation, long regarded as the final arbiter of quality in European restaurants, finally acknowledged the globalisation of high-end gastronomy when it published its first ever guide to New York, also the first in the US. There were four restaurants in the city awarded three stars, the highest ranking in Michelin's gift, plus four more with two stars. This immediately placed the city second only to Paris in the Michelin stakes. The New York guide was to be followed, we were told, by guides to other parts of America – San Francisco and the bay area would be next – before Michelin expanded into Asia.

The Man Who Ate The World

I was in New York the day the stars were announced and the next morning went to see Mario Batali, the Italian-American celebrity chef made famous in the US by his television cookery show *Motto Mario*, and renowned as the owner of a crop of generally well-regarded restaurants across the city. We met at his casual Italian place, Otto, down at the southern end of Fifth Avenue, and he arrived wearing cut-off chinos that dangled just below the knee.

Batali is not like most modern chefs, who tend to be lean and bony and pale-skinned from too much time spent in their windowless kitchens. Batali is soft and round. His arms and legs are built of long, fleshy ovals, and he has big, flat hands and a huge head, made to look larger still by the pasture of closely cropped beard and the way his sandy hair is permanently styled into a ponytail. We both perched on the bar stools, bits of us overflowing, and ate silky pieces of prosciutto with our hands. We ate sweet rock shrimps with a sprinkling of red chilli, and marinated artichokes, and slices of his famous thin-crust pizza.

Batali ate angrily and waved bits of food at me as he spoke. He had acquired two Michelin stars in the results announced the day before and he was not happy about it. Everybody knew that his pride and joy was the high-end Italian restaurant Babbo, down in the West Village. Babbo had been awarded just one star when he had hoped for two. The second of his stars had gone instead to the Spotted Pig, a New York take on the British gastropub, of which he was co-owner.

'I love the Spotted Pig,' he said. 'I adore the Spotted Pig. But a Michelin star? Geddoutta here.'

I asked him what he thought of the awards in general.

He shrugged. 'What you have to understand is that in the late 1980s three Michelin stars became nothing more than a guarantee that the ultra-rich could eat the same food anywhere in the world.'

I liked Batali. I particularly liked the smooth olive-oil gelato he now served me. But I didn't want to believe him. Surely this was just sour grapes. Surely the revolution in high-end gastronomy that was sweeping the world was about more than merely satisfying a particular clientele's hunger for nothing more interesting than consistency. It had to have produced some truly fantastic restaurants. Didn't it? Why would those chefs go to all the trouble of opening all those restaurants and sourcing all those ingredients and taking all the time it required to run a kitchen if it was just to serve safe food? There had to be more to it than that.

That was when it struck me. Somebody needed to chronicle what was going on by mapping this revolution. I had to find out for myself and, in doing so, I realised, I might well find the perfect meal I had dreamed about. This wasn't the only reason for going out there. There was another motivation, one that, if I'm honest, it had taken me a while to face up to. I had just turned forty and, reaching life's midpoint, I had begun to wonder seriously whether being paid to eat was a proper way for a grown man to make a living. If I had found the job even occasionally onerous, I could have convinced myself that the thing from which I took so much pleasure also involved sacrifices, but the truth was, my job had never been a burden. I enjoyed all of it, even the really bad restaurant experiences. They gave me great things to write about. Occasionally I was asked if there were any downsides to being a restaurant critic and I would reply that anybody who moaned about doing my job deserved a smack in the teeth. I meant it with perhaps a little too much vehemence. The puritanical part of me, the part that had worn down shoe leather as a reporter covering the evil that men do, wanted to be the one to do the smacking.

In the task I had set myself I sensed a certain redemption. By setting out to investigate the burgeoning new restaurant world, I could stop being an itinerant eater merely pleasuring his taste buds and become something else: an explorer, the one to record an entire movement. That had to be a virtue, didn't it? Plus I could try to answer a few questions about high-end dining. For example, is cookery a craft or an art? How much can we really learn about the world in which we live from the food that arrives on our plate? Is it moral to eat well while others starve? And is globalisation, as Mario Batali claimed, threatening to extinguish the flame of unique creativity that has for so long burned in the hearts of the world's great chefs?

Justifications aside, I couldn't think of a better person for the job. At six I had picketed the family home over a lacklustre meal. At eleven my enthusiasm for snails had almost led me to burn down a hotel. I had spent my entire life campaigning for proper dinner. I was the ideal candidate.

What I needed now, though, was a starting point. I wanted to begin somewhere that encapsulated the modern age. It had to be vibrant, innovative and open to gastronomic ideas. It had to be a city of appetite. It had to be a town that really, really loved restaurants.

There was only one candidate. It had to be Las Vegas.

1. Las Vegas

The first time I visited Las Vegas it was to interview a man who was famous because his wife had cut off his penis. It says much for the shape of my career back in the mid-1990s that I regarded the assignment as light relief. For the previous week I had been in Toronto investigating a particularly grisly set of murders. A young, middle-class couple – all white teeth and glossy hair – had dragged young women to their pastel-coloured house down by Lake Ontario, videoed each other sexually assaulting them, then chopped up their bodies and set them in concrete.

The court cases were still ongoing when I visited Canada in February 1995 to report the story and, because the accused were being tried separately, there was a lockdown on the reporting of the details until both trials were concluded. Nobody in Canada was meant to know anything about what had been dubbed the 'Ken and Barbie Murders' and, if they did know anything, they certainly weren't meant to talk to reporters like me. This forced silence only added to my gloom. Everywhere I went the ground was crusted with ice.

Snow blew against my cheeks like so much grit on the wind, and in a restaurant in the city's theatre district I acquired food poisoning courtesy of some spare ribs, which hadn't been particularly good on the way down and were much worse on the way up. I couldn't wait to escape Canada for the sudden sunshine and warmth of Vegas, even if it was to interview a wife-beater called John Wayne Bobbitt, who had achieved notoriety only because, one muggy summer's night, he and his penis had managed to arrive at hospital in different vehicles.

Bobbitt had gone to Vegas in search of an honest man to manage his career, because he felt he had been deceived by his previous manager. While it might seem odd that anybody should go to Vegas – a place long famous for its store of shysters, con men and career hoods – in search of honesty, it was no more peculiar than that Bobbitt should have been in need of a manager at all. By then he had parlayed the knife attack on him by his then wife, Lorena, into a thriving career. On my first full day in the city, enthroned at the huge, black glass pyramid that is the Luxor Hotel at the north end of the Strip, I got to witness that career for myself. Bobbitt had starred in a video called *John Wayne Bobbitt Uncut*, which was, depending on your taste for euphemism, either an adult movie or a desperate skin flick.

The shoutline on the video cover said it all: 'Ever since this whole thing happened all everybody wants to see is my penis . . . Now you can.' Indeed I could. It was a living monument to the powers of cutting-edge micro-surgery, and looked not unlike a tree that had been doctored by a tree surgeon or as if it were wearing a tiny lifebelt. It also functioned pretty well, as the video let me see in more detail than could ever be necessary.

Las Vegas

This was the image that was burned into my mind when I went off to meet Bobbitt and his new manager for dinner, which may explain why I cannot for the life of me recall a single thing I ate that night. I know we discussed Bobbitt's plans for a range of branded merchandise, including a 'penis-protector' – an autographed hollow tube – because you don't forget that sort of thing in a hurry.

I do remember that he came across as spectacularly stupid, and grunted his words rather than spoke them. I also recall that outside in Caesar's Forum, the covered shopping arcade where the restaurant was located, dusk fell every half-hour courtesy of some clever lighting effects. Of the meal itself I can tell you nothing at all. This is something I regret, for the dinner took place at a seminal restaurant in the history of modern Las Vegas dining: a branch of Wolfgang Puck's Spago, which opened at Caesar's Palace in 1992.

Before Spago opened (and for a good few years afterwards), food in the big casino hotels of Vegas was regarded only as an amenity, something the gamblers needed to keep them going while they emptied their pockets at the blackjack tables. It was the city of the all-you-can-eat $4.99 buffet and very little else. It's true that in the mid-1990s enterprising hoteliers were beginning to experiment with the notion that there might be sources of income in Vegas other than gaming. Hotels like the Luxor and the Arthurian-themed Excalibur, complete with theme-park rides for the kids, had been put up with the self-declared aim of rebranding the city as a family resort.

It was, however, a half-hearted project, which would eventually be abandoned in favour of a strategy aimed solely at adults (complete with the advertising slogan 'What happens in Vegas stays in Vegas'). Certainly in 1995 it was still the sort of place where an emerging porn star with no discernible talent for anything, like John Wayne Bobbitt, could get a table at Spago without a reservation, despite a queue out of the door.

It is really no surprise that Wolfgang Puck should have been the first into town. He had long displayed an uncanny nose for the next big thing. I had met him for the first time a few months before my return to Vegas and, now that I was here, gawping at the mammoth hotels and the hard-jewel lights, it struck me that he was very much like the city itself: on the surface frivolous, light, apparently obsessed with the ephemeral, but beneath that was a core of steel.

Puck was famous because he decided to put smoked salmon and cream cheese on a pizza. He was seriously rich because he had worked out how to sell that pizza again and again. Likewise, Vegas plays the good-time girl, apparently obsessed only with the here and now, but at heart it's a dollars and cents town. Pleasure – like the smoked-salmon pizza – is simply its product.

Puck – Austrian-born, Michelin-trained – knows how to market pleasure. In Los Angeles, at the original Spago on Sunset Strip, he created an environment where movie stars could feel at ease while eating Jo Schmo food. Then he replicated the experience time and again so now Jo Schmos could eat the same Jo Schmo food and feel like movie stars. Some of his food was interesting. Though he did not invent it, Puck can reasonably claim to have popularised Californian-Italian cuisine, and his fusion of Asian and European flavours at Chinois ushered in an era when it became a crime to cook a piece of fish all the way through.

Las Vegas

His real talent lay elsewhere: firstly, in his ability to replicate his good ideas and, secondly, in having absolutely no shame. Long before other big names of American cooking – Emeril Lagasse, Bobby Flay, Mario Batali – had cottoned on to the notion of themselves as brands, Puck was selling himself remorselessly. He published books, starred in his own TV series and opened a chain of expresses at airports that serves one of the worst Caesar salads it has ever been my misfortune to eat. It is the second of these characteristics, this willingness to plunge so far downmarket so fast it's a miracle he didn't get a nosebleed, that is the most important; it was this instinct that enabled him to take on Vegas.

In 1992 only the corporations wanted to be there. No self-respecting chef or restaurateur would go near the place, unless they had a sideline as a high-roller. Apart from Puck. As America rose out of the recession of the early 1990s, he recognised the growing power of the leisure dollar. For many years, though, he had the city to himself. Then, in October 1998, the Vegas hotelier Steve Wynn opened the $1.7 billion, 3,000-room Bellagio Hotel on the former site of the legendary Dunes Hotel and Golf Course, and everything changed. The city had never seen anything like it, which is saying something for a town that has seen most everything.

Inspired by the Lake Como resort of the same name, Bellagio was at the time the most expensive hotel ever built, only later to be trumped in cost by another hotel built by him, Wynn Las Vegas. Bellagio came complete with a multi-million-dollar fountain display out front that danced to piped music. There was an art gallery bulging with works by the great Impressionists from Gauguin and Monet to Van

Gogh and Renoir. It also happened to have eleven new restaurants.

Although Wynn paid the bills, it was the then food and beverage manager of the Bellagio, an Egyptian called Gamal Aziz, who came up with the idea. He had worked in grand hotels all over the world and, when he arrived, was shocked to discover just how lousy the food in Vegas could be. He had stumbled across those buffets and realised that this was where ingredients went to die. 'I wanted to signal a change,' he told me. 'To say there was something new and different about Las Vegas.'

Restaurants weren't just places you went to eat. They were to be signifiers, statements about the city's newfound confidence and sophistication. It helped that the US had seen a restaurant renaissance during the 1990s, and that media interest in food had exploded. The US cable channel the Food Network, founded in 1993, had come of age by 1998, after being brought under new ownership the year before. The names of top chefs were now familiar to people who were not in regular striking distance of their restaurants.

At the same time journalists like Ruth Reichl, then restaurant critic for the *New York Times*, were reinvigorating food writing and championing cooks who might otherwise have been ignored. Into the Bellagio therefore came a restaurant by the Alsatian *über*-chef Jean-Georges Vongerichten and a new outpost of the legendary Le Cirque from New York. Big-name American chefs like Michael Mina, Todd English and Julian Serrano were offered deals.

And what deals! Generally there would be an annual consultancy fee, plus 5 per cent of the gross. All they had to do was fill the tables and, if they wanted to, forget about the bottom line. As long as there was money coming in, they got a cut of it. Plus, if there was a profit, they got 10 per cent of that too, and there was a lot of profit. Suddenly people were no longer coming to town merely to throw their money away in the casinos while surviving on desiccated shrimp or lumps of sweaty pork that had been festering under the heat lamps of the all-you-can-eat buffets for six hours. The tables they were coming to were covered not with green baize but crisp linen. Every hotel on the Strip had to have a superstar chef in residence or, better still, six of them, or twelve – and it wasn't just the big US names; the French boys with the Michelin stars were starting to pay attention as well.

In 2004 non-gaming revenues in Las Vegas – from high-end hotel rooms to glossy arcades of shops stuffed full of Cartier and Chanel, and, of course, those restaurants – overtook non-gaming revenues for the first time. This wasn't because gambling had suddenly fallen out of favour. Gaming was still a roaring express train that was pouring cash into the city. It was just that more money was being spent on all the other stuff. If you were interested in restaurants, you had to be there.

I am interested in restaurants. Ergo, I had to be there. Plus I needed to do something to exorcise the memory of John Wayne Bobbitt and his damaged appendage.

Before I could begin, though, I had an appointment to see Freddie Glusman at his restaurant down on Convention Center Drive. Piero's is old Las Vegas and so is Freddie. He used to feed clams to Moe Dalitz, the original Las Vegas mobster who founded the Desert Inn and the Stardust. Frank Sinatra was a regular at Piero's too. Once, when he was out of town, Sinatra sent down to Piero's for dinner, so Freddie plated up some of his famed *pollo vesuvio* – chicken, tomato, fried aubergine and mozzarella – made sure it looked nice, put it on the Learjet and flew it over to the old man on his estate in Palm Springs.

When Martin Scorsese came to town to shoot his movie *Casino* and needed somewhere as the setting for Joe Pesci's restaurant, the Leaning Tower, he knew exactly where to go: Freddie's place down on Convention Center Drive.

Me? I had absolutely no intention of eating at Piero's. I was looking for transcendent meals and I really didn't care whether the food came with Sinatra's approval. He was a fantastic singer but no restaurant critic. Anyway, I had just four nights in town, and none of them was going to be wasted on *pollo vesuvio* or *saltimbocca alla romana*, however good Freddie insisted they were. Still, in the clichéd way of nice middle-class boys who have never punched anyone and who would run a mile from a real Mafia hood if ever they met one, I've always had a thing about the old Vegas of the Rat Pack.

One of my favourite recordings of all time is *Sinatra at the Sands*. Not vintage Sinatra vocally – he was only a few years from the nightmare of 'My Way' by then – but the Count Basie Orchestra is as tight as ever and from Frank's opening line – 'Who let all these people into my room?' – to the very last crack of the snare drum, you know who's in charge. I was about to submerge myself in the complete artifice that is twenty-first-century Vegas; before I did that, I wanted to go back a bit. I wanted to live a little of that recording. It felt like I was coming to pay my respects.

Piero's is a low-slung, dirty-pink building, opposite the Convention Center. Glusman's office is reached through the back car park, past the sort of garbage dumpsters that would be good for dumping a body in, if you were in the body-dumping business. The office is a windowless box on the first floor at the back. Naturally, it's carpeted in tigerprint. On the desk in the middle there's a wide dish of black jelly beans. Neither of these things are as interesting, though, as the walls. They are filled with photographs, all the same size and each with the same simple black frame. At first I assumed they would be friends of Freddie's and some of them are. Many are not. Here's a picture of Bugsy Siegel, the old hoodlum credited with turning Las Vegas into a gambling Mecca by opening the Flamingo, before taking a bullet in the eye. There's one of Jack Kennedy with Sinatra, and not far away a portrait of Nick 'the Greek' Dandalos, the professional poker player famed for having taken part in the greatest card game of all time, against Johnny Moss, a five-month marathon of Texas hold 'em, held at Binion's Horseshoe in 1949.

Freddie comes in as I am studying the wall.

'This is a tribute to old Vegas?' I ask, indicating the pictures.

'Yeah,' Freddie says. Now in his seventies, he has dark-brown, leathery skin, big hands and a voice like he gargles daily with gravel. He's wearing a black sweatshirt and various bits and pieces of gold jewellery, and he has those large, dangly earlobes that some people acquire in old age. 'There's Al Dorfman,' he says, pointing with one stubby finger at a black-and-white photograph. 'He got shot dead in Chicago. Here's Priscilla and Elvis. Here's Elizabeth Taylor. Here's Harry. He was a Nevada Supreme Court judge. Had to resign because of some bullshit or other.'

'And here's Jimmy Hoffa,' I say enthusiastically, pointing at a picture of the Teamsters' boss who went missing in mysterious circumstances in 1975, presumably because he had displeased his friends in the mob. 'I wonder where he is now.'

Freddie stares at me. 'How the fuck do I know?' He trudges off behind his enormous desk.

Glusman has been in Vegas for over forty years. He started out in the 'schmatte business', selling womenswear from concessions within hotels. Back then there was only one big-ticket restaurant in each hotel.

'Vegas is an entertainment town,' he says. 'And people in the entertainment business, they want somewhere good to eat, but there weren't that many places. The Flamingo had the Candlelight, at the Sahara it was the House of Lords, and the Sands had the Regency Room.'

These were old-style joints, where the boys on the floor always dressed in a tux, and almost nothing was served unless it had first been flamed tableside in imported cognac.

For years Freddie had been interested in restaurants, so, in 1982, he found a chef called Piero and put him in business.

'What happened to him?'

'He left,' Freddie says. 'After six months.' And then, as if I had asked why, 'Because I wanted him to leave.' So now he was running a restaurant called Piero's without a Piero. It seats 350 people and is only open for dinner.

His place, he says, has always been a local place. Nobody gets hassled at Piero's. As it says on his website, 'It quickly became a hangout for Las Vegas locals and celebrities like the Rat Pack, politicians, and some of those businessmen in the casino industry with Italian surnames, the "local colour" guys.' All of this plays up to the myths, of course – by 1982 the Rat Pack was probably talking hip replacements and pensions – but it's clear the restaurant has had an interesting clientele over the years.

Just a few years ago one of the big casino developers was beaten up at his table over dinner by a bunch of other casino guys because of an argument over $250,000 of chips, all of which redefines the term 'floor show'. Later Freddie told the press and the police he hadn't seen anything. Or heard anything. At all.

He hands me a tightly printed list of the celebrities who have eaten in his dining room downstairs, with its beige leather banquettes, cosy booths and low ceilings. Some of them mean nothing to me. Who is 'Too Tall' Jones? Just how magic was Lady of Magic? But others – Muhammad Ali and George Clooney, Brad Pitt and Sammy Davis Junior – are obviously familiar. On the wall behind his desk is a photograph of Sinatra signed, 'Hi, Freddie. Great as usual, Frank.'

I ask him what he thinks of the new breed of hotel and restaurant.

'The hotel owners are different today,' he says. 'In the old days they took care of the customer, and not just the high-rollers. Now it's just too impersonal. Unless you're a giant player. Then they'll kiss your ass. As to the restaurants, most of the big names above the door, they aren't ever there. The chefs just have to be in town maybe a week a month and that's it.'

'And yet they do well,' I say. I want him to moderate his

view. After all, I haven't even started eating yet. I want the place to be good. I don't want to hear this old guy's cynicism.

'Sure they do well,' he says. 'There's three thousand, four thousand people staying in the hotels. Where else they gonna go? Wolfgang Puck's got five or six locations in Vegas now. He's a good guy, but it's a little commercial, isn't it? That's not about the food. It's about the name.' He goes off on a long rant about the outrageous mark-ups on wine in the city – which I will discover to be the case in some places – and the way some of the fancier restaurants just plate up 'three beansprouts' and call it dinner. 'You used to get a hotel room for ten dollars. Now it's seven hundred. It's crazy.'

I look back at the wall of photographs. 'You used to feed the mob guys?'

He shrugs. 'They weren't them. They represented them.'

'Do they still eat here?'

He shakes his head, like I'm an idiot. 'They're all dead.'

So the old Vegas really has gone: not just dead, but buried too. Instead I need to discover the new Vegas, which, naturally enough, means going to Paris, though only that bit of Paris located at the Venetian Hotel. I have a table at Bouchon, an affectionate rendition of the classic French brasserie by Thomas Keller, widely regarded as the best American-born chef in the world.

I always knew that Keller would be a part of this journey of mine, and more than once. At the French Laundry in Napa Valley and Per Se in New York, he partners soft-boiled eggs with black-truffle purées and makes a millefeuille of crisp green apples. He puts thyme ice cream together with extra-virgin olive oil and makes sorbet out of hibiscus. Anybody in search of the perfect meal will want a piece of that. Here at Bouchon, however, he (or his team, for Keller is either in California or New York tonight) does straight-up French brasserie food, which is something I have always loved. Asked once what type of food I would choose if I could eat that and only that for the rest of my life, I chose a menu of French brasserie classics: *fruits de mer* and *steak-frites*, cassoulet, *pot au feu* and rabbit in mustard sauce. Nothing else seems to me to speak so loudly or clearly to the appetite. I was excited about eating at Bouchon.

The walls of the restaurant are a studied shade of nicotine in a room where very few people smoke. There is a tiled floor. There is wood panelling and engraved glass and mirrors and, before me, there is a perfect dish of fresh oysters on the half-shell with a ramekin of shallot vinegar.

Of course, the whole thing is as authentic and cheesy as a movie set but, having wandered the Venetian Hotel for an hour before coming upstairs to Bouchon, I have concluded that notions of authenticity are a distraction in Vegas. Complaining that everything is artificial here is like wandering into a nunnery and chastising the residents for praying too much. You either engage with it or you go home, and I wasn't about to go home. That said, it is possible to acknowledge that a lot of modern-day Vegas is Olympic-gold-medal-standard silliness – though you can still enjoy it.

In the foyer of the Venetian Hotel, another 3,000-room megalith, men in red and white striped shirts wearing straw boaters float about playing accordions, as if it were a reasonable thing to do. There may be a travelling exhibition of works by Rubens, on loan from the Guggenheim, here at the hotel, but most people make do with the intricate murals on the walls and ceilings: of fat-clad cherubs and sunlit clouds and melon-breasted ladies in diaphanous gowns looking slightly startled to find themselves here.

Naturally, it is all irredeemably camp. Indeed, as I wandered the city over the next few days – past the centurions with their breastplates at Caesar's, the intricate marble floors and stuffed sofas at the Wynn and the display of giant hand-blown glass flowers by Dale Chihuly at Bellagio – I was constantly pursued by that C-word. Vegas redefines camp. It's camp on anabolic steroids. Vegas, I eventually concluded, looks like it has been designed by a battalion of gay interior designers who were never allowed to hear the words 'Enough, already!'

Try this: at the Bellagio there are stripy gold and copper awnings over every card table, like the place is the set for a Little Bo Peep story. I was dying to meet the hard-knuckled high-roller who specifically wanted to drop a few grand at the Bellagio just because 'They got them pretty awnings.'

During my pre-dinner journey around the Venetian I stumbled across the town square, a wide, open cobbled space meant to replicate the feeling of Venice at dusk. It comes complete with water-filled canals that teem with gondolas for hire, so that tourists who can't make it to the real Venice can slip gently under fake bridges and past crowded pavement cafés and feel pleased with themselves. In the square, rather good opera singers are performing for the crowds, each dressed in a sofa's worth of brocade and velvet. All of this is far away from the chuntering slots and card tables of the gaming floor.

Las Vegas

It is a different place, filled with corridors of shops and restaurants, and it is blisteringly expensive. Exploring the hotel, I come across the Pinot Brasserie, serving a surf and turf of filet mignon and Maine lobster for $65. There's a big-ticket fish joint called Aquaknox offering a $68 dish of whole lobster stuffed with crab, which strikes me as indulgence squared. There's a Chinese place specialising in 'six-hour' spare ribs, and Emeril Lagasse's Delmonico, where a New York Strip steak will cost $42, which in this setting is a bargain. Curiously, in this Venetian-themed hotel, it takes me half an hour to find a restaurant serving anything approaching Italian food. Finally, on the square, I come across the Ristorante Veneto.

The first dish on the menu that catches my eye reads, 'Hormone-free chicken roasted on the rotisserie.' I know the reference to hormones is meant to sound like a good thing. I know they want me to think well of this chicken and the blameless life it has led, so far from the medicine cabinet. But the truth is, I don't want to hear about hormones on a menu, even if the reference is in the negative.

So I head upstairs to Bouchon. I suck those sweet oysters off their shells and taste the sea. I try their snails in garlic butter and this time, without a burner, I put nobody's life at risk. Instead of shells, they come with tiny, crisp puff-pastry hats, which is a shockingly good idea. One of the reasons I have always loved escargots is because, at the end, you get to slurp the remaining garlic butter from the shells. I always find myself trying to get my tongue into every nook and cranny to remove the last crisp, salty bits of parsley. As the dish is carried away, I am haunted by the fear that somewhere, lurking at the bottom of a shell, is the mother lode, a fantastic explosion of garlicky, buttery flavour that I hadn't made enough of an effort to find. The puff-pastry thing gets round that. You use them to soak up all the sauce. Yes, it removes some of the fun, and the commitment, but the rewards are greater. I make a mental note to tell a London chef friend about the idea so he can steal it.

I eat long-braised beef short ribs, in a rich bourguignon sauce with lardons and wild mushrooms, and finish with a crème brûlée, which is let down by the burnt-sugar topping. It is soft rather than crisp. Still, there is a floor show to make up for it: at the table across the aisle is a large, bearded man accompanied by a Japanese girl with the sort of cleavage small children could get lost in. He has ordered the caviar at a breezy $125 and is showing her how to eat it, not off the ball of the hand, but from small blinis and with a little chopped onion.

I am intrigued by her body language. Maybe I'm just traditional, but I don't expect women to put all that embonpoint on display on a first date, and yet, over the caviar, she behaves as if she has only just met him. She watches him studiously, almost respectfully, and pays attention. There is nothing giddy about it, as there should be when $125 of ebony fish eggs are about to be licked up in just a few seconds. For her, it is a serious business, which seems a shame.

The grey-haired Australian man sitting on the banquette next to me – collar, tie, brass-buttoned blazer – who is also eating alone, has seen me watching them. He says, 'By the hour.'

'I'm sorry?'

'Those two.' He nods across the aisle. 'She's his date for the evening, if you get what I'm saying.'

Las Vegas

'You mean . . . ?'

He nods. After all, in Nevada prostitution is legal. 'I always stop in Vegas for a few days to get a little R & R when I come on a business trip,' he says. And then, 'Isn't Las Vegas a great city?' He doesn't wink at me, conspiratorially, but I get the message. He could be that guy over there, and tomorrow night he probably will be.

My instinct is to dismiss his take on the matter, not least because of his enthusiasm for it. Just because a woman is wearing a low-cut dress doesn't mean she's available to anybody by the hour, and yet it makes a kind of sense. I had watched her laugh at his jokes just a little too keenly and then seen her face fall dead as she stared off into a corner of the restaurant, as if distracted by an unrelated thought. I am comforted by the idea that if she is a hooker, the sex, almost inevitably mediocre, will at least have been preceded by good food, and that, long after she has showered to remove his smell, she will still be remembering the way those salty little eggs burst against the roof of her mouth to release their rich, oily taste with its ghost of fishiness.

Because, that brûlée aside, the food has been good. Even so, I'm not entirely convinced by the experience. Bouchon looks out over a carefully tended courtyard garden. Adolescent cypress trees spear the sky, and there is a studied elegance and maturity about the view. This room is about as far away from the Vegas of slot machines and blackjack tables as it is possible to be. That – combined with jet lag and four glasses of good Californian wine – has, I think, created in me a sense of dislocation. I don't entirely know where I am. Or, to put it another way, I could be anywhere, which may be their intention. What I want is a Vegas experience. I want the kind of experience I couldn't have anywhere else in the world. Happily, I have a reservation for just such a place the following night.

In 1996 Joël Robuchon turned fifty and, as he had always said he would, retired. That year he was named 'Chef of the Century' by the (then) highly regarded French guide *Gault Millau*. He is a small, odd-looking man with a squashed face, as if somebody has inadvertently folded away the middle. He favours black, collarless shirts and has a monkish air, as if part of his personality has also been folded away. Anybody who meets him will not be surprised to discover that, as a boy, he trained for the priesthood until lack of funds forced him to leave the seminary and take a job in a hotel kitchen.

Those British chefs I know who have worked for him – Gordon Ramsay and Richard Neat – attribute to him the qualities of the mystic, and those who work with him now also often resemble members of a priesthood. A couple of years ago Robuchon was hired to cook a one-off dinner at the Connaught Hotel in London. A small advance team of his cooks was to bring a van of ingredients through the Channel Tunnel, because they did not trust any of the ingredients available in Britain. The French cooks insisted that they be met at the British end of the Channel Tunnel in Kent by cooks from the Connaught, who would then drive the van up to London. None of Robuchon's team was used to driving on the left-hand side of the road and they believed the effort would destroy their Zen state of concentration for the cooking of the meal to come. Naturally, the British cooks thought this was the funniest and the most precious thing they had ever heard, but complied with their wishes.

Fans of Robuchon refer to his extraordinary palate and his innate ability to know when a flavour combination is absolutely right. Ask them to name a perfect Robuchon dish and they may well mention his cauliflower panna cotta with caviar *en gelée*. They might talk about his black-truffle tart. But there is one creation they will all mention: his mashed potato.

Joël Robuchon revolutionised the making of mashed potato. He did this by putting less potato in it. Instead, he made it with half its own weight in butter. The result is a dish so rich, so luxurious, so completely outrageous it ought to be illegal. I have eaten it just once – at that Connaught dinner – and my arteries were still complaining. The method has been so regularly copied since he introduced it to his menu in the 1980s that it has essentially become the accepted modern method for making pommes purée in top-end restaurants. To change the approach to something so basic and so simple as mashed potato seems to me as good a test of greatness in the chef world as any other.

Tragically, after 1996, the chance to eat it as made by Robuchon himself was reduced almost to nothing. Then, in 2003, came the announcement that had high-end foodies beating their *poulets de Bresse* with feverish anticipation: the chef was returning to the stove. Former colleagues of Robuchon wanted to open a restaurant of their own but the banks had refused them money. They asked him if he would join the venture and he agreed, as long as the restaurant that resulted was not the classic three-star, high-end, gastronomic temple that he had left behind. He wanted to do something more casual. He wanted to do the kind of place where diners would sit round an open kitchen at a bar.

There would be simple plates of the best Spanish hams, as well as more complex dishes reminiscent of Robuchon in his prime, a tiny langoustine ravioli with black truffle, for example, or the sweetest chops of Pyrenean milk-fed lamb with thyme. It would be the kind of place you could come to for just one or two plates, as well as a full meal. The emphasis was on informality. The first L'Atelier de Joël Robuchon opened that year on Rue de Montalembert in Paris. It was followed by another in Tokyo, the beginning of what would turn out to be a chain.

Then came the big surprise. For years Gamal Aziz, now president of the MGM Grand, the biggest hotel in the world, had been trying to lure Robuchon to Las Vegas. Thing is, he didn't want a branch of L'Atelier. At least not at first. The MGM Grand had launched a new, upscale wing to the hotel, the Mansion, and for that he wanted the full-on Robuchon. The big-ticket Robuchon. He wanted every bell and whistle in the marching band.

'I said no,' Robuchon told me, when I met him in London in spring 2006. 'The problem is, Gamal Aziz is a very charming man. He was just too persuasive. Plus he said I could have anything I wanted. He never talked about profitability. He just wanted the best.'

In October 2005 Joël Robuchon at the Mansion duly opened inside the MGM Grand, and now I was going to eat there.

Unlike with Bouchon, there is no attempt to hide Joël Robuchon's restaurant, or restaurants, for it was eventually decided that there should also be a branch of L'Atelier and the two sit side by side, next to the entrance to the Mansion, but still on the gaming floor of the hotel. The entrance to the high-end restaurant – two huge, floor-to-ceiling curving doors – is just twelve paces from the last slot machine. Inside, though, every part of the restaurant has been so heavily engineered that you can't hear any of the noise from outside.

In the dining room, which seats just forty people, there is a $28,000 chandelier by Swarovski. There are vases by Lalique and an outside 'garden', which isn't outside at all, but which takes $8,000 of plants a month to maintain. There is a trolley with twelve different types of bread at the beginning, and another with twenty-five different types of petits fours at the end, plus a wine list as thick as a paperback book. Everything is dressed in 'regal' shades of purple, and a specially commissioned interlocking pattern is repeated from the handles on the cutlery to the carpet and the curtains.

Although there is a standard menu, Joël Robuchon at the Mansion specialises in multi-course tasting menus. I sat down at the table. I was handed a folder made of thick, glossy card, which I opened. I began reading. The sixteen-course tasting menu, the one I wanted, the one I was determined to try, was listed at $350 a head. Before drinks. Before tax. Before service.

I blinked.

The money thing

A few years ago I spent £49 on wine in a restaurant. Not impressed? You should be. It wasn't for a bottle (let alone for two). Nor was it for some fancy-pants champagne. It was for a single glass, and not a very big glass at that. I know what you're thinking. If you're polite, you're thinking, 'More money than sense;' if you're not polite, you're swearing at the page. It's OK. I can deal with it. Because the honeyed amber fluid in that glass, served to me at Restaurant Gordon Ramsay in London's Chelsea, came from a bottle of Château d'Yquem, perhaps the greatest white wine on the face of the planet, and it was worth every penny. Or, at least, it was to me, which is the same thing.

The fact is, I have no problem with the notion of spending large amounts of money on hugely expensive restaurant experiences. I make no apologies for this, even though our puritanical culture so often demands it. Lunch for £200 a head? Yes, please. How about £50 for a starter? Seems fair enough to me. And £75 for a main course? Bring it on. In France I would not need to explain myself. There, spending serious volumes of cash on dinner is a national spectator sport.

Elsewhere, behaviour like this puts you in the same grim league as politicians and muggers. It's regarded as an obscenity, an experiment in excess as filthy and reprehensible as snorting cocaine off the flattened bellies of supermodels or slaughtering white Bengal tigers to provide the fur trim for your panda-skin gloves.

There is one reason for this and one reason only: we need food to survive. Therefore it is a necessity, and to crash the plastic until it smoulders on a necessity – one that some people don't have enough of – is regarded as wrong. That is to completely misunderstand the point of restaurants and high-end gastronomy. For a start, modern famines are not generally caused by a capricious Mother Nature, denying food to some people here, while others over there have plenty. As aid organisations have long said – and continue to say – they have man-made, political causes, such as the ill-considered land-reclamation policies in Robert Mugabe's corrupt Zimbabwe that have pushed its population to the brink of starvation. You foregoing dinner in a restaurant will not resolve that problem.

By the same token, nobody goes to restaurants for nutritional reasons. Nobody eats hot smoked foie gras with caramelised-onion purée to stave off rickets. They go for experiences, and what price a really top experience?

Let's put it another way. How much would you be willing to pay to see your football team play in the FA Cup final? Would you pay £100 a ticket, or £200? How about £500 for a really good seat? You wouldn't think twice about it. A place in the front row for Robert De Niro on the stage? A few hundred quid, easy. The chance to see Sinatra in his prime? Hell, you name the price.

What does that money buy you? Nothing but memories, and the right to say you were there. Serious gastronomy is no different. An example: a little while ago I was invited to eat at the Auberge de l'Ill in Alsace. Restaurants don't come much more haute than the Auberge. It has been owned, and the kitchen run, by the same family, the Haeberlins, since 1884. It has had three Michelin stars since 1967, and some of the dishes have been on the menu for over forty years. Among them is a black truffle the size of a golf ball – not shavings, the whole thing – wrapped in foie gras, bound in a buttery pastry, baked and served on a rich, meaty truffle *jus*. Yours, back then, for 125 euros (about £87; it costs more now).

It was served to me with a 1994 Cos d'Estournel, a big-fisted Bordeaux listed on the menu at 330 euros (or £230). A total cost of 455 euros for the ten minutes it took me to eat the dish; that's over £30 a minute (50p a second. Can I stop now?). It was ear-poppingly expensive. It was also sublime: there was the heady, dense aroma of the truffle as I cut in, a smell that I could taste it was so intense, and the back-kick of the sauce, and then the red wine reminding me of the soil.

True, I wasn't paying for this myself. But would I have done so? Happily. And could I justify the price? Of course. This wasn't simply about sitting down at a well-laid table and being served a set of ingredients cooked in a particular fashion. It was the Auberge de l'Ill truffle dish, cooked by one of the Haeberlins, eaten overlooking the River Ill. It was about the moment, one I'll never forget.

That's the thing about expensive restaurant experiences. They have to be worth it. A couple of years ago there was media outrage when a new restaurant opened in London called Sketch, where dinner would cost £500 for two. The pundits were right to be outraged, but for the wrong reasons. It wasn't the price that mattered; the problem was the person setting it. The fact is, you have to earn the right to charge top dollar. The overseeing chef at Sketch is a Frenchman called Pierre Gagnaire. In Paris he is a superstar. There, they queue to give him their money. In London (where he isn't even at the stove) none but the obsessives like me have a clue who he is. You have to be a legend – a Frank Sinatra, a Robert De Niro – before you can start squeezing wallets dry.

France is littered with culinary De Niros and Sinatras: at Alain Ducasse's restaurant in the Hôtel Plaza Athénée in Paris, he serves a caviar and langoustine dish costing just over £100; the late Bernard Loiseau's restaurant, Le Côte d'Or in Burgundy, serves a chicken dish costing £175; and *über*-chef Marc Veyrat will sell you a chocolate pudding for £50. I'd willingly shell out for them all, if I had the cash to hand.

In Britain the choices are more limited. For example, at Restaurant Gordon Ramsay, on Royal Hospital Road, the top-rated restaurant in London, the basic menu is still a mere £85 for three courses: the tortellini of lobster with herb velouté, the sautéed loin of venison with a bitter chocolate sauce and a gravity-defying coffee soufflé. No worries: there's always the Château d'Yquem by the glass to help you top up the bill. The thing is, a whole bottle of d'Yquem will set you back hundreds of pounds at the very least. A big vintage – a 1928, say, or an 1880 – can cost as much as £30,000 on a restaurant list and, while I may be keen on big-ticket dinners, there are limits to what I can afford. Frankly I'd given up all hope of ever getting to taste the stuff. So that Château d'Yquem by the glass was practically a social service on Gordon Ramsay's part. Indeed, at £49 a pop it should really have been regarded as a bargain. And I never could resist one of those.

The confession

Except that, when I went to Joël Robuchon at the Mansion, just as when I went to the Auberge de l'Ill in Alsace, I wasn't the one picking up the bill. In fact I wasn't expected to pay for anything much in Las Vegas. It was all on the house.

It is not always like this. Whenever I review restaurants for the *Observer*, the newspaper reimburses me for all the meals I eat. I book tables under a pseudonym and, while I have never gone as far as Ruth Reichl, who used to review for the *New York Times* disguised as her own dead mother, I try not to draw attention to myself. We never accept freebies for review.

Meals eaten for features have always been a different matter, however. At the *Observer* we are allowed to accept 'hospitality' where the experience would inform what we are writing about, and that pretty much covers all eventualities, including gluttony.

Within hours of contacting the Las Vegas Visitors' Authority, which has offices around the world, I was being pelted with offers of hospitality. I was being hosed down with them, assaulted by them. My email inbox filled up with suggestions for meals I could eat, and places that would love to have me, and ones that would be mortally offended if I didn't at least drop by for cocktails and canapés. (The most worrying was the offer direct from Freddie Glusman at Piero's, but only because he is a known associate of convicted killers.) I could have survived in town with an empty wallet for a fortnight on the offers I had received. Instead, all I had was a few nights and an appetite that, while enthusiastic, had its limits. Choices had to be made. Selflessly I had chosen Joël Robuchon at the Mansion to be among those restaurants where I ate for free.

At first I was a little uncomfortable about this, not least because I wasn't entirely sure what category my efforts at the table would be falling under. No, I wasn't reviewing for the paper. Some of my experiences would end up in its pages, but not all of them. I just wanted to pursue my perfect meal and that meant eating in a whole bunch of really good and improbably expensive places as cheaply as possible. As ambitions go, it's hardly up there with 'cure the world of all known diseases' and 'usher in an era of global peace'. When I had eaten the £300 truffle–wine combo at the Auberge de l'Ill, my wife had told me that the only thing which mitigated what would otherwise have been morally reprehensible behaviour was the fact that I *hadn't* paid for it. There was, she said, a smear of virtue in freeloading. I wasn't convinced.

Within a day or so of arriving in Vegas, however, it became clear to me that freeloading really was the only way to go here. So much money washes through the city, courtesy of the casinos, that *not* adding to the cash pile seemed to me to be a genuinely responsible thing to do. After all, it wasn't like I was hurting the chefs. They were on such sweetheart deals that one meal to a journalist on the take was neither here nor there.

Anyway, everybody was doing it. The night I ate at Joël Robuchon at the Mansion, one table was occupied by a group of journalists from San Francisco who were hardly fighting to protect their anonymity – they kept posing for photographs – and another was being hosted by Gamal Aziz, who certainly wasn't expecting a bill. The next day a group of seventeen other freeloading hacks was due in, and none of them would be paying either. And it's not just the media that gets the treatment. A few weeks before my visit a Chinese businessman had lost $7 million in the casino at the MGM Grand. As a courtesy, the sort of courtesy offered to all high-rollers in Vegas, the hotel had then invited him to eat for 'free' at Joël Robuchon. It struck me that I was actually being smarter than that guy because I was getting a free $600-a-head dinner without, up to that point, having lost a single cent. I concluded that I really didn't have anything to feel guilty about. I had beaten the house, and in Las Vegas that is something worth boasting about.

And so, accompanied by the public relations executive for the MGM Grand (a committed, valiant and remarkably slender woman called Jennifer who would do all sixteen courses again the following night with that party of seventeen), I ate.

At the start there were crunchy pearls of green apple, with a vodka granita to cleanse the palate. There was the famed caviar *en gelée* beneath a musky cauliflower panna cotta, the surface of which was decorated with tiny dots of a deep-green herb purée (applied from a pipette, we were told proudly; there were exactly the same number on every dish). We had a millefeuille of unagi – glazed savoury eel, Japanese-style – and foie gras, the flavours of these two ultra-rich ingredients playing tag with each other in the mouth. There was, as there was at almost every restaurant I visited in Las Vegas, a tuna tartare followed, as there wasn't anywhere else, by a coin-sized langoustine ravioli, with a little sautéed cabbage. We were served a bowl of a soft, luscious sweet-onion custard on to which was ladled an intense lettuce soup. And then a sausage fashioned from a scallop mousseline, encased beneath tiny slivers of raw scallop, which tasted tantalisingly of the sea.

While we were awaiting the arrival of course eight, the halfway mark, a waiter brought another chair to our table. We looked quizzically at him, and he nodded to the back corner of the restaurant, to where a small, grey-haired man in a black collarless shirt was standing talking to Gamal Aziz. Joël Robuchon was in town and he wanted to join our table.

Las Vegas

I had eaten food in front of the chefs who had cooked it for me before, but none had been of Robuchon's calibre. I regarded the man as a legend and, even having interviewed him once already, I remained in awe of him. This was the 'Chef of the Century', the guy who revolutionised mashed potato! Plus there was the language barrier. My French is atrocious, his English not much better. In London we had communicated through a translator. Here there was none. Now, as he sat down at our table, his face fixed in a crooked grin, I couldn't think of anything to say other than 'Mmmm' and 'Lovely' and 'How do you do it!'

He smiled.

I smiled.

I told him in dysfunctional French that the food had been '*fantastique*', and hated myself for not coming up with anything better. The next dish arrived and he indicated that we should eat. In the middle of the plate, sitting on its sawn-off end, was a hollowed-out bone. It came, he told us casually, from a wagyu; wagyu is the most expensive breed of cattle in the world. Inside the hollow was a mixture of crisp, green fava beans and wild mushrooms, in this case girolles, bound by a fava bean purée. Perched on the top was a jewel of bone marrow.

We had our forks raised and were about to begin when Robuchon announced proudly that this was a new dish. He was keen to see what we thought of it. So, no pressure, then. He watched me eat. He watched me more intently than I have ever been watched before. He watched me like a cat watches a mouse. I knew now what it was like to be stalked; all pleasure was leaking out of this meal very quickly. Naturally, we thought 'Mmm' and 'Lovely.'

I turned to my companion and said, 'How does he do it!'

I wanted to savour the forest flavours of the mushrooms and the beans, but I was too intimidated to do so. I just wanted to finish the dish and get it off the table.

He watched as we tried the abalone, in a viscous broth of ginger and artichoke, a symbol of his growing love affair with Japan. He watched as we attacked a piece of Japanese snapper, which had been flash-seared with the scales in place, so that they were crispy. He watched as we studied a lobster claw, in a saffron and seafood bouillon. Desperate now to make conversation, to do something, anything to stop him staring, I said, 'Maine lobster?' This hardly required great connoisseurship. All the lobster served in Las Vegas was from Maine.

'*Non, non*. Bretagne.'

'Brittany?'

'*Oui*. Bretagne.' He thought for a moment, summoning the vocabulary. 'It is better.'

I stared at the plate. My dinner had travelled further to be here than I had.

This single dish represented the one great argument against restaurants in Las Vegas: that, while there may be a lot of places to eat in the city, not a single thing they serve comes from nearby. Everything has to come from elsewhere, a tiny minority by road from Los Angeles, over four hours away, but most of it by air. In London, when I had mentioned my coming adventures in Las Vegas, friends of mine hadn't even tried to hide their disdain. How could Las Vegas be regarded as a great restaurant city when it had no local food culture upon which to draw?

I see the appeal of the cult of locality, the idea that for a restaurant to be any good it must draw its produce from nearby. I cannot deny that, over the years, I have eaten some fantastic meals that took their ingredients from as close by as possible. I remember once eating a plate of shellfish at a restaurant in Scotland, while outside, just a few feet from my table, the small boat that had landed them bobbed on the ebb and flow of the tide. There is no doubt that the location added to the experience. And location was all at the Auberge de l'Ill. But a commitment to locality, to what in its truest form the French refer to as *le terroir* – the land – can also lead to an ossified gastronomic culture. Visit Toulouse and every restaurant will offer cassoulet; in Marseilles it will be an endless list of expensive but mostly indifferent bouillabaisses; and in Strasbourg you can eat anything you like, as long as its choucroute. It is provincial pride for pride's sake.

The definition of local also seems to be surprisingly elastic. The country inns of France might well get their ingredients from within a 5-mile radius. Chez Panisse in Berkeley, California, which for over thirty years has noisily pursued a doctrine of organic produce grown by local suppliers, expands the concept of local to include the Chino Ranch in San Diego, 500 miles away. The fact is, most of us in the developed world live in cities, and the ingredients we eat are always going to have to come from somewhere else.

Very early one morning during my stay in Las Vegas, I went out to see the cargo operation at the city's airport, which is housed in a set of steel sheds off a dusty avenue on the edge of town. In the cold rooms of the cargo-handlers I saw boxes of prime fish from the Pierless Fish Corporation in Brooklyn. There was meat from Hawaii, and oysters and clams from Boston. There were boxes of tuna and sea bass. There was food from everywhere. And every few days or so a box would arrive containing lobsters from Brittany because the man once named the chef of the century thinks they are better than the ones from Maine. As he sees it, once the lobsters are in the air it doesn't matter how far they fly, so he might as well have the best. That, it seemed to me, was the most important thing about restaurants in Las Vegas. All the ingredients might come from elsewhere but they are of the highest quality available. It's all the best non-intensively reared, free-range, organic meat, fish, fruit and vegetables.

Alongside this admirable commitment to quality is another concern, however, about the impact of all that air-freighting on the environment. I want to say it's something that doesn't bear thinking about, but, of course, it does, and at some point I will have to think about it.

For now, though, I am being stared at by one of the world's leading chefs as they bring me a slice of his thinly cut veal, which, unlike the lobsters, has come from only a few states away. It is a fantastic piece of meat, soft, sweet, velvety.

Just as we finish the veal, Robuchon indicates a black-and-white photograph sitting on the shelf beside my shoulder. There is Robuchon, grinning madly, and next to him is a tall woman with shiny hair and more than her fair share of teeth.

'Céline Dion,' Robuchon says enthusiastically.

I look at the picture again and of course it's her: she has a residency at Caesar's Palace, in a theatre specially built for her. The table we are sitting at, Robuchon says, is Céline's table. It's where she always sits when she comes, which is often. She always comes in the back way.

Céline Dion! Oh, God! Why couldn't it have been someone else? Elton John would have been fine. I wouldn't have minded sitting at his table. Or Wayne Newton. Or the guy who plays the crab in the Cirque du Soleil production that is running at the theatre just outside the restaurant. But Céline bloody Dion? If it had been my call, I wouldn't have built her a theatre; I would have built her a maximum-security cell for crimes against music. Clearly Robuchon loves her. He adores her. It is proof, if proof were needed, that you should never get to know your heroes.

Thankfully, a short while after our Céline Dion moment, Robuchon is called away to meet a table of Japanese diners who, remarkably, are not only paying for dinner, but have bought a bottle of 1957 Château Latour. We can relax at last, but, however ungrateful it sounds, the joy has gone out of the meal. Partly it has been the stress of sitting with the chef. Partly it was our own fault. Our booking was for 8 p.m., which was too late for a menu this long, and now, close to midnight, we are both flagging.

We consider commandeering the petits-fours trolley and riding it out through the doors, but there are just too many staff working the room. We'd never make it. We even suggest we'll give the petits fours a miss, but the waiters look appalled. They promise it will only take a minute or two. It doesn't. They insist upon introducing every single one of the twenty-five options: the sake meringues and the red wine tuiles, the caramel chocolates and the macaroons and the nougats. I have no recollection of what they are like. By that point all I wanted was to sleep.

The next morning I awoke and spotted at the end of my bed a vast breast of brioche. This, a loaf the size of my own head, was the going-home present, a perfect symbol of the excess of Joël Robuchon at the Mansion: after the meal of the night before, I can't imagine anybody being able to do justice to a brioche this big. Still, I like to show willing. I pull off a lump and chew. It's pretty good.

Over the following days I work my way around the restaurants of Las Vegas. I go to Bartolotta at Wynn, which will soon be named one of the best new restaurants in America, and have fillets of red snapper with miserably small clams and dried-out mussels for $32. I visit the Mesa Grill at Caesar's Palace and try a fine spicy tuna tartare with hot sauce and avocado relish, and an uninspiring Caesar salad. One morning I am taken on a tour of what will eventually be the site of Guy Savoy Las Vegas, the first restaurant from the Michelin-starred chef outside of France, which is also at Caesar's. It will be managed by his son, Frank, who takes me to a dusty corner of the building site and points to a spot that, he says, will be occupied by the best table in the room.

'Why will this be the best one?'

Frank, who is a tidy young Frenchman and is wearing a pastel-coloured jumper despite the Vegas warmth, smiles excitedly. 'My father's restaurant in Paris is only two miles from the Eiffel Tower but you cannot see it.' He points out of the window. 'But from here you can.' I look up. We are just across the road from the Paris Las Vegas Hotel, complete with a half-sized replica of the tower. It is clear that Frank Savoy loves Las Vegas.

That evening I take the lift to the sixty-fourth floor of the Mandalay Bay Hotel; not long afterwards, I am considering throwing myself off. Suicide might seem a drastic response to a bad restaurant – and Mix at the Mandalay Bay is very, very bad; it's a jazz riff on bad, a masterclass in the finer points of bad – but at least the sight of a diner plunging to earth would wipe the smirks off the waiter's face.

Mix belongs to Alain Ducasse, who is the only chef to have had a trio of restaurants with three Michelin stars, in Monte Carlo, Paris and New York. (He has since closed the New York outpost.) He has a couple of dozen others too, in Switzerland, London, Beirut and Hong Kong, among other places, plus here, at the top of this tower.

It is so high up that the stove had to be flown in, slung beneath the belly of a helicopter. There is a long shiny bar area with the best view of the city, and beyond that a huge white space, hung with glass baubles, with, at one side, an open kitchen so you can watch the chefs do terrible things to fine ingredients. Allegedly, the restaurant and bar cost over $20 million to create. Now they have to recoup that investment, by charging astonishing prices. Personally, if I had been paying, I would have preferred a mugging; at least when you're mugged, you aren't left with a nasty taste in the mouth.

I take an instant dislike to Mix, not least because it saves time: I hate the moodily lit white-out of a space. I hate the barman who can't mix a good cocktail, the booming music, and the homemade peanut butter that comes with the bread and makes me think the poor cow was milked unnecessarily.

I hate the white cube that houses the men's toilets, which is dirty and scuffed, and littered with discarded paper tissues. Mostly I hate the food. In the middle of the menu is a list of 'Alain Ducasse Classics', which, allegedly, are served at his restaurants in Paris and Monte Carlo.

A tranche of seared foie gras is so overcooked it crumbles away in the mouth. Lobster is served '*au* curry' in a sickly sweet sauce, flavoured with something that reminds me of the seasoning mix from a pot of instant noodles. Tasting it, I think the entire Indian subcontinent would have grounds upon which to sue the restaurant for defamation of its good name. Starters at Mix cost around $25. Mains are priced between $35 and $50 and top out at $75. I know I said I don't mind restaurants charging big money for high-end experiences, but the food does have to be edible. It's a minimum qualifying standard.

I check out the wine list, which is full of big-name wines at bizarre prices. For example, there is a 1961 Château Latour. It's listed at $8,416. Why not $8,400 or $8,450? Where did the random $16 come from? I call over the sommelier.

'We just mark up everything three hundred per cent,' he says, with a 'what are you going to do about it?' look on his face.

'What? Even the big stuff?'

Generally in restaurants wine mark-ups decrease the more expensive they become. A 300 per cent mark-up would be standard for the $30 bottles, but with the big numbers it's just about realising a reasonable cash sum.

I look at him, slack-jawed. 'How do you get away with this?'

He shrugs. 'What can I tell you? It's Vegas.'

I want to punch him. By now, I want to punch a lot of people. Mostly I want to punch the other customers, not just for being stupid enough to eat here – and on a Wednesday night the place is packed – but simply because of who they are. I survey the room and, not for the first time, I find myself wondering gloomily about the types who go to expensive restaurants, and whether I might be one of them.

The next evening I was to eat at the Vegas branch of Nobu, where, I had heard, they serve Château d'Yquem by the glass for $65. I wanted to order it but, despite having paid for very little so far, I decided it would be poor form to suddenly put my hand in my pocket. This, after all, was Vegas; if I wanted to taste one of the greatest white wines in the world, there was only one way to go: I had to win it. I would do so at the poker table.

A part of me knew the scheme was doomed from the start, and had been even before I arrived in town. Every Friday night in our house our elder son, Eddie, gets to stay up late and eat dinner with his parents. It was part of a cunning plan to inculcate him into his parents' obsession with food. Aged six, we had introduced him to a classic daube and to a pork and chorizo stew. In the course of many Friday nights he had eaten a rack of lamb roasted with honey and toasted almonds, and the finest egg pasta with clams and flat-leaf parsley. There had been roast duckling in a red wine and blackberry sauce, pizzas that we had made from scratch ourselves and skewers of grilled octopus. He had eaten the lot. We were creating a monster in our own image.

The Friday night before I flew to Las Vegas had been a particularly important one as far as I was concerned. It was the first night Eddie ate real steak, served medium rare, so it was good and pink in the middle, and he had loved it. He had even shown up my wife's phobia for fat, which I have always told her is where the flavour is in steak, by enjoying not only his own piece of lean rump, but also some of my richly marbled rib-eye. I was very proud.

Afterwards, as all responsible parents do, we set about teaching Eddie to play poker. The game was seven-card stud and, sadly, I cast a pall over the evening by beating everyone. It really wasn't my fault. It was the cards. In three hands I ended up with four aces, a hearts flush and a king-high full house. After the third of those hands I turned to my wife and said, 'And those are going to be the best cards I will see for the next ten days.'

So it proved, or almost; the one good hand I got, I threw away because I was so overwhelmed by the speed of the game. In 1995 when I had played poker in Vegas it had been a laid-back affair; it was possible to stay at the table for a few hours with just $20 of chips in front of you. It was also a game of marginal interest as far as the casinos were concerned, because their cut was so small. Now, though, poker is huge business, and in the vast poker room at the MGM Grand, where I was staying, pale young men in baseball caps, who spent the rest of the year playing poker online, hunkered down behind piles of chips so high they recalled Devil's Mountain from Steven Spielberg's *Close Encounters of the Third Kind*.

Back then, the game of choice had been seven-card stud, which I knew well. Now, it was Texas hold 'em, which requires both greater experience and skill, neither of which I had. The betting can also be complicated. On my first hand, remarkably, I pulled a diamonds flush and was so startled that, with just one guy left in, I flipped my cards before the last round of betting.

'That's a hell of a tell,' one of the others said, referring to the involuntary movements that inexperienced players make to give away a good hand.

The other player folded and, blaming fatigue for my error, I pulled in a pot that was about half the size it should have been. After that it was all downhill. Within minutes I lost every cent of those winnings, as well as the $100 I started with, most of it to an Australian who, back in Sydney, was press officer for a well-known politician.

I told him I was a journalist and he said, 'That makes it extra sweet. What's your beat?'

'Mostly I write about restaurants.'

He looked me up and down with disbelief. 'That's a job?'

Quickly I left the table.

So I did not get to drink Château d'Yquem that evening, but I did get to drink chilled sake. I ate paper-thin slices of Kobe beef, which had been seared and dressed with yuzu and chives. There were oysters with salsa and yellowtail with jalapeño, a tuna tartare – but of course – and their famed black cod, marinated with sweet miso, served in my honour with a tranche of foie gras, the two buttery ingredients proving excellent companions. I decided I liked this Nobu very much. I had eaten at the London branch a couple of times and, while the food had always been good, there was something about the fashionista and international celebrity crowd who thronged about it that made the experience dreary. In Vegas, Nobu is located in the Hard Rock Hotel, which is away from the Strip, and the room, with its wooden fretwork screens, has a cosy, intimate feel. It's a place you go to eat rather than a place you go to be seen to eat.

Part of the pleasure of the evening was my companion, a veteran professional poker player called Eric Drache, whom I had hooked up with through a mutual friend. Eric, now in his sixties, has won millions and lost millions. These days he makes his money producing poker tournaments for television, and scouring the footage for hands that will make good TV. In the old days, though, he liked to live by the seat of his pants and, alone among the poker pros on the circuit, liked to spend his winnings in good restaurants. He was the kind of man who would buy himself a first-class plane ticket even though he couldn't afford it and then pay for it at the other end when he had won the game. He almost always won the game.

Once, he found himself flying alone to Europe in first class. 'Nobody else had bought a ticket, so I got the entire stock of caviar to myself. I ate the lot.'

Eric was my kind of guy. He told me about his favourite restaurant experiences, compared the carpaccio to others he had eaten elsewhere, swooned over the king crab tempura and nodded approvingly at the curl of gold leaf that decorated one of the dishes. Eventually, though, I realised that underneath all this talk of restaurants visited and winnings spent and dishes eaten, there beat a true gambler's heart.

We had just finished our chocolate cake with green tea ice cream.

'Have you ever eaten fugu?' he said, referring to the Japanese blowfish whose organs contain a deadly poison, tetrodotoxin, which every year kills a number of diners. Nobody is sure how many. In 1958 over 150 people were reported to have died as a result of fugu poisoning. More recent studies have claimed that only one or two people now succumb to its effects annually.

I told him I hadn't.

'What do you think it would be like?'

I shrugged. 'I don't know. I think it's a macho thing. I don't think people eat it because of the taste. They eat it because they want to show how fearless they are.'

Eric nodded sagely and thought for a moment. 'What are the odds?'

'What do you mean?'

'I mean, is it a thousand to one that you'll die? Is it two thousand to one?'

'I don't know. I suppose the odds are even longer than that. A huge number of people in Japan eat it every year and the number is growing. Relatively few of them die, so . . .'

He called over the maître d', a Japanese-American woman called Jo, and asked her if the restaurant served fugu.

She shook her head. 'You need a licence to serve fugu and we don't have a licence.'

'So I'd have to go to Japan?'

'I guess so,' Jo said, humouring him.

Eric smiled. 'What do you think the odds would be on dying?'

Only in Las Vegas.

I had one last stop before returning home, a place called Lotus of Siam, which is reputed to be the best Thai restaurant in America. Weirdly, the best Thai restaurant in America is not located in one of the over-stuffed, marble-clad hotels on the Strip. Instead it's in a mall on East Sahara Avenue, fifteen minutes away. Still, if it was the best of anything, I surely had to be there. I checked my bags in at the airport, picked up a cab and, declining the driver's kind offer to supply me with a hooker for the night from the glossy catalogue he kept on his dashboard, drew up outside Lotus of Siam.

It reminded me of the car park at the back of Freddie Glusman's place: it was another lovely spot in which to dump a dead body. Apparently, in the 1960s, when this low-rise mall was first constructed, it was the height of fashion. Retailers were desperate to be there. Now most of the shop units, which occupy a long, inward-facing square, are dilapidated and broken down. Lotus of Siam is a little better appointed than most, but even so it is hardly a classy spot. This made a curious kind of sense to me. It is in the nature of any ethnic restaurant in America named the best of anything that it should be in a hard-to-reach spot in an unlikely town. There was indeed something absurdly intrepid about making the cab ride out here, just to check on the quality of a Thai green curry. Unsurprisingly, this had led to a certain kind of hyperbole, some of it absurd.

A couple of nights previously I had mentioned that I was going to Lotus of Siam to the maître d' of a restaurant where I was having cocktails.

'Is it the best Thai restaurant in America?'

He looked at me very seriously through his wire-framed glasses. 'It's the best Thai restaurant in the world.'

I took a deep breath. 'Don't you think,' I said carefully, 'that the best Thai restaurant in the world might actually be in, say, Bangkok?'

He shook his head slowly. 'You'll see.'

After that conversation I wasn't expecting much and, inside, I wasn't disappointed: scuffed carpets, polystyrene tiles on the ceiling, a little varnished wood which was in desperate need of a touch-up and, in the middle, a large buffet, with dishes kept warm in aluminium containers over guttering flames. Because of the time of my flight, I had decided to go early, but even at the ludicrous hour for lunch of 11.30 a.m. it was packed.

To be fair, I can see why. I had a lovely crunchy salad of minced sour sausage, peanuts and puffed rice, dressed with chilli, ginger and lime juice. I had thin, dark, chewy slices of marinated beef, which they described, reasonably enough, as a homemade jerky, and then a pork stew in a dense sauce with the fiery heat of chillies. It was all very nice. But the best of anything? Just to be sure, I ordered a chicken green curry, a dish I knew well. It was as good as many I had eaten in London, but it was no better and certainly not the best. There were only two options: either Thai restaurants in the US are staggeringly poor or Lotus of Siam, an admirable restaurant serving very good food at reasonable prices, had been hyped beyond all human understanding. I tend towards the latter.

And yet I had enjoyed my meal here more than almost any other in Vegas, and for two distinct reasons. Firstly, I could not escape the fact that it had been eaten in a dusty town in the middle of the desert. Lotus of Siam felt like part of Las Vegas – not the Vegas of slots and showgirls, but the other one, which lies beneath all of that, the old-fashioned, hot, sweaty frontier town where everybody is striving to make a go of it against the odds. It had struck me, as I moved from linen-covered table to linen-covered table, that the success of the new breed of Las Vegas restaurant now lay in its ability to transport you from the city in which it was located to somewhere else entirely, by sheer weight of excess. That dislocation I had experienced so acutely at Bouchon had actually been present at all the places in which I had eaten. In order to make you think that Las Vegas was now a really sophisticated place, they had to make you stop thinking about Las Vegas altogether, and they had done so pretty successfully. Lotus of Siam wasn't like that. You could never forget it was in a crappy old Strip mall on the edge of town.

The second reason I had enjoyed my meal was rather more basic than that: I had paid for it myself. I had slipped my credit card out of the warm leather slot where it had sat unmolested for so many days, and used it to settle the bill of $38.72, including tip. Freeloading might have been entirely justified in Vegas. Doing anything other might well have seemed foolish. But the mechanics of it couldn't help but detract from the experience. It made me a supplicant. It robbed me of control.

When I was eating on the house, I was always somebody's bitch.

That was something I didn't like. Somehow, from now on, I would have to pay for every meal myself. Of course, it would be expensive, but if I didn't do that, I would never find the type of experiences I was hunting for. I would never understand what was happening out there. The journey would be wasted. It was time to return to London, consider the finances and then head off again in search of dinner.

I couldn't just go to any old place, though. Yes, I had already identified lots of cities that were worthy of my attention, but if I was going to start lifting my own credit card in anger, I needed to head somewhere where money was what mattered, where money was the universal language. I thought about this but knew pretty quickly what I was going to do.

A little over a century ago my forebears had fled the Russian steppes pursued by the Cossacks. Well, now I was going back. I was going to Moscow. Everything I had read of those years had led me to understand that the Jews of Russia ate very badly around the turn of the last century – a diet composed mainly of sugar beet, potatoes and, if they were lucky, chicken fat. That was something for which I intended to make amends.

2. Moscow

My plan to pay my own way was not going well. I had been chauffeured to the Kempinski Hotel hard by the Moskva River in a shiny black people carrier. My suite there boasted a bed the size of Kansas, and from the windows I could see both the Kremlin and the absurd onion domes of St Basil's Basilica. I had hot and cold running concierge, access to the indoor swimming pool and a free newspaper every morning. It should all have been costing me $1,500 a night. Instead I was getting it for free.

This had not been my intention, or at least not at first. I really did mean to pay. Then, while still in London planning my trip, I was invited to meet Janina Wolkow, and it all went wrong. Janina is the twenty-something daughter of Alexander Wolkow, a Muscovite restaurateur who owns the three most expensive Japanese restaurants in a city so obsessed by sushi that even the Indian restaurants serve it.

In London's Mayfair, Wolkow owns Sumosan, which his daughter manages. A mutual friend said she was the person I should talk to about Moscow. Janina invited me to lunch at her restaurant. She fed me lobster salad, and sushi rice topped with seared foie gras, a desperate combination of carbohydrate and luxury fat that made me mourn the unnecessary sacrifice of a blameless goose. Janina told me she would be happy to help. She proffered another plate of sushi, this time topped with truffle mayonnaise, and said she could direct me to all the best restaurants in the Russian capital and that her father would be delighted to introduce me to the city's leading restaurateurs. Without pausing for breath, she said, 'And when are you going to review my restaurant?'

I chewed on the swab of warm rice and buttery, truffled salad dressing. I understood that she was looking for some form of quid pro quo. I could see her point. I explained gently, swallowing hard, that Sumosan, at an easy £70 a head, might be too expensive for my newspaper's liberal, often puritanical readers.

'We do a cheap lunch,' she said quickly, and fixed me with a fierce glare.

And so, a few weeks later, I found myself in Sumosan with a friend, reviewing the cheap lunch. Happily, there was no more foie gras sushi. Instead there were bright, clear broths with thick, slurpable noodles and crisp tempuras. There were pristine sushis and sashimis, black cod in miso, a white chocolate fondant and green tea ice cream, and I liked it all very much. I said so in my column. At £22 a head, I said it was good value.

It was the day the review appeared that I began to worry. What was I doing reviewing Sumosan? The restaurant had been open for four years, and many of the reviews were less than admiring. (One said the food was generally 'without merit or taste'; another described the 'funeral pall' of the room; a third said it was the kind of place frequented by 'young girls and older men'.) Had I been dishonest, then, when I said I liked the Sumosan lunch? No, I was certain of that. I really did like it. But would I have bothered to review it had I not been looking for some sort of assistance? Again, the answer was a firm no. Finally I faced up to the truth: the moment I became involved with the Moscow restaurant business I had started working to a different set of principles; unconsciously or otherwise, I had recognised that accommodations needed to be made, that it was not a place for scruples. I had become Muscovite in my methods.

I certainly knew by then that Moscow was not like other restaurant cities. I had spoken to a French chef who, for a few years, ran the kitchen of a high-end Muscovite restaurant, the kind of place where, he said, 'it wasn't uncommon to see someone drop a five-hundred-dollar tip'. He told me about the armed security men outside the doors and said that, while he had never experienced any problems, he knew the owner had been pressurised by criminal gangs. 'The place was a money machine,' he said. 'It was turning over eleven million dollars a year, and a million of that went straight to the Mafia.' For obvious reasons, he asked not to be named.

An experienced London restaurateur told me (again on condition of anonymity) that he had investigated setting up in Moscow but had quickly abandoned the idea. 'I got pressure when I went there. People came to see me. They said, "You will use us as your suppliers or else." I left town.'

Others told me that Moscow was nothing like this any more, that it might have been chaotic back in the mid-1990s, when the crime syndicates were fighting each other for control of the city, but it was a different place now. Just to be sure, I entered four words into Google. They were 'restaurant owner', 'Moscow' and 'murdered'. The result was startling. In the previous few weeks two restaurant owners had been shot dead. Pavel Orlov, the owner of a chain of restaurants, had been found murdered in his apartment on Udaltsova Street, two bulletholes in his back. Ilgar Shirinov, the owner of a restaurant called Olymp, had been killed with his bodyguard when the Toyota Landcruiser they were travelling in was sprayed with bullets. Law-enforcement officials said Mr Shirinov's death was linked to his 'professional activities'.

It spoke volumes to me that these killings warranted no more than a paragraph each in the Moscow press. Around the same time the campaigning Russian journalist Anna Politkovskaya was killed by a hit man, as were a bunch of bankers. The *Financial Times* was moved to run a long report about the return to the bad old days of business motivated assassinations.

I became nervous. The plan had been to go to Moscow for a bit of dinner. I was thinking blinis, smoked fish, maybe a little vodka. I wanted to see how the cheerful new capitalists of the new Russia liked to eat out. Instead, it appeared I was heading to Chicago circa 1929. It became clear to me that I needed a good hotel, ideally one with scary armed heavies at the door. The problem was that the authorities in Moscow had gone out of their way in recent years to close down all the mid-range places, so they could be replaced by expensive business hotels. Those were way out of my league.

Fully inculcated now into the ways of Moscow, I knew

immediately what to do: I had to make use of my connections. I asked Janina Wolkow if her father might be able to get me an advantageous 'press rate' at one of the hotels where he had a restaurant.

She called me two days later. 'He has a permanent suite at the Kempinski,' she said, naming the most expensive hotel in town. 'But he doesn't need it while you are there. You can have it for free.'

In Las Vegas I had worried that receiving free meals might make me a creature of the restaurateurs. Now, in Moscow, I was allowing one of them to put a roof over my head. Weirder still, it seemed like the only sane thing to do.

The Moscow that I was to encounter, as I searched its new breed of fine-dining restaurants for the perfect meal, would indeed live up – or down – to the stories I had been told about it. No, nobody was shot on my watch. But the city's big restaurateurs really did have bodyguards, and almost everybody seemed to have a chauffeur-driven four-by-four or a Mercedes limo, some with bulletproof glass. The doors to all the big-ticket restaurants really were protected by huge security men, and it became clear that the Moscow restaurant business was fully plugged into the very highest echelons of the Russian government.

What I hadn't expected to find was that the restaurants themselves would be rooted in a strain of moist-eyed sentimentality. Nor that they would indulge a passion for kitsch that would have left the Walt Disney Corporation feeling like rank amateurs.

And I certainly didn't expect to come face to face with it all on my very first night in town.

Café Pushkin, a 350-seater restaurant less than a mile from Red Square, occupies an eighteenth-century mansion a short walk from the statue of the great Russian writer from which it takes its name. The statue's head is bowed, and it is easy to imagine that Alexander Pushkin, the author of *Boris Godunov* and *Eugene Onegin*, is mourning the commercialisation of his reputation, although he should be used to it by now. Only a few years after he died, in 1837, from wounds acquired during a duel, merchants were already selling Pushkin-branded vodka and cough mixture.

In 1999, to mark the bicentenary of his birth, Pushkin and his famed mutton-chop sideburns were used to advertise everything from cigarettes to knickers, chocolates to more vodka. That was also the year in which a young Muscovite called Andrei Dellos opened Café Pushkin. It looks the part. Candles gutter in wood-lined salons and waiters wear beige moleskin waistcoats, as if they have just stepped off the pages of a nineteenth-century novel. There are cracks in the old brick walls, and the flagstoned floors are smoothed to a shine by centuries of Russian feet. On the first floor is a library packed with leather-bound volumes of Tolstoy and Dostoyevsky, and Bibles in every language, should you wish to repent over dessert. It is a cosy and beguiling environment.

It is also a complete fake. Café Pushkin was built from the ground up in just six months in the late 1990s, and nothing about it is real: not the cracks in the plaster, nor the intricate cornices on the ceiling, nor the polish on the flagstones. They have even given the restaurant what screenwriters like to call a backstory. 'At the end of the eighteenth century some

Germans opened here a pharmacy,' I was told by the manager, who said her name was Anastasia, 'like the youngest
daughter of the Tsar', though I wondered if that too was
something she had put on for the evening, much like the
high-waisted, ankle-length, lace-necked frock she was
wearing.

She showed me around the ground floor. 'Behind the bar,
you see the pharmacy bottles. Here they would cook the
medicines and, while you wait for your medicine, they make
coffee and tea and snacks, and this is the beginning of the
restaurant today.'

On our tour we pass a distinguished elderly gentleman,
dressed in appropriate vintage costume, with a carefully
cropped white beard, wire-framed round glasses and leather
book in hand, who is strolling the dining rooms. 'The
pharmacist,' Anastasia says casually; this backstory even has
a cast.

She leads me to the basement, which, she says, 'is the
laboratory. You see the equipment?'

Ancient and dusty glass bottles and test tubes are lined up
in cabinets. Down here, she says, the food is traditional
Russian. Upstairs, where we are sitting, it is modern Russian.
Pushkin is open twenty-four hours a day, seven days a week,
365 days a year.

Back at our table, we are presented with the menu. It is
long. Not just 'gosh, what a lot of choice there is' long. Not
even 'my, how busy the kitchens must be' long. It's long as in
'if I read all of this, will I have any time left for dinner?' At
Pushkin there are forty starters not including the pies and
pickles (and in a Russian restaurant, one must always include
the pickles). There are twenty-nine main courses, thirty

desserts and twenty-one honeys, should you want twenty-one honeys, and I wasn't sure I did.

There are also twenty-four waters. At Pushkin they not only have mineral water from the usual suspects – France and Italy – but also from the Czech Republic, Slovakia, Russia and Wales. I had flown for nearly four hours, queued for forty-five minutes at passport control for the pleasure of being stared at as if I was attempting to import anthrax, had been driven through Moscow's evening traffic jams for double that length of time and, living dangerously, walked for thirty minutes through the city's streets only to be offered mineral water from a country so close to where I live I make a point of never going there. I considered ordering it, and then noticed the price. At Pushkin water from Wales – where it is either raining or about to start raining – costs almost £10 a bottle. Perhaps it had flown business class to be here. Instead I ordered a Russian mineral water at a mere £8. It was wet and had bubbles.

The water prices, however, were nothing compared with those on the wine list. It wasn't just the big-ticket bottles of Bordeaux and Burgundy, the prices of which often read like telephone numbers in whatever currency they happen to be expressed. It was all the other stuff, the bottles that were meant for the civilians like me. Not for the first time I felt like a fraud, an impostor who had pulled up to the table on false pretences. I simply couldn't afford this restaurant, not properly.

The food wasn't (and never has been) the problem. It is always possible to find out in advance how much a menu is going to cost, and there has never been any shame or embarrassment in not ordering the most expensive dishes or set menus (however much I might yearn to do so, and I always do). As long as you do your research properly, the food could generally be regarded as a fixed cost, which, poor cooking and gastric distress aside, was unlikely to throw up any terrifying surprises.

The wine list, however, was – and always has been – a different matter entirely.

Costing a bunch of grapes

For years in London, while eating on my newspaper's not unlimited expense account, I had wasted little time studying what was actually in the restaurants' cellars, putting my energy instead into looking at the numbers in the far right-hand column, in pursuit of something that I knew would be acceptable, if only to the accountants signing the cheques. As a result I had become a connoisseur of wine lists, though not of the wines they contained.

I had come to hate the ones that, quite logically, arranged their bottles according to region so that the cheaper (read 'cheapest') bottles would be scattered randomly across the pages, and hard to find. Conversely I had come to love those that began with a 'house selection'. (Translation: 'a few cheap bottles for those schmucks who shouldn't be here'.)

I had also become geographically savvy, focusing on parts of the world that could be relied upon to be cheap – Argentina, say, or Croatia – and then despairing when the caprices of fashion served to make what had once been a bargain-basement wine-producer suddenly achingly hip and therefore wallet-punishingly expensive. In the mid-1990s, for example, Australia had been my wine country of choice, always good for a wide selection of bottles in my price range.

I had drunk gallons of huge oaked Chardonnays, wines that left you feeling like you'd spent the evening sucking tree bark, not because I had a particular weakness for tree bark but because I could afford them.

Then bang! Australia was declared the land of quality wines and it was out of my price range. New Zealand fell next, then South Africa. The way things were going, I'd soon be drinking the wines of Moldova or Tajikistan and praising their youthful vitality and power. Certainly, with years of practice, I had managed to make ordering the second-cheapest bottle on the list look like the decisive act of a man who knew his own palate.

At Pushkin, though, the 'second-cheapest bottle on the list' act wasn't going to cut it. That cost nearly £50. Before I arrived I had read that Moscow was now the world's most expensive city – 23.9 per cent more expensive than New York, apparently – but as I lived in one of the other top-five cities and always managed to find something in my price bracket at home, I hadn't taken it seriously. Friends had also told me that the prices were only punishing if you tried to live like one of the oligarchs, the hyper-rich Russian industrialists who had come to wield power over the Russian government; that otherwise prices – rents, transport, meals – were perfectly reasonable.

The problem was that in touring the world's high-end restaurants, I really was attempting to live like an oligarch, if only for a few hours at a time. I was at the restaurant with my newspaper's Moscow correspondent, who had made huge if fruitless efforts to get media accreditation for me from the Russian Foreign Ministry so I might visit the Kremlin kitchens. (Official response: 'A restaurant critic? I don't think so.') Tom spent a lot of his time in godforsaken corners of the Southern Caucuses, a long way from the nearest restaurant, and I wanted to show him a good time. The least he deserved was some wine, but this list was the enemy.

I knew that for sure when, thinking I had finally found something I could afford – it was the rouble equivalent of £30 – the waiter leaned over and, in hushed but clipped tones, said, 'You do realise that's a half-bottle?' I settled on a rosé Côtes-du-Rhône at a mere £45 and tried to pretend it was worth it even though I knew that, in France, it would retail for less than a fiver.

The wine pricing was a particular issue because, even on my brief acquaintance with this restaurant, it was clear to me that the food would best be enjoyed drunk. Modern Russian apparently means complicated and architectural: every dish looked like something a small mammal could nest in. We had starters of smoked eel and rare, thinly sliced lamb, and both came in rings round the plate, surrounding huge carousel-like flounces of salad or pickled vegetables, which rose at the centre to volcanic peaks.

Tom ordered a main course of salmon, which was arranged to look like some mutant sea creature that had swum too close to the outflow of a nuclear plant: a tail of mangetout, the head and arms of a crayfish and, between them, a half-cylinder of crisp (and inedible) salmon skin shielding the body of salmon beneath.

Mine read like three dishes in one: confit of rabbit leg wrapped in slices of slab bacon and baked in the oven with a pâté of rabbit meat in a box of puff pastry with raspberries, baby vegetables, cream and morels sauce. Fresh raspberries sat on top of the whorls of claggy rabbit pâté, making it look like the onion domes of St Basil's Basilica realised in food, and not very good food at that.

These dishes were to subtlety what Paris Hilton is to chastity. It was pantomime food, slapstick modelled in protein and carbs. Around me large tables of American men, in white shirts and red braces, clanked bottles of wine into ice buckets and laughed loudly at each other's jokes. Almost everybody here seemed to be anything but Russian.

As I paid the bill for nearly £200, for a meal which in London would have cost perhaps a third of that, I brooded on the artifice around me. Of course, high-end dining in Las Vegas had also been constructed around artifice, but it was artifice with its own internal logic, built partly on the lack of context of a desert town created from scratch, and partly from the worship of Mammon. Nothing was out of place because it had no place in which to be.

Moscow was different. Tom told me that the capital's restaurants were currently in the grip of an outbreak of nostalgia for food of the Soviet era, which was apparently now more popular than sushi, though I doubted what we'd eaten had borne a resemblance to anything served under Communism (save for a bowl of pickled cucumbers). This was a city wallowing in history. It was drowning in the stuff. And yet the 'historical' restaurant that Moscow had taken to its heart was such a weird, modern caricature that surely only Walt Disney could have been proud of it. It was clear to me that I needed to get to grips with what had gone before. I wanted to trace the journey from the Communist restaurant table to the fiction that Pushkin never wrote. And I knew there was only one place to start: the restaurant that Stalin built.

In 1950 Joseph Stalin and Mao Zedong marked the birth of the People's Republic of China by signing a treaty of Friendship, Alliance and Mutual Assistance. Naturally, to celebrate this bond, work began on a new restaurant, the first Chinese in the Russian capital. The Peking, inside the Peking Hotel on Bolshaya Sadovaya Street, was decorated in shades of imperial red and gold, and in the dining room the pillars were painted with ox blood. The hotel was a gargantuan building, which, for the short period before the completion of the Stalinist-Gothic superstructures known as the Seven Sisters – huge, multi-tiered, multi-spired edifices that ring the city – was Moscow's tallest building.

It was so tall that Lavrenty Beria, the founder and head of the KGB, and the man who oversaw the latter stages of Stalin's purges, was said to have a glass-walled office at the very top from where he could keep watch on the city below through binoculars.

The Peking is not the only example of a Moscow hotel or a restaurant created in this way. For the political strategists in the Soviet-era Kremlin, restaurants weren't places to go for dinner; they were a means by which to express solidarity with their allies. Moscow is littered with hotels and restaurants named after both the republics and capital cities of the Union. There's the Hotel Ukraine (which occupies one of the Seven Sisters). There's the Prague and the Warsaw and the Budapest. Each has its restaurant.

As I learned about this, I became rather fond of the old Soviet Union, or at least the idea of it. Who could not love a political system that didn't merely see restaurants as places in which to do deals, but as a means by which to express social and economic progress? The obvious answer is the poor benighted citizens of the Soviet Union, most of whom were never allowed access to those restaurants or who found few menu items available if ever they did make it inside. The premise, though, was a great one. If the British government had scrapped the lousy notion of a Millennium Dome when it was on the drawing board and instead spent the better part of £1 billion on a gastro-dome, packed with the very best restaurants the world had to offer, I for one would have welcomed the twenty-first century with open arms, and lent the Labour Party my unstinting support for evermore.

Of all the politically motivated restaurants in Moscow, the Peking (never, it seems, to be renamed the Beijing) was the most intriguing because it depended for its success on chefs supplied by China. As a result, the fortunes of the restaurant came to mirror those of Sino-Soviet relations. During the 1950s the Peking thrived, and became regarded as the height of fashion: party apparatchiks couldn't get enough of their sweet and sour pork and their spring rolls.

In the 1960s, however, when ideological differences between China and the Soviet Union led to bloody territorial disputes, all the Chinese chefs were called home to be replaced by Russians. For years afterwards the Peking served cabbage and Russian sausage, though diners were given chopsticks with which to eat them. There were décor problems too: the walls were decorated with murals of Stalin and Mao meeting in hearty handshakes of mutual admiration, and they regularly had to be doctored to keep pace with political change. After Khrushchev denounced him in 1956, Stalin was painted out. Mao went a few years later.

It took twenty years, and the accession of Mikhail Gorbachev to the Soviet leadership, for relations between China and the Soviet Union to begin a long thaw, the impact of which was not lost on the city's Chinese food lovers. 'Some people say that when they ship in a good Chinese cook to the Peking Restaurant,' the *New York Times* reported one China watcher as saying in the spring of 1985, 'that will be a sign that things are really beginning to change.'

Despite the end of Communism, little has altered in the way the Russian government works. In 2006, when relations between Russia and Georgia soured, the Moscow authorities knew exactly what to do. They closed down all the Georgian restaurants, claiming they had breached hygiene codes.

Elsewhere in Moscow during the Soviet period, the ability to eat out was dependent simply on status. There were restaurants, but some were open only to Communist Party members. Others were located in the headquarters of the various trade organisations – the Union of Writers, for example, or the equivalent unions for actors or film-makers – and you had to be a member or related to one to book a table.

Stepan Mikhalkov was one of those who could always get a table. Mikhalkov, now in his forties, is as close to cultural nobility as it comes in Russia. Both his father and uncle are film directors who either won or were nominated for the 'Best Foreign Language' Oscar. His mother is a famous actress, and his grandfather wrote the lyrics to his country's national anthem not once but three times, changing them when Stalin was denounced and again, as an old man, when a new version was needed to mark the end of Communism.

Mikhalkov met me at his restaurant, Indus, where Indian

food by the highly regarded London chef Vineet Bhatia is served, but stripped of all its grace and power because the Russians have no palate for spice. They like the blander, softer concoctions, of the sort that Mikhalkov got to eat as a child because of his family connections.

'I always ate well,' Stepan says, recalling his visits to the House of Writers. 'But for seventy years all the menus in the restaurants were exactly the same because there was only one cookbook, the state cookbook.' There would always be a version of salad Olivier – cubed chicken and vegetables bound in a slick of mayonnaise – named after Chef Olivier, who owned the Hermitage restaurant in Moscow in the 1860s. There was smoked fish, and the vivid beetroot soup borscht, and a remarkable selection of very different but surprisingly similar types of stuffed dumpling, be they boiled, baked or fried: there were *pierogi*; there were *pelmeni*; there were *varenyky*. Whatever they were called, it could all be guaranteed to be heavy food with its own gravitational field. 'It was homely food,' Mikhalkov said, picking at an emasculated samosa.

When Communism ended, in 1991, and the Soviet Union collapsed, many of these old restaurants closed, unable to cope with the demands of the market. Many of the new ones that opened soon found themselves the focus of the Mafia gangs that proliferated in Moscow in the early 1990s. At one point it was estimated there were 8,000 different criminal syndicates working in Russia and over 100,000 people claiming allegiance to them, and many of those ran protection rackets of one kind or another.

In the years before he came up with the idea for Café Pushkin, Andrei Dellos was running a club in Moscow.

'Twenty times a day I received threats and promises and from very serious people,' he told one magazine journalist. 'Soviet people were peaceful, educated and nice-looking, and then suddenly from the depths of the earth came these Mafia demons. I didn't sleep because I was so afraid.'

Eventually a number of the criminal syndicates took to running their own restaurants so they had somewhere to meet and launder money, though they rarely lasted long. Either there were shoot-outs inside, which forced the police to close them down, or they withered for lack of investment.

In the early days what the restaurants were not about was the food. Often it was simply about the ability to have money and to spend it as one wished. In her book *Sale of the Century*, about the rise of the oligarchs, journalist Chrystia Freeland describes the scene at Serebryany Vek, a grand restaurant in a converted bathhouse not far from the Bolshoi Theatre. There Moscow's newly emergent demimonde would gather nightly beneath chandelier-encrusted ceilings to gorge on 'mountains of caviar'.

One popular event at Serebryany Vek was the auction every night of a single red rose, which began at midnight. There was nothing special about the red rose – stem, thorns, petals – save that it was for sale to the highest bidder. On the night Freeland went, it was sold for $110. 'It could have been a nauseating moment,' she wrote. 'But there was something glorious about it too. The man in the suit that was a little too shiny and the tie that was a bit too wide bought that rose just because he could. Because there was no central planner, no head of the factory Communist Party cell, no stern censor of morality in the workers' state, to tell him not to.'

In time the determined restaurateurs, the ones who knew

how to work the system and get for themselves the necessary *krysha*, or 'roof' – patronage of the right people, be they politicians, businessmen or hairy-knuckled Mafia hoods – were able to prosper. Andrei Dellos, for example, was soon launching Shinook, a re-creation of a Ukrainian farmhouse, complete with live animals, separated from diners by a glass wall, and a lift so that the horse could be exercised in the street outside. Nobody I spoke to about Shinook had much to say about the food, but they all talked about the animals and the happy horse. It was the same as the sale of the rose. They appreciated the right to spend their money on it, however ludicrous and bizarre it might seem to others.

What of the Peking Hotel? How had that fared in the transfer to a market economy? It had not been without its troubles. In January 2002 Konstantin Georgiyev, the general director, was gunned down – one shot to the chest, another to the head, bang, bang, in classic-hit style – while leaving the orthopaedic clinic where he was being treated for injuries incurred when he had been run over by a car a few months before.

In 2004 control of the lower floors was sold to Storm Entertainment, a casino company, and by the time of my visit the renovation was all but complete. Richard Kveton, the casino's food and beverage manager, took me into what was once the Peking Restaurant. Kveton, a Canadian who has been in Moscow for over ten years, looks like something out of Martin Scorsese's film *Goodfellas*. The day we meet, his hair is slicked back. He is wearing a sharp suit with a pin-stripe of crimson and, beneath it, a crisp shirt in a matching shade of pink.

His Little Italy 'made-man' look is appropriate for the

space because the murals that once depicted Stalin and Mao shaking on the deal are no longer visible. The columns painted in ox blood are also gone. Instead the restaurant created to celebrate the victory of Communism is now called the New York Casino, and in the middle of the room is a model of the Statue of Liberty, rotating in a clockwise direction to survey the slot machines, flame aloft. On the carpet is a skyscraper motif. The pillars have been made to look like the supports to the Brooklyn Bridge, and there are fake street signs to Broadway, Times Square and Fifth Avenue.

When Kveton arrived two years before, the Peking Restaurant was still functioning, but only just. He shows me the current menu in the Peking's new restaurant, which is called the Manhattan Bar and Grill. Given the name, it is an unsurprising mix of Caesar salads, burgers and club sandwiches, plus a page of Russian standards, including salad Olivier, to appeal to the Soviet-nostalgia market. There is also a Chinese menu. 'But we've closed the Chinese kitchen,' Kveton says. 'In Russia everything used in a restaurant has to be officially approved and most of the things we use, by necessity, come from unofficial sources. We're due an inspection very soon so we thought it was better to close that kitchen down.' They'll open it once the inspectors leave, he tells me.

Then he says, 'There's something amazing I've got to show you. It's the room where Beria used to watch the city. You want to see it?'

Usually the room, on the very top floor of this thirteen-storey hotel, is locked off, but Kveton negotiates with the building's managers and soon the five of us – Kveton, his

Austrian executive chef, two executives from the building and me – are crammed into a rattling lift. Up above the cheesy glamour of the casino, the Peking is still very much an unrenovated Soviet-era hotel. It is gloomy and dour and decorated in four shades of brown.

We reach the eleventh floor, from where we take the stairs. Finally, at the top of a sweep of curving staircase, we reach two locked double doors, which open on to a huge open space, swamped with light from the floor-to-ceiling windows. Below us is the spread of Moscow, and we pad about trying to imagine Beria keeping watch on his people below with binoculars slung at his neck.

I look up. On the ceiling is a well-executed if garish mural of a young Chinese woman crossing a wooden bridge and being welcomed into the Soviet Union by what I assume are meant to be the flower of Russia's youth. It is the last reminder in this building, save for its name, of the past, though it is oddly positioned and I find it hard to work out how best to view it, and say so. Richard moves me to the top of the stairs and, his hands on my shoulders, tells me to look up.

'You stand there,' he says, 'and it would probably have been the last thing you would have seen before you got a bullet in the head.'

Everybody laughs.

One thing is now clear to me: in Moscow nobody cares about chefs. There are no superstar cooks, no masters of the stove, no Gordon Ramsays or Wolfgang Pucks or Joël Robuchons.

'In Moscow it's all about the restaurateurs,' says Guillaume Rochette, a French-born, London-based recruitment consultant, who makes a nice living supplying Moscow – and many of the other cities on my global haute cuisine trail – with the Western European chefs and maître d's they all need.

The biggest of the Moscow restaurateurs, he says, is Arkady Novikov. 'You have to meet Arkady,' says Rochette, who is a large, soft-cheeked man with big hands and tidy hair. Rochette is in Moscow drumming up business and is keen for me to interview his star client. Novikov trained as a chef in the Soviet era, at the romantically named Culinary College No. 174. He was turned down for a job at the first branch of McDonald's in Moscow and so moved into the business side of restaurants.

The week I am in Moscow he has forty-six of them, but he was due to open eight more before the end of the year (and it was already October). Rochette tells me that people go to a new Novikov place simply because he's involved, that they love his roquette salad with shrimp and Parmesan, which is available in most of his restaurants, or the indecently young burrata, a fresh, milky-tasting cheese much like mozzarella, that he has flown in every day from Italy.

For the first time on this trip, I feel a surge of optimism. My experience at Pushkin had made me fear that Moscow would be an awful eating city, that there was nothing here for a man in search of the perfect meal, but the burrata thing has excited me. This Arkady Novikov really might be my kind of guy. He goes to huge efforts to score good cheese. Rochette tells me he even does some of the catering for the Kremlin, that he's very well connected, though he doesn't like to talk about it. I love the image of Vladimir Putin eating soft, milky cheese and roquette salad, while he wages war on the oligarchs. At the moment, I'm told, Novikov is somewhere in his car, roaming his city, overseeing his new restaurants, working the phones, working the Moscow traffic.

While I wait to meet the man himself, I decide to try the first restaurant he opened, back in 1992. In a very Moscow fashion Sirena is famous not so much because of the fish and seafood it serves but because of the floor: it is made of glass, and beneath it, in a tank, swim sturgeon and carp. From what Rochette has told me, I am expecting something sleek and chic, a shiny joint for shiny people, but I have forgotten about the Russian taste for sentimentality.

Sirena is located on a drab residential street, just on the edge of the city centre. Inside, it is entirely wood-panelled. The dining room is an arched space with portholes behind which water gurgles, as though you are eating inside a galleon that has been upended on the seabed. Garlands of plastic laurel leaves, dotted with fairy lights, stretch across the room, the waiters all wear sailor outfits, and on the stereo an instrumental version of Chris de Burgh's 'Lady in Red' is playing. It is one of those songs that is appalling when you can hear the lyrics, worse still when you can't.

It doesn't help that, on a Thursday lunchtime, I am the only diner. Eventually there will be others, big Russian men with thick necks and cropped hair, drinking vodka and ordering the oysters at £5 each. For now it's just me and Chris de Burgh and the waiters and the stonking 3-foot sturgeon, with their familiar ribbed backs and pointed noses. Beneath my feet they swim in long, lazy circuits as I study the menu. I consider having the barbecued sturgeon, because I think it would be cute to eat the siblings of the tank's residents. Unfortunately it's not available.

Instead, in celebration of the other species in there, I order the 'fillet of carp in the Jewish style with ruby jelly'. What arrives is a solid chunk of cold skin-on fish, complete with bone, itself stuffed with more minced white fish. There is beetroot jelly on the plate and a little horseradish, and the moment I taste it all I am a child again, though not in a good way. For what I am eating reminds me, in a visceral manner, of a dish my mother used to cook, one which I always hated. But the sudden taste memory goes so much further than that.

For days, wandering Moscow, I have been intrigued by the Soviet-nostalgia menus of pickled vegetables and smoked fish, of cakes made with poppy seeds, and now this lump of dense carp on the plate before me. I have been intrigued by it all because every single one of those tastes has been so familiar and therefore a reminder to me of what I really am: not the savvy, cosmopolitan Londoner; not the Englishman, raised on Dickens and Shakespeare, soothed by Edward Elgar and Ralph Vaughan Williams. Instead, I am just a big-bellied peasant of Jewish stock, with a taste for chicken fat, salt beef and new green pickles, who happened, by good fortune, to end up living a bloody long way from here.

Worshipping at the fridge

When I was thirteen years old I was bar mitzvahed and, though I recall none of the Hebrew I read that day in synagogue, I do remember the dessert that we ate at the party afterwards: it was blintzes stuffed with thick, sweetened cream cheese. There were also, after dinner, platters of fruit-laden Danish pastries. There were biscuits and outrageous cream cakes and, with the coffee, chocolates, both plain and milk.

This suggests the main course had been fish of some kind for, while my parents didn't give a damn about religious observance, even they would not go so far as to bust Jewish dietary laws by serving milk and meat together at a bar mitzvah. My mother, to be fair, was so antagonist towards any form of religious observance she would quite happily have foregone the whole affair. However, my father, though no great believer, insisted that we would only regret that which we hadn't done. He told us that afterwards we could decide for ourselves if we wanted to take Judaism further.

He was the one who made sure I got to Hebrew classes and who, pressing into service his experience in the menswear trade, chose my outfit for the big day: houndstooth trousers, white ruffled shirt, black velvet jacket and a flowing red silk cravat held in place by a silver ring. It was not a good look for a fat thirteen-year-old; I appeared to have taken fashion tips from Tony Curtis in his plump, 1970s phase.

It is curious that it should have been my father who took responsibility for my Jewish education because, while he gave me the knowledge, it is actually from my mother that I take almost all my Jewish identity, though only because she fed me. I have always thought that I am almost entirely Jewish by food, and have long joked that I worshipped at my mother's fridge. She made a mean chopped liver, and there was always matzo in the house to spread it upon, not just at Passover.

She knew how to boil a fowl to make the most soothing of chicken soups, and liked to fry eggs with wurst, a kind of beef salami, which always stained them pink. Most of all she made gefilte fish, both boiled and fried. The boiled, which she loved, I hated. The mix of sweetened white fish (in some recipes ground almonds are added, giving an unpleasant crumbly feel) would be formed into balls, boiled, then allowed to cool and served with a clear fishy jelly. I thought it was disgusting, a creation that should go from pan to bin without troubling the plate, and it was that dish which the stuffed carp at Sirena most reminded me of.

Her fried gefilte fish, though, was something else, the crisp, salty exterior giving way to light, fluffy insides. The only peculiarity was that my mother insisted it should be eaten cold rather than hot. This was a relic from the days of observance that she so firmly rejected. Fried gefilte fish would have been made in advance of the Sabbath and then eaten cold when cooking was forbidden. We ate bagels and onion platzels, garlicky new green pickled cucumbers (which she sometimes made herself) and salt beef, which ideally came with its own ribbon of amber fat.

When I left home, and moved even further away from my roots, I came to think that the only thing which defined me as a Jew was my love for these dishes. All of this food marked my family out as Ashkenazi Jews, who came from the Pale of Settlement, those parts of Poland, the Ukraine, Lithuania and Byelorussia annexed in the late eighteenth century by Catherine the Great of Russia (a country which, until that point, had been closed to Jews).

Throughout the centuries of wandering, the Jews had been famously good at adapting the local culinary traditions to the demands of their religious dietary laws, and because they settled for so many centuries in the lands of Mittel and Eastern Europe, and became so established, they appropriated an awful lot of what was there. As a result, many of the things that I had always associated with the Ashkenazi – the use of soured cream and dill, of caraway and poppy seed, the chicken soups and dumplings and pickles – were really just the foods of the Slavic peoples (minus, tragically, their love of all things pig, a relationship I have since put a lot of effort into rekindling).

In London, where I grew up, my taste for schmaltz – literally, for chicken fat – was the last remaining vestigial stump of all those historical and geographical associations. My need for a regular fix of salt beef on rye was like the phantom itch from a long ago amputated limb. My wife, Pat, who is not Jewish, hates this stuff and says I would too, were it not for the cultural attachments. She also says that Jewish cuisine is an oxymoron. On this we are agreed. The word 'cuisine' suggests finesse, and if there's any finesse in Jewish food, it isn't being done right.

A few years ago a cousin decided to trace our family tree and, though I had not looked at it in any detail, I had brought the documents with me on this, my first trip to Russia. It begins with my ancestor Boruch, born near Lublin, Poland, in 1796, a major achievement of genealogy for the Jews, who, notoriously, can claim thousands of years of collective history but none of the paperwork to back it up.

From Boruch it works forward through nine generations to describe a family, mostly unknown to each other, that now spans the world from London to Jerusalem, from Canada and the US to Brazil and Argentina. My line of the family comes from Josef Boruchowicz, my mother's grandfather, who was born in Sarnaki, Poland, in 1882 and died in London in 1942, having changed his surname to Berk.

What intrigues me most is not what happened to the ones who left Poland but what happened to those who stayed. Obviously, large numbers were murdered during the Holocaust. The accounts of the fifth, sixth and seventh generations, who were still living not far from Lublin at the outbreak of the Second World War, are littered with the names of concentration camps like Sobibor and Majdanek. At least eighteen of my relatives on this side of the family were killed by the Nazis.

Then there are the ones who survived and their offspring: the children of Icek and Valentina Sherman, Tanya and Ira, who now live respectively in the Russian cities of Kurgan and Nizhniy Tagil; the children of Rita and Boris Gillman, Edik and Gennady, and of Moisey and Sima Sherman, all born in Slavuta, Ukraine, and where the extended family lives still. The 'what if?' school of history can be terribly unconvincing, because of the myriad possible outcomes to any given situation. But here, spread out on the counterpane of my expensive hotel bed in my expensive (if free) hotel suite in Moscow, was a clear path I genuinely could have followed. Had I been on another branch of this family tree, the funny Jewish food I liked to force upon my wife would not have been an occasional culinary diversion. It would not have been the focus of my fragile cultural identity. It would just have been dinner, and for some reason I found that terribly chilling.

A wet weekday night and I am in an expensive black four-by-four barrelling past a line of stationary traffic on the outskirts of Moscow. Next to me is Katya Dovlatov, daughter of the late Sergei Dovlatov, a highly regarded Russian writer who was forced to emigrate, unpublished, to the US in the 1970s and who only found a Russian readership in the 1990s, long after his death. The car we are in, and its driver, have been borrowed from Katya's flatmate, an executive with the oil company British Petroleum, who is away on business (for in Moscow all executives have cars and drivers on twenty-four-hour call). Katya says nothing as the car speeds past the other vehicles, but leans forward a little in her seat to see what awaits us. This spur of road ends at the motorway, where we find a single policeman holding back the traffic. I feel Katya stiffen in her seat.

Our driver, Alexi, winds down the window and barks something at the policeman, who stares back at him impassively.

'He's telling him that we are foreigners and that we are late for dinner,' she says with a bitter laugh.

Katya left the USSR when she was eleven and lived amid all the other Russian émigrés in Queens – her accent when she speaks English is pure New York – where her father edited the Russian-language newspaper the *New American* and wrote stories for the *New Yorker*. She first revisited Moscow shortly after the collapse of Communism and, after studying Russian literature in London, has increasingly made Moscow her home.

Now she runs a charitable foundation in her father's name, though she makes no attempt to hide the fact that the way the city operates drives her nuts. On our journey we had seen big black cars simply drive down the pavement to escape the traffic, and others with blue lights flashing driving on the wrong side of the road. 'Under Yeltsin anybody could get a blue light for twenty thousand dollars,' she told me. 'Now you still have to pay, but they only go to certain people.' This, she says, is a city that functions according to status, and it does not surprise her that the driver should be trying to get us on to the closed motorway by intoning our position as foreigners with restaurant reservations. It's usually a killer combination.

Tonight it makes no difference. Our driver is 'fined' the equivalent of £10 (in reality, a bribe to keep him out of the judicial process) and we are told to wait in line. Then, out of the darkness, its red and blue lights flashing against the wet surface of the empty motorway, comes a police car moving at serious speed, a thick mist bursting from its back wheels. A few seconds later comes the reason for this traffic jam: a long, shiny black limo, low to the road, the flag of the Russian Federation flying on its bonnet. President Vladimir Putin is being driven to his country residence outside the city and, as always happens when he makes the journey, the security services have shut down the motorway to let him get there as quickly as possible. His people must wait.

Katya watches him speed past. 'Welcome to the Rublevskoye Highway,' she says.

Rublevskoye, she tells me, is the Beverly Hills of Moscow, only with less taste, and more Armani; once a place of modest country dachas, forty-five minutes outside the city, it is now where the seriously rich live in their enormous houses, behind high walls 'patrolled by scary men with Kalashnikovs'. It's home to the politicians, and the oligarchs, and the new Russians for whom money is just a way of keeping score.

Recently a new shopping mall was opened alongside the

highway. It is populated only by the likes of Prada and Ferrari, Maserati and Gucci, temples to luxury built out here on a wooded hillside, a short drive in the Merc away from the compounds. It is also home to our destination, an Arkady Novikov restaurant called Tsarsky Okhota, or Tsar's Hunt.

I play with the idea that Putin would have regretted making us late for our table, had he known, for cooking and food are a part of his heritage. In his authorised biography, *First Person*, published in 2000, he revealed that his grandfather was a chef who had been brought to Moscow to cook at one of Stalin's dachas and that, as a boy, he also prepared food for Lenin. But you only need to look at Putin, at his skin the colour of porridge and that waxy sheen he has, to know he doesn't do food, not even Novikov's burrata or his roquette, shrimp and Parmesan salad. Quietly, the Wolkows like to boast that the Kremlin orders their sushi to go, but then sushi has always been the fallback for rich people who like to pretend they have taste when they have no interest in eating at all.

No, the last real eater in the Kremlin, the one who would have understood our eagerness to get moving, was Putin's predecessor. Boris Yeltsin apparently liked a bit of food with his vodka. He was a man of prodigious appetites and he often liked to satisfy them at Tsar's Hunt; photographs of Yeltsin and Jacques Chirac eating like tsars hang on the walls. If it's good enough for two presidents, it must be good enough for us.

When it first opened, Tsar's Hunt sat alone with only the trees for company, a faux hunting lodge in a perfect setting, but development is fast out here and now it is adrift on a tundra of tarmac, with a shopping development on one side of the car park and an apartment complex across the road. Inside, though, the fantasy is intact. There is a waterwheel and a babbling stream, which you cross on a little bridge. There is, naturally enough, a wishing well, and the walls are hung with animal heads and antlers and furs, because many creatures had to die to furnish this place.

Everything is panelled in dark wood, and the waiters are dressed as Cossacks, which I find unnerving. Once I became a father, my wife would often suggest we go camping. She was sure the kids would enjoy it, and I was sure that I wouldn't. I told her Jews didn't do camping, that the last time my people had camped was when they were fleeing a pogrom and that, if ever I found myself under canvas, I was sure the Cossacks were coming. I thought this was very funny.

Now, though, I am being served by a bunch of them: big, stern men, with short-cropped blond hair, solid brows and smile-bypasses. I decide it is best to get the orders in quickly in the hope that they might go away. At Katya's insistence we avoid the £50-a-head buffet and choose instead some *zakuski* (from the Russian verb '*zakusit*', meaning 'to take a little bite'), the Russian 'tapas', which traditionally start every meal. We order a plate of sliced pig fat, and another of Russian charcuterie, which is almost the same thing. We have assorted pickled mushrooms, a basket of uncut vegetables (starring a whole skin-on onion) and another of bread, including toasted *borodinsky*, a coal-black rye bread with heavy molasses flavours, which Katya tells me to rub with a cut clove of garlic. I do as I am told.

It is only when this food arrives that Katya lets me know that she actually hates it all and that she merely wants me to have an authentic experience, which seems like a victory for hope over expectation in this pelt-heavy room.

'Nobody ever cooked in my house when I was growing up,' she says, picking at the mushrooms. 'It was all these little plates of . . .' she hesitates, hunting for the right word '. . . stuff,' she says dismissively, waving at what has been assembled before us. 'It was not real food. I always wanted proper plates of things.'

In response to my panic about wine prices, she orders a bottle of vodka – 'In Russia vodka is still cheap' – and insists we toast each other over the pig-fat and raw-garlic tang. Behind us a fire burns fiercely, filling the room with the smell of woodsmoke and rendering animal fats. The meat menu is solid and masculine: there are lots of things on it that needed shooting before eating. There is slow-roasted brown bear with turnips. There is wild boar with a pomegranate sauce.

Then there is what I order: the back of dappled deer, roasted on a brazier. What arrives is just a couple of chops with a dark slick of a sweet reduced sauce made from local berries. It comes away easily from the bone and is – praise be! – one of the best pieces of venison it has ever been my pleasure to eat: intense, deep with the flavour of an animal that has lived a good life high on the windswept hill. More than anything, it is a surprise. Granted, there's nothing ambitious going on here. It's barely a dish, more a thing on a plate. But here in Moscow, surrounded by wishing wells, under-floor sturgeon and fake nineteenth-century mansions, I had begun to despair of ever having a good meal, or even a good course, yet here it was: two pieces of deer, roasted to perfection. Sure, these two chops, dispatched in four mouthfuls, had cost more than £20, but compared with the play food at Café Pushkin it felt worth it. Despite the best efforts of the Russian president, the great Arkady Novikov had managed to feed me well.

The next day I go to eat sushi with the man who had given me his suite. Alexander Wolkow has invited me to lunch at the original branch of Sumosan in the Radisson-Slavyanskaya Hotel. This being Moscow, lunch is at 3 p.m., and he will not be eating.

The Radisson is notorious in Moscow because, in 1996, its American co-owner, Paul Tatum, was shot eleven times in a nearby metro station, in what was assumed to be a Mafia hit. It was widely known that Tatum had been in dispute with his Chechen business partners and at the time of the killing he was wearing a bulletproof vest. It was assumed the killer was aware of the precautions he was taking because every shot was fired either to the neck or head. In the early days the lobby and restaurants of the Radisson had swarmed with gold-encrusted 'businessmen' and their bodyguards, and there had even been a shoot-out inside.

It was sitting in that same hotel lobby with his daughter in the late 1990s that Wolkow had decided to open Sumosan. At the time he was an executive with the energy company Lukoil, working mostly in Kazakhstan, with a taste for fine Japanese food that he felt could not be satisfied in Moscow. 'It was Janina who said I should open a restaurant here. So I did,' Wolkow says.

A varnished-wood picket fence marks off the section of the lobby set aside for Sumosan, which stretches away via a fairy-tale wooden bridge over a stretch of dry marble floor into a set of private rooms at the back. Wolkow orders me a plate of his reassuringly expensive sushi – £12 for two pieces of tuna nigiri – and sits watching me eat while he chain-smokes.

I can't argue with the quality of the fish in the beautiful lacquered box in front of me. I had been told that much of the cheap sushi served in Moscow arrived pre-sliced and frozen, which sounded like a recipe for the worst sushi in the world. They might as well have put the poor fish up against the wall and shot it. This, though, has that reassuring bite which speaks of freshness. The knifework is also exquisite, the surface of each lozenge of fish delicately marked with the finest of lacerations to create a greater surface area for the tongue. Each piece of sushi is beautiful to look at, even through the ribbons of tobacco smoke that slip around me, and I realise I would prefer to study my lunch than my host. I feel like I am looking upon a tiny patch of purity, in a city that is seriously short of it.

That, I decide, is why Muscovites so love sushi, why it must be on the menu of every restaurant, regardless of what other food they serve. The city is a place of barely concealed chaos. Bad things happen here all the time, and not only to bad people. Sushi is anti-chaos. It is order, fashioned from raw fish and rice. It is tranquillity in a box.

I find it curious that my host should be so in love with sushi, because he doesn't look a particularly tranquil chap. Wolkow is short and round and improbably hairy – even the backs of his hands could do with a comb – and I find the thought that I am now sleeping in his bed troubling. Despite the fact that he has given me his hotel suite, he seems less than eager to indulge in pleasantries, as if it would be undignified for a Russian to indulge a Western European with politeness.

When I ask if he had found it tough getting top-quality ingredients into Moscow, he snorts with derision. 'It was easier than bringing them into London,' he says. (This I know to be rubbish: every other restaurateur has told me about the red tape they endured when importing ingredients.)

I ask if the Muscovites had needed educating about quality sushi.

He takes extravagant offence. 'Russian people are gourmets, probably much more so than in France. You eat in France and you don't remember the tastes. And in England there are too many tourist restaurants. There, the food is not for eating.'

Feeling guilty for hurting Wolkow's feelings, I swallow hard on my foie gras sushi, which is no better here than it had been in London. I ask him where he got the idea for foie gras sushi.

'Some ideas, they come at night,' he says, and he sucks another cigarette down to the filter. I prefer not to think about Alexander Wolkow at night.

Finally, after three days of phone calls and waiting and more phone calls, I am invited to meet Arkady Novikov at a restaurant he would soon be opening opposite the Defence Ministry. 'My guests will be the general staff of the army,' he tells me through my translator, and he looks very pleased at the thought of all the military men he might soon be feeding. He is a small, tidy man with tiny feet and close-cropped greying hair and is wearing a dark blazer over jeans.

The new restaurant, which is on the third floor of an anonymous building, will be called Next Door. As he leads me around, it is not entirely obvious whether Novikov has decided anything else about it. I ask after the menu.

'There's kind of a menu,' he says, without looking at me. 'It's French. Sort of French. Not really French.'

It will probably include roquette salad with Parmesan and shrimp. I look around. It's dark and subdued in here, almost funereal, and not just for Moscow. This would be funereal for anywhere, including a funeral.

Though the restaurant is a few weeks from opening night, Novikov has insisted not only that the tables are in place, but that all of them are laid. The restaurant is set for over 300 non-existent people – glasses, napkins, cutlery – as around us carpenters fix wood batons to the walls and electricians fiddle with down-lighters. Various Novikov assistants – young, thin, taller than him and female – wander about looking busy and willowy.

'I want to understand how this dining room will be. I want to see how it works,' he says, when I ask about the ghost table settings. 'You need to feel the colours.' In this dining room there are no colours.

Looking for a way to compliment him, I say, 'Your restaurant is big.'

He says, 'I like money.'

Eventually, after fifteen minutes of a curiously random guided tour, as though he is re-acquainting himself with a house he used to visit as a child, he sits down and, fidgeting with his mobile phone, agrees to talk. He describes his early culinary training in the Soviet period and how there was never any point worrying about the quality of the ingredients because often there weren't any. He talks about setting up Sirena and, when I ask where he got the idea for putting sturgeon under the floor, he shrugs. 'Oh, you know. I have so many ideas' – like we all might think of building a restaurant on top of a giant fish tank. He tells me that Muscovites like sushi because it is 'exotic'.

What about the Mafia? Did he have problems with the Mafia?

He leans towards me and solemnly knits his fingers together. 'Yes,' he says, 'I did have problems with the Mafia.'

I am excited. I am going to get something of substance from this man. I am hoping to hear about threats and danger and bribes.

His mobile rings. He takes the call and sits bolt upright. 'Mrs Putin is here,' he mutters. 'I must go.' He darts from the room, barking instructions to his assistants as he runs.

Ten minutes later the doors to a lift at the far end of the room open. Inside are Novikov and a small middle-aged woman dressed in a brown A-line skirt and a bulging, brown Pringle sweater. 'It's her,' says my interpreter, with a mixture of wonder and disgust.

I had been told about the connections between restaurateurs and the political classes. On the way out of the Radisson, for example, Wolkow had made a detour simply to shake hands with the brother-in-law of Moscow's mayor, a major power in the city. The president's wife is a much bigger catch. Novikov is clearly not just connected to the Kremlin. He's hard-wired.

Behind Novikov and Ludmilla Putin is her bodyguard, a tall man with chiselled features, a blond flat-top and, trailing from his crisp white shirt collar, a curly pig's tail of cable going to an earpiece. For the next thirty-five minutes we watch as Ludmilla Putin is shown every single detail of the restaurant, her bodyguard never more than a few steps behind, scanning the embryonic dining room for threats (or admiring the understated interior design. Who's to know, with an Easter Island expression this impassive?).

Ludmilla looks at every piece of crockery and cutlery, at every architectural flounce and flourish. I ask an assistant why she is here and I am told it is because she has an office nearby, which doesn't quite explain this level of interest. She looks like she's thinking of buying the joint. I ask if she has money invested in the business. Novikov is known only to put up a small amount of the capital for each restaurant – usually less than 10 per cent – raising the rest from investors who know that his name alone is enough to bring in the crowds and guarantee a return. Nobody here seems to know whether the wife of the president of Russia has a financial stake in what's going on here. Or if they do, they don't want to talk about it.

All I know is that once again the first family has contrived to derail my plans. A few nights ago I was late for dinner because of the president of Russia. Today, because of his wife, the time I had in which to speak to Novikov is gone, and I definitely don't want to be late for my next appointment. Novikov may be a restaurant mogul. He may be Ludmilla Putin's go-to guy for tips on cool modern interior design. But the next man on my agenda is the chef of a restaurant that celebrates an organisation famed for its involvement in persecution, repression, torture and murder. That demands a little respect, not to mention punctuality.

The Shield and Sword is named after the emblem of the KGB and, fittingly, is located just up the road from the Lubyanka, where the state's feared security service was based and which is now home to its successor, the FSB. Inside, there is no doubting the restaurant's commitment to its theme. The walls are crammed with portraits of the great leaders of the Soviet Union and the KGB, including Beria.

There are medals under glass and a large statue of Felix Dzerzhinsky, the founder of the Cheka, the Soviet Union's first secret police force. On a television old films of great Soviet military victories play. Apparently many former members of the KGB like to come here to eat the house speciality of meat *solyanka*, a thick, spicy and sour soup, and to talk about the old days.

We are led through the restaurant and into the office of the head chef, Nikolai Morozov, who was head chef at the Kremlin for thirty years during the Soviet era. Morozov, now in his seventies, sits stiffly behind his desk staring straight ahead, wearing one of the tallest chef's toques I have ever seen. It is at least 2 feet tall. He has a big, solid face, held down by luscious, white, bushy eyebrows, as though he had inherited them in Leonid Brezhnev's will. More intriguing even than the chef is the wall next to him. Arranged neatly in an arch are photographs of those he served, and the heroes of the Soviet Union that preceded them. Here, indeed, is Brezhnev. Here is Khrushchev, here is Andropov, and here, in pride of place, is a picture of Uncle Joe Stalin. I ask about the pictures.

'These are all the people I worked for,' he says proudly. 'Apart from Stalin, but I was lucky to be the successor of the people who cooked for Stalin.'

I ask about all the delicacies he cooked for these great men.

He shakes his head. 'If you looked at the menu of what they ate and what a regular Soviet worker ate, you would see it was just the same.'

I am surprised by this. I had read an interview with Mikhail Zhukov, another senior Kremlin chef, who had rather different memories. 'We worked like crazy under Brezhnev,' said Zhukov. 'We cooked for congresses, for meetings, we cooked for him at his private residence, we literally worked nonstop. Back then, we were asked to prepare a lot of whole suckling pigs, whole sturgeons, whole partridges, whole crabs.'

Morozov is having none of it: 'It was simple food. Nothing special.'

I push him. Surely there must have been special occasions, banquets perhaps, or state visits?

Morozov fixes me with a glare, as if he thinks I am trying to catch him out. 'They ate exactly the same as everyone else,' he says. 'Only presented a little more beautifully,' and he pushes across the desk an album of photographs. Inside are pictures of whole sturgeon baked in pastry, the golden shell decorated with a lattice of mayonnaise. There are boned suckling pigs, glazed in aspic with cherries for eyes. There are watermelons hollowed out and filled with fruit. There is a hedgehog fashioned from chicken liver pâté and a giant golden melon carved to look like a swan.

'I have worked for fifty-two years,' Morozov says, nodding at the photographs. 'All this beauty is the treasure of our country. What the guest first sees is the table, and how the table looks reflects the importance I associate with your visit. Nowhere in the whole of Moscow is there anywhere doing food as tasty and beautiful as mine.' He pauses. 'I am the last of them.'

What immediately strikes me, looking at this gallery of food sculptures, is that I was completely wrong about Café Pushkin. I had laughed when they had brought out the salmon dish with the head of crayfish and the tail of mangetout. But now I could see there was a direct line between the Soviet-era creations in the photo album in front of me and that mutant fish at Pushkin.

'Only God knows how long I will go on cooking,' Morozov says. 'And as long as I have the energy, I will continue passing on the information.' He tips his head on one side, to consider the picture we are looking at. He nods slowly. 'You can do amazing things with a melon,' he says, and he sounds sad and wistful.

I am convinced now that the most outrageous, lunatic and completely over-the-top restaurant in Moscow is Café Pushkin, the one I had visited on my very first night in town – apart, that is, from the restaurant right next door to Café Pushkin. Turandot, which cost $55 million to build, is probably the single most expensive restaurant in the world. It opened in December 2005 and, like Café Pushkin, is owned by Andrei Dellos. It is more outrageous, more lunatic, more over the top.

Here, the theme is the Chinoiserie style of the eighteenth century. At its heart is an enormous eggshell-blue dome, crusted with gold-leaf detail. It looks like something the producers of the film *Les Liaisons Dangereuses* would have rejected as a location for being too ornate, just too damn gilded. There are cherubs and faux-Chinese figures in relief around the fringes of the dome, and songbirds and tendrils of wispy plants, much of it created by the scenic designers at the Bolshoi Ballet.

Around the huge, galleried, circular dining room are intimate private salons and, in the middle of the ground floor, a string quartet plays Mozart, wearing period costumes and high white Rococo wigs. It is both intoxicating and far too much, the visual equivalent of eating a whole box of Turkish delight.

For the food, Dellos took his cue from the word 'Chinoiserie' and hired as his consultant the London-based Chinese restaurateur Alan Yau, who has two Michelin-starred restaurants, Hakkasan and Yauatcha, in the British capital. Yau happened to be in Moscow when I was there, so we met for tea one afternoon at Turandot and it quickly became clear that he was not happy with the way things were going.

The first time he had worked in Moscow, he said, it had been under duress. 'I was approached by some Russians who said they had a restaurant in Moscow called Shatush which they admitted was a blatant rip-off of Hakkasan. Now they wanted the food to go with it and wanted to know if I would help. At first I refused. I kept turning them down. But eventually I gave in.'

It was after the Shatush experience that he was approached by Dellos, who said he'd been working on Turandot for six years and had a team of eighteen craftsmen on full salary creating the interior. He needed the food to match the ambition of the building.

'But it wasn't easy,' Yau said. 'Chinoiserie is Chinese-ness based on French attitudes. It's a parody.' To reflect that Asiatic theme, they wanted both a Japanese kitchen – 'because all Muscovites love sushi' – and an Imperial Chinese kitchen. 'A lot of the food here is what I call classical chop suey,' he said, with little enthusiasm.

The real problem was getting the staff. Turandot has eighty chefs, of which fourteen are his people – expatriates from Singapore, Malaysia and Hong Kong – though he'd already been through two teams and was about to move on to a third. 'It's very hard working here. The weather is appalling. There's also the Soviet mentality which still holds on. Here, the chefs aren't allowed the keys to the storerooms because of the old Soviet fear of the staff stealing from the management.'

I told Yau that I had heard Russians didn't have much of a palate for spicy food. Some had even told me spice was actively hazardous to human health, which told me everything I needed to know about Muscovite attitudes to eating.

He nodded sadly. 'It's true. Wait till you see what they've done to my food.'

The dishes I eat that night, in the company of Katya Dovlatov, are much better than I had been told to expect, though the chilli heat that I am familiar with from Yau's restaurants in London is indeed completely absent. It is as if a whole colour with which the kitchen can paint has been removed from the palette. The reds are gone. There are flavours, but they have no depth or clarity.

The most reassuring thing we try is a platter of dim sum, and I find it reassuring because it is familiar to me from home. Alan Yau revolutionised Chinese food in the British capital by insisting that dim sum didn't just have to be daytime food. He said it could be eaten anytime, including the evening. Then he employed chefs who did dim sum better than almost anybody else: the slippery rice-flour casings were lighter than anybody else's; the seafood with which they were filled was fresher and more skilfully seasoned.

Clearly whoever is in the kitchen at Turandot is from the same school of dim summery, for here comes the prawn dumpling with chives, and something with scallop, and something else with unctuous minced pork in a savoury sauce, and it is all lovely.

The food at Sirena had reminded me of home in a bad way, the carp in the Jewish style leading me towards uncomfortable truths about my origins. The dim sum here at Turandot are reminding me of home in a good way. What is not reminding me of home is the waiters, because, as far as I can recall, there is no Chinese restaurant in London that insists the men wear knee britches and the girls wear huge, shiny taffeta ball gowns in shades of ivory and amber. If there were, they would be laughed first out of the dining room, then out of town and finally out of the country. This, though, is Turandot, where dinner for two costs £300 at least, and all of these things are being taken terribly seriously by the moneyed new Russians who fill the tables crowding the gallery.

It strikes me that for this place to work, for any of it to make sense, this restaurant would actually have to be rather *more* decadent than it currently is, not less. If I were told there were orgies going on in the various anterooms ringing the rotunda, that the diners were first eating dinner and then each other, perhaps while snorting arm-lengths of cocaine off silver platters, proffered by bare-chested dwarfs wearing brightly coloured turbans, it would all be totally of a piece – and not just because I have a sordid imagination. Instead, it feels like a stage-set filled with actors who don't yet know their lines and are awaiting direction.

This is partly due to the ham-fisted service. Faced by noodles and steamed rice and dumplings, Katya becomes the New York girl through and through, and insists, as I do, that the dishes are just placed on the table so we can help ourselves. This is what we do in Chinese restaurants and it makes no difference to us that we are in a Chinese restaurant in Moscow.

We gently shoo the waiters away whenever they attempt to serve us. The waiters, in turn, look completely flummoxed, as if we have disenfranchised them cruelly. One girl, apparently searching for something, anything to do, takes it upon herself to refill our water glasses if we take the slightest sip. The same happens with the wine. We are no longer being served. We are no longer being looked after. We are now being stalked. Sip, fill, sip, fill, sip, fill, it goes, until we start muttering to each other about how much effort it would take to tip the poor woman off the gallery and into the musicians below, where she might be speared on the powdered peaks of their white wigs.

To subdue our homicidal thoughts, we turn our attention

back to the food. We try jasmine-tea-smoked ribs, which taste exactly the same as the ones in London, though they are much fattier. For some reason, this doesn't surprise me. On Yau's recommendation we order the long-braised beef ribs in red rice sauce, which has a tiny echo of chilli heat. Finally, they bring us a dish of steamed king crab legs in black bean sauce, which costs £45. I have seen king crab on the menu in many of the restaurants I have eaten in, and it seems to me now the quintessential Moscow ingredient. It is like the huge four-by-fours that any businessman worthy of the name has to drive in this city. The king crab is huge, unmissable and bloody expensive. You order it not because you particularly have a taste for king crab, but because its appearance on your bill says something important about you, which is 'I can afford it'. At Turandot it comes in a light black bean broth, which, combined with the briny flavour of the crab itself, makes for a salty plateful.

After puddings from Turandot's French-patisserie kitchen – a silky crème brûlée, an assiette of lovely chocolate things, scattered with fragile curls of gold leaf as though the décor had fluttered away from the ceiling – we escape the waiters to do a little window-shopping. Downstairs, in the colonnaded lobby of Turandot, there are a set of jewellery and antique shops, placed there, Katya tells me, 'So that stupidly rich drunk men will come out and buy their girlfriends presents.'

It is close to midnight but, seeing us staring into the shops, a woman appears and opens them all. We wander from one to the other, making what we hope are the appropriate noises.

'A girlfriend of mine was actually given a ring by her

boyfriend which he had bought here,' Katya tells me. 'The next day she brought it back to exchange it for the cash and discovered it had cost twelve and a half thousand dollars. She was outraged.'

Of course, I say. I can see she would be.

'Yeah,' says Katya, deadpan. 'It was the cheapest in the shop. She was really pissed off.'

Back in the bar of my hotel, a slender Asian woman – Korean, perhaps, or Vietnamese – is singing power ballads to a computerised backing track. It is late and the few men watching her are drunk, as indeed am I, on a heavy-bottomed tumbler of Russian Standard vodka. It is not helping my mood. Before I left London, a colleague who reported from Moscow for many years had described the city as being 'full of bitterness and anger and undiagnosed psychosis', and I am coming to agree with him.

The restaurants here do not feel like somewhere you go to eat, not even the ones like Tsar's Hunt where the food can be better than average. They feel like a redoubt, one built against a surfeit of politics and history at the door. In the restaurants of Las Vegas the fantasy was by turns charming and ludicrous, but never sinister. At the end everyone went home. Here, the fantasy restaurants feel necessary, a place of escape and therefore a vital resource for those who can afford them, and that in itself is troubling. No one cares about the food. Just as in Soviet times, they only care that they are part of an elite who can visit them.

Or maybe it is just that I am reminded too much of my

own family's history by being here. Maybe I was never going to be happy in Moscow.

I wander downstairs to the wide, open hotel lobby, vodka in hand. In one corner is a model of the next project by the Kempinski Hotel Group. It is called the Emerald Palace Kempinski and, when it is completed, will occupy a prime site on a set of man-made islands now being built in the shape of a palm tree off the coast of Dubai. The model is very detailed. It shows the hotel's two main buildings, with their shiny sea-green windows and, in front of them, around two dozen individual villas. There are huge outdoor swimming pools, children's play areas and, fringing the site, beautiful custard-yellow beaches. It is only mid-October, but today in Moscow there were snowflakes on the wind and all the Muscovites I had spoken to talked ominously of the winter that was to come, as if the thought of it had taken them by surprise.

I look again at the model, and then at the glossy presentation photograph alongside, which shows the exact location of the hotel when it is completed a year from now. I conclude that a place like Dubai, that would choose to build islands in the shape of palm trees, sounds like an awful lot of fun.

3. Dubai

It is just before seven on a damp winter's evening, and I am sitting outside the most expensive restaurant in Dubai, watching the queue. There shouldn't be a queue outside the most expensive restaurant in Dubai. It costs £150 a head to eat at Al Mahara, more if you hit the caviar list, and among the things that money should buy you is the right not to stand in line.

Ever since my bruising experience with the wine list at Pushkin I have been thinking hard about the purpose of big-ticket restaurants. I have concluded that I am not the only one attempting to live life like an oligarch by dining in them. It is part of what they are about: for the price of dinner, we get to experience life as a wealthy person, only without having to sell our souls as investment bankers, rape and pillage developing nations or exploit the downtrodden. It doesn't matter how long it took you to save up (and how low down the wine list you have to shop); if you can pay the bill, you become one of them.

Few luxury services are like this. You can hire a limo for

an hour or two but you will never have the ease, or sense of entitlement, that owning those wheels brings. You can spend three months' salary on a designer outfit but every time you look at it you will be reminded only that all your other clothes are cheap and tatty by comparison.

Expensive restaurants are different. They operate a deformed kind of democracy. In Moscow the point had been made most acutely as we left Turandot. Inside, we had been the same as everybody else: big-ticket diners with a leasehold on prime eating real estate. Outside, we were scum. Turning right from the front door, we walked past a sleek £300,000 Maybach idling at the kerb in wait for its owner. There was no shiny Merc or BMW for us, let alone a Maybach. This being Moscow, we couldn't even telephone for an ordinary taxi; they don't do licensed taxis in Moscow. Instead we went to the corner, stuck out our hand and hailed a gypsy cab, a romantic name for a sooty, clapped-out private car, whose driver just happened to be passing and thought he'd make himself an extra couple of quid. It smelled of old dog. We had gone from first to cattle class in minutes.

Now, of course, I was back in first class, or meant to be. I watched the line of diners continue to build, with a grim fascination. I knew why the queue was there. Al Mahara is reached by a submarine simulator designed to suggest that your table is not really on the ground floor of the hotel in which it is located, but 90 metres out across the seabed. It is the simulator – in truth just a lift that travels down one floor – which everybody is waiting for.

Apart from me. I refuse to queue. I look up. The 180-metre-high atrium of the Burj Al Arab Hotel towers away from me, pinpricks of light glinting in the boldly coloured ceilings of each open floor. The sail-shaped Burj Al Arab, the tallest hotel in the world, is built on its own man-made island 100 metres out to sea, as if it is about to float away on the breeze. It is also reputed to be the most luxurious in the world.

Shortly after it opened, in 1999, a British journalist declared it the only seven-star hotel on the planet. There is no such thing as a seven-star hotel, because the ratings stop at five – it was a tidy bit of journalistic hyperbole – but the label stuck and, having been given the tour that afternoon, I could see why. The hotel employs 1,700 staff for a maximum of 500 guests. One hundred and sixty of those staff are butlers, so there are at least fifty on duty at any one time. There aren't mere rooms at the Burj, only 202 double-floored suites ranging in price from £1,000 a night for a basic one-bedroom to more than £6,500 a night for the 780-square-metre royal suite (breakfast not included).

The décor follows the 'soon to be deposed murderous dictator' school: too much 24-carat gold leaf, too much thick blue velvet, more gold, a bit of shiny black stuff, marble, tassels, curtains, gold, chandeliers like giant crystal tits, gold, glass-topped coffee tables and leather armchairs upholstered in human skin. All right. I made up the armchairs, but not the gold. There really is a lot of gold. At the very top of the hotel, just above the bar with its view out over the city, is a circular helipad (where, famously, Andre Agassi and Roger Federer once played tennis).

At the bottom is the fish and seafood restaurant, Al Mahara, which I have been told is the best in the city, and if it's the best in the city, obviously I have to eat there. And I will do, just as soon as the bloody queue subsides.

Eventually I am loaded on to the submarine with a crowd of Japanese tourists who only stop photographing each other when the Indian captain insists they sit down and strap themselves in. Then off we go: the cabin, with its electronic display up front and bucket seats in the back, vibrates and rolls as we apparently set off into the shallows of the Persian Gulf. Through the 'windows' we see the 'seabed'. Fish swim by. Seaweed waves. The captain maintains a listless commentary, which clearly he has performed a dozen times already this evening: 'Oh, here's a turtle come to say hello, and there's where I crashed yesterday . . .' Finally, with a judder, we are there and the video images fade. To celebrate, my companions photograph each other.

I am led into the dining room and have to stop to scoop my jaw up off the thickly carpeted floor. Al Mahara is to good taste what Adolf Hitler was to world peace. The entrance is through a gold-leaf, multi-ridged opening that reminds me of nothing less than a giant vulva (an image not helped by the fact that, behind it, is a womb of an antechamber in crushed red velvet). The dining room is one long curve with, on the ceiling, huge mirrored panels so you can watch yourself gawp. In the middle, dominating the space, filling your field of vision, is a back-lit 80,000-gallon aquarium, complete with moray eels and leopard sharks and flamboyantly coloured parrot fish, the it-girls of this neighbourhood, loitering by the glass as if aware of their good looks.

The fish have been forced on to a reverse sleep schedule, so they are asleep during the day but raring to go at night, when people like me are staring at them. What is it about expensive fish restaurants that they feel the need to show you your dinner while it still has a pulse? At Sirena, it was underfloor sturgeon; here, it's everything else. At Sirena, I had imagined the sudden sound of cracking, snapping glass as the floor gave way beneath me; here, all I can think is that I am now on the set of a 1970s disaster movie, before the interesting stuff happens and Jason Robards dies an heroic death.

I am waiting for a pair of spring-loaded lobster crackers to go flying across the room, smash the glass and send out the sharks, ideally in pursuit of the party of ageing Canadians from Montreal who are talking in loud voices about the luxury cruise they are on from Istanbul to Singapore, and how their home town has just been recognised by *Gourmet* magazine as one of the great food cities of the world. I quickly decide I'd pay good money to see them eaten by sharks.

As I am led to my table, a harpist strikes up. 'Yesterday' floats across the room, followed by George Michael's 'Careless Whisper' and, because it is now only a few weeks until Christmas, 'Walking in a Winter Wonderland', a natural choice of song for a restaurant in a city perched on the eastern tip of the Arabian Peninsula. I am handed the obligatory water menu and notice that here, water from Wales is half the price it is in Moscow, which almost makes it a bargain. They compensate for this outbreak of sanity by the inclusion of Chateldon, a mineral water that costs £12.50 a bottle. Apparently it was big with Louis XIV and 'is also a curative for nerve and skin problems'. I consider my complexion in the bowl of a spoon and decide I am not yet in need of Louis XIV's favourite water.

By now, unsteadied by my submarine ride and baffled by

the décor, I am expecting heroically bad food and the first dish I order doesn't disappoint. The menu is divided into 'classics' and 'modern' and, being an idiot, I order a starter from the latter. It is listed as soya mud crab ravioli with truffle mango mayonnaise. What arrives is two piles of crabmeat, beneath not pasta, but a flap of amber jelly, which reminds me of something you would put on a burn victim's wounds to soothe the pain. The sweet, sickly mayo doesn't help matters. I stare at the aquarium and wonder whether the sharks will forgive me for the waste of such prime seafood when those lobsters crackers go flying and the waters break.

After that I start eating from the classics menu and things improve greatly. There is a rich lobster bisque heavy with brandy (because, in Muslim Dubai, alcohol is legal in five-star hotels and private clubs), which is spooned from a silver tureen at my table. There is a piece of John Dory, with a light sage sauce, and then a solid piece of turbot in a ripe, gratinated seafood sauce full of mushrooms and prawns. Even allowing for the model of the Burg Al Arab Hotel realised in puff pastry that arrives with it, this dish is a wonderfully old-fashioned piece of work. It's the sort of thing that would have appeared in the dining rooms of Paris before nouvelle cuisine took hold in the 1970s and creamy cheese sauces like this went through the culinary equivalent of ethnic cleansing.

There's something sweet about it. They have a state-of-the-art simulator, a fish tank that is a wonder of engineering, and a modern menu full of foams and jellies and weird flavour combinations. But here, where summer temperatures often reach 45 degrees Celsius or more and rarely drop below 21 degrees Celsius even in winter, what they do really well is soups full of brandy and cream, and white fish in cheesy, flour-based sauces.

Driving around Dubai, I keep recalling an old Frank Zappa song called 'Cocaine Decisions'. It's about fat-wallet businessmen spinning mega deals while speeding on the white stuff, and if that was how this city had come into being, it would make sense. It feels like a giant game of *Sim City* made real, created by someone who has been up for a month bingeing on chemical stimulants. Except that Dubai is madder than that, because the decisions that have shaped this place were made by Sheikh Mohammed, a good Muslim boy who doesn't drink, let alone bury his face in piles of cocaine like Al Pacino did at the end of *Scarface*.

Presumably the head of the Dubai ruling family was unmedicated when he decided that his kingdom needed an entirely new Downtown area of fifteen skyscrapers, all to be built at exactly the same time, including the Burj Dubai, which will eventually be the tallest building in the world (though nobody would say how tall; they didn't want anyone else to build something taller before they had finished).

He must have been in control of his senses when he chose to build the Jumeirah Palm, the man-made island in the shape of a palm tree measuring 5 kilometres by 5 kilometres with room for 1,500 villas, where they are putting up the Kempinski Hotel that I saw the model of while I was in Moscow. And another palm double the size with more fronds. And a third, complete with an island in the shape of Arabic script which spells out a line of the poetry he likes to write: 'Take wisdom from the wise – not everyone who rides is a jockey.' They are the only words in any language that can be read from space.

Plus there are the developments still to be completed: Falcon City of Wonders, with its full-size replicas of the Eiffel Tower, the Pyramids and the Leaning Tower of Pisa; or the Dubai Waterfront, which will help extend the coastline from a mere 70 kilometres to over 1,500 kilometres; or the World, another set of man-made islands in the shape of the globe, so that you could buy Australia or France or Germany and build your dream house on it (though not Israel: there is no Israel in the Dubai world).

Before arriving, I had looked at the place on Google Maps and, from 50 miles up, it had a twisted kind of logic. Now, on the ground, there is no logic at all. It is a chaos of cranes and car-clogged motorways and construction workers in blue and orange jumpsuits working night and day. The population of Dubai is now around 1.5 million, and only 15 per cent of that is native Emeratis. The rest are immigrants, here to build the dream.

I am aware that the same friends who were appalled by the notion of me going to Las Vegas to eat would be equally dismayed by the thought of coming to this massive building site for dinner. I, however, have decided to be optimistic. After all, great restaurants are an invention of cities. Conventional wisdom has it that they were born in Paris after the revolution when the chefs to the newly beheaded aristocracy found themselves in want of employment. Recent scholarship, most notably by Rebecca Spang, author of *The Invention of the Restaurant*, has argued that this was just another example of the legend-making in which the world of gastronomy so easily indulges, creating kitchen heroes from lowly cooks and imbuing humble ingredients – the mushroom, the oyster – with quasi-mystical significance.

Spang traces the word 'restaurant' back to a restorative medicinal dish rather than a physical institution where people were fed. All interesting enough, but she still allows Paris its central significance, and rightly so. It is not in the fields where the raw materials are farmed that the largest number of great restaurants have ever been found. It is in the cities, where people with spare cash congregate. That is one reason why, as a city boy down to the last knotty, twisted helix of my DNA, I am fascinated by them. I have always seen the restaurant as a mark of civilisation. As Sheikh Mohammed is attempting to build a great city here on this narrow stretch of sand tucked in between Saudi Arabia and the sea, it seems reasonable to hope that it will also be a good place for a man like me seeking good food. Or at least food.

In the 1950s, long before anybody had thought of serving lobster bisque in the Middle East, only 6,000 people lived in Dubai. It was little more than a trading post, with a reputation for the wild pearls that once grew in the oysters on its seabed and for the smugglers who liked to sail dhows full of contraband up the creek. It was the ruling Maktoum family who decided it could be much more than that. Though oil was discovered offshore in the 1960s, it was in relatively small amounts. Instead the Maktoums decided to focus on trade. In the 1970s they dredged the creek and built a huge docks, and set up free-trade zones to attract invest-ment. None of this softened its rough edges. Dubai still had something of the frontier town about it, and continues to do so.

Dubai

When the Soviet Union collapsed, the Russian Mafia poured into the old town, recognising it as a place where they could buy and sell anything. In 2004 when news broke that a Pakistani government scientist, Dr Abdul Qadeer Khan, had been selling nuclear secrets to North Korea and Iran, it was discovered that many of the deals had been made through front companies in Dubai. It is still rumoured that containers full of contraband – gold, weapons, narcotics – flow through its docks every day, and terrorist money trails have regularly been traced into the city and back out again.

This is not the Dubai that Sheikh Mohammed wants you to think about. He doesn't want you to come to Dubai for a little light arms dealing – or at least not *just* for that. He wants you to come here for dinner. He has declared that by 2010, 15 million tourists should be coming every year to experience capitalism's unfettered bounty. In service of that aim, Dubai's massive construction companies, which are all either fully or partly owned by the royal family (despite the fact that they compete with each other), are building ever bigger apartment developments and shopping malls and five-star hotels. The Jumeirah Palm alone will, when it is finished, be home to thirty-two new five-star hotels. And every one of those will, in turn, be home to multiple restaurants.

This is why I have a free suite at the five-star Grosvenor House Hotel down by the marina, my very own white Mercedes limousine to drive me around town and a butler called Rajesh. I can't claim this was unplanned. Startled by the prices in Moscow, I had decided to look closely at my finances. I had concluded that if I really was to avoid taking complimentary meals, I would have to make a few policy decisions. Firstly, I would have to eat by myself in the seriously expensive places, as I had done at Al Mahara. Secondly, I would have shamelessly to take any other non-food freebies that came my way, and the hoteliers of Dubai, desperate to promote themselves, hadn't been slow to come forward with generous offers.

Granted, the butler was a bit unnecessary. I really didn't need him to deliver up the fresh trays of canapés every afternoon (though I did like the foie gras pâté on toast), and there was no way I was going to let Rajesh polish my shoes, however much he begged. The moment he clocked my cheap man-made soles he would have had me for a fake. Still, it was nice to have the sitting room and the two plasma-screen televisions. It was also handy to have the big white car to take me to the Mall of the Emirates so I could have a look at the 400-metre indoor ski slope, complete with real snow, and study the menu at St Moritz, the Swiss café at the bottom. Although I had come to Dubai in winter, the temperature was still in the mid-twenties. And yet, at St Moritz, you could get a fondue.

Before my trip I had met chefs across London who were working on ventures in Dubai or who had been approached about sweetheart deals. Guillaume Rochette, the catering recruitment consultant who had been supplying chefs to Moscow, now had an office in Dubai too, and talked excitedly of the money to be made there and the deals to be brokered. Dubai, he said, was about a commodity called lifestyle, and an expression of that lifestyle was restaurants. Alan Yau said he had plans for four or five places in Dubai, and the British celebrity chef Gary Rhodes had just signed a deal, regardless of the fact that his whole career was based on a style of hearty cooking – Lancashire hotpot, oxtail stew, mutton pie – that drew on the traditions of a temperate northern European country.

It didn't matter that there was less access to local ingredients here than in Las Vegas. It made no difference that the place was bereft of cultural context, that even the rare examples of Arabic architecture felt as artificial as the ski slopes. Dubai had a hunger for wealthy people and wealthy people have a hunger for food.

For one British chef, none of this was news. He had spotted what was happening in Dubai years before anyone else, opening his first restaurant outside Britain in 2001 at the Hilton Dubai Creek. By all accounts Verre wasn't bad either. The local edition of *Time Out* had given it numerous awards, and whenever I asked locals to list the best restaurants in the city it was always among the top five. As a result, bookings were notoriously hard to come by. Happily, though, I had managed to secure one. It was time to visit a Gordon Ramsay restaurant.

I first ate Gordon Ramsay's food in 1995 when he was cooking at Aubergine, a restaurant in London's Chelsea. It would suit the narrative if I could now claim it was the best meal I had eaten up to that point, but it wasn't; a remarkable place called Le Champignon Sauvage in Cheltenham still held that honour. (Oh, that mint chocolate soufflé!) But there was no doubting the talent at work. I remember a single, fat lobster raviolo in an intense shellfish velouté, versions of which would become one of the chef's signature dishes.

At the end of the meal there were three tiny crème brûlées,

flavoured with thyme, marjoram and basil, though the waiters did not announce this. They insisted we had to guess what the flavourings were. I thought this more than a little cute: I didn't go to expensive restaurants to guess my pudding. Still, they were good.

A few years later Ramsay had an argument with his employers and walked out, taking the entire staff with him. Backed by £1 million of his father-in-law's money, he reopened at the site of a nearby restaurant called La Tante Claire on Royal Hospital Road, which had boasted three Michelin stars. In 2001 Ramsay won his own third star and, while he had not embarked on his full-blown TV career by then – he was still slagging off chefs who dared to moonlight on the small screen – he was already gathering notoriety. He had appeared in a fly-on-the-wall documentary series, *Boiling Point*, in which he managed to use the word 'fuck' as a noun, verb, adverb, adjective and, just occasionally, as an expletive. He threw Joan Collins out of his restaurant for the sin of being in the company of the scabrous restaurant critic A. A. Gill. He telephoned newspaper gossip columnists to tell them exactly what he had just done.

It was later the same year that the scale of his ambition became obvious: he announced he was taking over the dining room at Claridge's, arguably London's grandest hotel. The Claridge's restaurant, which was derided by some critics for having too many tables and for turning them too quickly in a desperate grab for profit, never managed to go beyond a single star, but Ramsay seemed unconcerned. He began eating up the hotel dining rooms of London, using the cooks who had been with him since Aubergine days until, by 2007, he had interests in eight (plus two pubs).

Ramsay published cookbooks. He wrote newspaper cookery columns. He took up sponsorship deals with everyone from crockery manufacturers to high-street liquor retailers, and discovered that television wasn't so bad after all. He fronted the reality show *Hell's Kitchen* both in the UK and the US, and made multiple series of *Ramsay's Kitchen Nightmares*, in which he went into failing restaurants, turned them round, stripped off to the waist and said 'fuck' a lot. His face, which didn't so much look lived in as under multiple occupancy, was everywhere.

Inevitably questions began to be asked about how much cooking Ramsay now did. The chef had a stock answer: 'People ask me who does the cooking when I'm not there and I tell them it's the same people who do the cooking when I am there,' he told me in spring 2006. 'I remember being asked that question by a journalist in a very expensive Armani suit. I asked her whether she thought Giorgio had stitched every single seam on her suit. Obviously not.'

There were also questions over the food itself. Back in the mid-1990s the appearance of herbs that would normally be associated with savoury courses, in desserts like those crème brûlées, was modish, forward-thinking, almost cutting edge. But even back then a new movement was developing quietly which would eventually make a basil crème brûlée look as staid as a rum baba. A few years before, a young Catalan chef called Ferran Adria had put a tomato on the end of a bicycle pump, blown it up and created, to his surprise, a tomato foam.

At his restaurant El Bulli, a gruelling two-hour drive north of Barcelona, Adria began experimenting. He investigated the science of food and the conventions of the restaurant. He created hot savoury jellies and aromatic foams that sparkled on the tongue before disappearing to nothing, leaving only the echo of flavour. He broke away from the traditional three courses to serve twenty, thirty, even forty tiny bites. He used *sous vide* machines to cook under vacuum, paired savoury with sweet and was hailed as the founder of a movement in cookery as groundbreaking as nouvelle cuisine had been in the 1970s. Almost a century after it had revolutionised literature, music and the visual arts, modernism had finally come to the kitchen.

Within a few years others were pursuing similar ideas. At the Fat Duck in the *über*-English village of Bray, the self-taught Heston Blumenthal put white chocolate and caviar together, served a pudding of smoky-bacon ice cream and made a dish of snail porridge, all of which eventually won him his third Michelin star. In the mountains of France, Marc Veyrat gave diners syringes with which to inject their food with sauces made from foraged herbs and wildflowers, and in New York, at WD-50, a chef called Wylie Dufresne made a deep-fried mayonnaise. No meal cooked by any self-respecting with-it chef was now complete without foams and jellies and savoury ice creams and meat and fish cooked at low temperature under vacuum.

Ramsay stuck rigidly to his neo-classicism, to his fillets of beef with Madeira *jus* and his caramelised tarte tatins of apples with vanilla ice cream. He was convinced there was a market for it, and it was hard to argue with him, as new projects were announced with dizzying regularity. In the autumn of 2006 he celebrated his fortieth birthday by opening a restaurant in New York and revealing plans for further restaurants in Florida, Los Angeles, Prague, Dublin,

Amsterdam, Paris and Australia. It looked like Ramsay was intent on conquering the world.

That summer his flagship restaurant, Restaurant Gordon Ramsay, on Royal Hospital Road, had been closed so the dining room could be renovated and the kitchen upgraded. Ramsay also announced he was putting in an £80,000 webcam system. 'That way, I'll be able to see what's going on in all my restaurants around the world,' he told me. 'We'll have clocks up for the different time zones too. It will look like a fucking investment bank in there.'

By then it was clear that the Royal Hospital Road restaurant, with its three Michelin stars, was no longer just an expensive place where people went for something to eat. It was the rock upon which an entire brand had been built. This made a kind of sense because the economics of the Michelin-three-star restaurants had become increasingly unsustainable. While Michelin was notoriously coy about the criteria upon which they based their awards, it was generally understood that, for a restaurant to win three stars, it had to have a staff-to-diners ratio of at least one to one. If there were forty-four seats, as there are at Royal Hospital Road, there had to be at least forty-four staff, as indeed there are. Making a profit with this sort of head count is very tough indeed, so for many three-star chefs their flagship restaurants had become loss leaders, out of which other profitable businesses – cheaper brasseries, outside catering operations – could be spun.

This made Verre in Dubai intriguing. After all, if a major factor in the luxury experience is the number of people you are able to employ, then in a place like Dubai, where labour is relatively cheap, it should be easier to deliver a high-quality experience. Shouldn't it?

Early on the day I ate at Verre, I went to meet the head chef, a bald-headed, cheerful Mancunian called Jason Whitelock. When Verre first opened, it was overseen by Angela Hartnett, one of the cooks from Ramsay's Aubergine days, who would eventually go on to take over the Connaught for the group. Whitelock had never worked for Ramsay before taking on the position at Verre, though he said cooking the dishes was not difficult. He was in constant contact with Ramsay's executive chef, Mark Askew, in London, and Ramsay himself came over twice a year. The real problem was the ingredients.

'Don't eat the veal tonight,' he said. 'My original consignment got rejected at customs because the labels weren't right.' Bureaucracy was the curse of his life, he told me. All meat coming into Dubai has to be halal, literally permissible under Islamic law, which means, among other things, that it has to be drained of blood (as with koshered meat). This may make it virtuous to Muslims, but to greedy men like me it's disastrous. Cooking halal meat so it is not completely tough or dry requires real skill.

'Under the Dubai rules it needs to go through customs no more than two weeks after slaughter so it also can't be aged,' Whitelock said, with a sorry shake of his big, domed head. Later he showed me a piece of beef that, he told me, was actually pretty good compared with some they had received. Drained of blood, it was a peculiar shade of pink, more like veal than matured beef.

He could use pork, but he needed a special licence for it and a separate kitchen in which to prepare it, plus everything had to arrive by air. Back in Britain, he was used to receiving shellfish that were still alive when they came into his kitchen. 'In the two and half years I've been here,' Whitelock said, 'I haven't seen a langoustine move.'

Then there was local taste. Some ingredients simply didn't sell. If he brought in pigeon, he told me, they would lie in the fridge for a week, neglected by the customers until, in desperation, he would turn them into a terrine. 'And then I would eat the terrine.' He also found himself serving a lot of meat well done. 'It kills us to overcook meat like that,' he said, 'but you have to give the customers what they want.'

What about the staff?

Bar the four or five Europeans supplied by Ramsay, the rest were generally from the Indian subcontinent. 'They are great,' he says. 'They are not like British cooks, who constantly want to change things. They have no interest in that. They just want to do it the same every time. Problem is, on their days off they go away and eat these serious curries. It blows their taste buds. You really have to watch the seasoning after that.'

It does not make me relish the prospect of the meal to come, and nor does the setting. Granted, the Hilton Dubai Creek looks better at night than it does by day but, even so, it still has something of the 1970s disco fantastic about it. Everything is chrome and angular black leather sofas and spotlights. All the lobby lacks is a mirror ball and Gloria Gaynor tottering on roller skates in tight Spandex. Upstairs, the dining room is reached through an automatic door that hisses and puffs on its hydraulics with such regularity during the meal that it begins to sound like a patient on a respirator in an intensive-care unit. Even allowing for the trademark Ramsay shade of purple, the dining room itself still manages to avoid exuding glamour, much as Dick Cheney has always studiously avoided exuding glamour. Above the main banquette is a shelf bearing a straggly line of white tinsel and miniature plastic Santas. It says much that, in this setting, it doesn't look out of place.

Mostly, though, I am struck by the people. Outside on the pavement, I had been in an Emirate on the eastern seaboard of the Arabian Peninsula. Inside, I might as well be in a small commuter town in southern England. There is one Emerati couple. He is in traditional white flowing robes and headdress. She is veiled over her head and up to her chin, revealing only the smallest patch of beautifully made-up face. Other than that, the dining room is full of the mousy, white, English middle classes sitting nervously opposite each other, speaking in hushed voices, as if terrified that an overly demonstrative Continental waiter is about to do something to them they will find humiliating or baffling or both. There is an uneasy stiffness to these couples. They all look like they think tonight will end in an argument.

These people had come for the Gordon Ramsay experience, and if the man himself had popped out of the kitchen and told them all to fuck off, just like he does on TV, they would probably have been quite happy.

Instead they have to deal with a tall, garrulous Italian called Lucca, who keeps clapping his hands together and jovially asking people how dinner is going. Clearly they hate it. They abhor it. They want Lucca to go away. This is a constant failing of the English in restaurants. They don't like being waited on. They find the whole process excruciatingly embarrassing, more akin to an internal examination by an unfamiliar doctor of the opposite gender than a part of the dining experience to be relished, as if every part of it was designed not to enable them to eat nice stuff, but to make them look like total idiots. An offer of bread is to be treated with suspicion, the tasting of the wine an obvious and blatant trap. (It's why the English middle classes don't complain when things go wrong in restaurants, preferring instead to whine incessantly only when they've left the place and there's nothing that can be done about it.)

Here they sit now, this type I know so well, eyes scanning the menus furiously in search of things designed to catch them out. They mutter at each other about the fortunes of Manchester United and the weather – really! They do! – and steer clear of any dishes using words they think they might mispronounce.

The food, though, is good. In places it is better than good. It is sparkling, in its unshocking, very familiar sort of way. There is a crystal-clear minestrone, bursting with flavour, over a single cheese tortellini. There is a complex dish of scallops and braised pork belly, a re-engineered surf and turf, with seared watermelon, which shouldn't work but does, on a bright, ginger velouté. There is a firm piece of halibut, with a risotto that is so little rice and so many other things it barely deserves the name but which holds its corner against a powerful lobster sauce. There is a fillet of that beef, which is surprisingly good, tender and flavourful, despite having been drained of its life force. It comes with a slab of seared foie gras and a few other things besides. At the end there is a crème brûlée – *sans* herbs – with leaves of dried strawberry tucked in under the crisp burnt-sugar top so it resembles a flower.

Noble to the end, I work my way through these last delicate petals. The unavoidable truth is, however, that I have been served an absurd amount of food and I am now very full. I'm not sure there was any way round this. Although I had insisted upon receiving a bill, I had secured my booking through Gordon Ramsay's PR company. This meant that, while they might not be comping me, they were determined I was going to get the works. At the beginning of the meal Lucca had handed me both the basic menu and the grandly titled seven-course 'menu prestige' at £67 a head. ('What a blatant, cynical piece of upselling,' wrote one British restaurant critic of the menu prestige when she came across it at the Royal Hospital Road restaurant in London. She described it as merely 'a way of making the punter who doesn't choose it feel like the poor relation. What are they getting? The "menu déclassé"?')

'If you don't order the menu prestige,' Lucca said, with what I thought sounded like a hint of menace, 'the chef's still going to send you out some extra dishes.' I had no reason to doubt him. The same had happened at Al Mahara and would, I was certain, happen elsewhere too. These extra courses, these chef's gifts, were unrefusable and unleavable. I had to eat them. Under the fierce glare of the kitchen's attention I had to eat everything. I ordered the menu prestige. After all, I told myself, compared with the same deal at Royal Hospital Road, where it was £110, this was practically a bargain.

It was still too much food. At the meal's end I felt not so much as if I had been served my dinner as assaulted by it, and dinner had won. All I could think about, as the artificial respirator of a door puffed me out into the hotel foyer, was just how much work I would have to do in the gym the next day.

I have never been thin. There is a picture of me taken shortly before my sixth or seventh birthday party, all toothy grin and flowing cravat (the bar mitzvah outfit was not without precedent) and, looking at it, I can see my weight was probably about normal. I don't recall feeling normal, even then. I did not come from a family of normal people. Normal people were thin and we were certainly not that. I would like to attribute this to something hidden in the genes: a couch potato of a metabolism specifically engineered to cope with the harsh winters of Eastern Europe whence we had come, by storing as fat any of the scarce calories that came our way. As various members of my immediate family have struggled with their weight over the years, there might indeed be something in this, but the truth is far simpler: we over-ate. Arguably my mother put too much food on the table at times, but she was pushing at an open door. In my family, when she lifted the serving spoon we all lifted our plates.

I recall dieting for the first time when I was about eight, a curious and mathematically taxing regime that involved giving scores to the various food groups and then attempting not to go over a given total of units for each day. At twelve I went on an egg diet, which made my breath stink. Only when I was sixteen, and my waist had topped 44 inches, did I achieve any measure of success, though not with a carefully designed programme. I simply ate less. Of course the weight crept up again and, over the years, I would have to intervene with my body much as the United Nations has had to intervene in chronic, intractable civil wars.

Eventually, appalled by the notion that I should find a

sensible diet for life as experts insisted – a diet for life? Give me death – I decided exercise was the solution. This was, frankly, bizarre. As a child, the appeal of sport had been lost on me. Partly this was because I was very, very bad at them. Everybody else knew it. Team captains didn't so much avoid choosing me as hope that if they didn't look in my direction, I might not be there. Back then I thought ball control meant wearing tight underpants, and took every opportunity I could not to run anywhere after anything.

In adolescence I bunked off games with like-minded friends and we hid in the woods, learning to smoke and frying cheap sausages over a camping stove. On the one occasion I was forced to participate in sporting activity, I was so appalled by the idea I signed up for golf. I was rubbish at it, of course, but at least I didn't have to take my clothes off.

One day in my late twenties, I went into the local gym, climbed on to a step machine and found I liked it. The step machine didn't judge me. The step machine didn't laugh at me if I fell off, or if I pressed out a paltry 80 calories of burn. Plus I could watch TV while I did it. This seemed the ideal solution and, with modest alteration to my eating habits, eventually had an effect.

Then I became a restaurant critic. You don't need to have a degree in physical fitness and nutrition to recognise this as a very bad idea. It was like putting a smack addict in charge of the medicine cabinet. I spoke to one of my predecessors in the job, who said he had put on 2 stone in three years, and attributed it all to the desserts. I knew another restaurant critic who did it for a dozen years and put on almost 8 stone. I comforted myself with the thought that these were previously thin people, who, like curious virgins unacquainted with the clap, had no idea of the consequences of the world into which they were diving. I was different. I was already promiscuous at the fridge. I knew what eating could do, understood the mathematics of calories and was determined not to let the bitter calculus of food get the better of me.

Still, it was a challenge. The main issue was time. Visiting the gym took so much of it that I had begun driving rather than walking there; in short I had started avoiding exercise to take exercise. So I cancelled my gym membership and bought a huge Nordic cross-tracker, a great chromium thing of handles and paddles with a digital screen that pulsed out flashing digits in diodes the colour of blood. I positioned it in my office at home behind my desk, as an encouragement. I asked my accountant if I could claim the substantial cost against tax.

'I'm afraid not,' he said. 'The truth is, you don't need to be thin to do your job.'

'Perhaps not, but I do need to be alive.'

My accountant laughed. 'The Inland Revenue doesn't care whether you live or die.'

I swallowed the cost and went to work. My day job was meant to have only two stages: eat, then write about it. To this I added a third: atone on the Nordic cross-tracker. I was and always have been godless. Nevertheless I now had my own confessional, a place where, instead of Hail Marys, I cracked out twenty minutes at level six, with another fifteen to follow. At the end, as the endorphins flowed, I slipped gently into a state of careless rapture.

By the time I had decided to investigate the globalisation of high-end restaurants, I knew exactly what the project meant and concluded that, wherever I went, I would need access to a gym. As a result, I was not only eating all over the world; I was also working out all over the world. Each gym had its own character. In Las Vegas, at the MGM Grand, it was full of flinty-eyed executives from the convention circuit, flicking through brochures as they used the treadmill. The Moscow gym had been an afterthought of a windowless box in the basement, and the only other users were late-middle-aged American businessmen, working the steppers tentatively, as though their medical history already listed three minor heart attacks.

In Dubai, where all the users were lissom and tanned young women, the gym looked out over the chaos of the building site that surrounded the Grosvenor House Hotel. New tower blocks were going up, crusted with cranes and warped, rusted steel reinforcements, and roads around them could only be readily identified by the lines of traffic cones that snaked about their fringes. The building sites were so chaotic, so brutal, that I found it impossible to imagine them as anything other than a work in progress. Completion was impossible to contemplate.

I felt something similar about myself. The meals I was eating were so full of hidden traps – unexpected courses, platters of unordered *amuse-bouches* and pre-desserts – that it seemed unlikely that I would ever catch up, however hard I worked out on the machine. Pieces of gym equipment – treadmills, steppers, cross-trackers – have always been about running fast to get nowhere. For me, it felt doubly so.

Still, the morning after my Gordon Ramsay meal, I boarded the Grosvenor House cross-tracker and went to work, determined to fight the good fight. Part of the concern was not just with what I had eaten at Verre but with what I was due to eat that lunchtime. I was very keen to try some Emerati food. I wanted to know what the locals ate. Sure, I could and would try Lebanese, which is to Middle Eastern food what French is to European, but I was certain Emerati would be different. Most people scratched their heads or laughed at me when I enquired. It was unlikely I would get to meet an Emerati person during my trip, they said, let alone eat a few of their specialities.

I was determined, though, and eventually found my way to the World Trade Center Club, perched at the top of the World Trade Center Tower. They had a restaurant up there on the thirty-ninth floor that served a menu of 'international cuisine'. That sounded terrifying, but it turned out they were also one of the biggest caterers for high-class Emerati weddings in Dubai, and traditional Emerati cooking was increasingly popular. They would love to serve me a banquet, I was told by Ed Barnfield, the club's British PR man. He told me this with such enthusiasm, such gusto, that I became anxious. The word 'banquet' sounded ominous. I suggested to him that the chefs really should not overdo it on my account. I was met by the email equivalent of hollow laughter. I had requested Arabic hospitality, and Arabic hospitality was what I was going to get.

I am standing in front of a camel-sized oven, in the aircraft-hangar-sized kitchens at the back of the World Trade Center exhibition halls. It is the only camel-sized oven in Dubai and the executive sous-chef here, a Jordanian called Khalel, is understandably proud of it. The oven, which was built to his design, is 12 feet long, 8 feet high and 6 feet deep. They can cook four camels in here at once, he says. He is a solid man whose face is heavy with geography – big cheeks, deep jowls, full lips, furrowed brow – all offset by long, feminine eyelashes. When I express surprise that they can cook four camels at once, even in an oven as big as this, he says 'baby camels'. Let them grow too old and the meat is as tough as shoe leather, apparently. The best meat, he tells me, 'is twenty-five centimetres under the hump'. I store this piece of information away. It might come in handy one day.

We have not eaten camel today, though it is just about the only thing we have not been fed. I feel a little queasy standing here in front of this oven. Every now and then the flavours of one particular dish from the banquet repeat on me, and not in a good way. I find this flavour so unpleasant, so repulsive, that I wonder whether I'll ever be able to rid myself of it. My mouth has been violated. To distract myself, I try to calculate how many people one could cook in an oven like this, and I conclude about eight, lying side by side. It doesn't help.

Most of the meal was fine, though hardly Emerati. The catering company, like so many of the businesses in Dubai, is run by two thrusting young Indian executives – Indians are the biggest ethnic group here – called Sethu and Rakesh. They are determined to show me a good time. They want me to know about the enormous weddings they have catered, the variety of foods they can offer – they have teams of chefs from China, Thailand and Morocco, among other places – and the enormous numbers of animals they have slaughtered. 'For the biggest wedding we ever did we had to slaughter nine hundred lambs, forty camels, ninety deer and twenty cows,' Sethu says proudly. That fed 7,000 people.

We had eaten lunch at the top of the World Trade Center, in one of the rooms behind the second-biggest advert in the world, which carries the face of Sheikh Mohammed and covers the whole building. Or, to be more precise, I got to taste a sequence of dishes that were so numerous the varied forkfuls added up to one meal. On the table, awaiting us, there were bowls of hummus, baba ganoush, a rich, long-simmered tomato paste flavoured with walnuts and chilli, home-cured salmon and seared prawns, an Iranian salad of cucumber and yoghurt, a bowl of tabbouleh, that traditional mix of chopped flat-leaf parsley dressed with lemon juice, and another of the Lebanese salad fatoush, in which the vegetables are layered with crisp, curling slices of toasted pitta bread. There were lamb and chicken kebabs roasted in Indian tandoors, dainty cheese or meat burrek – small pies – and vegetable samosas from the Punjab.

As each item was introduced to me, like honoured guests at a wedding, I noted with relief that nobody was finishing anything. Still, it didn't mitigate the volume of lunch that was coming at me in waves. I lost count of the platters at two dozen. There was a sweet and sour fish concoction; two biryanis, one with fish and one with chicken; various dense, meaty curries; grilled lobster; a few vegetarian stews; some kofte; something else involving rice and on and on it went. (At dessert the whole process was repeated, with little pots of things made with nuts and dates and honey and spices, with tottering Parisian-style gateaux and even a chocolate crème brûlée.)

There were just three Emerati dishes. The first, called Harris, demands that a cut of veal be cooked in wheat for so long that the meat has completely disintegrated into the grain, which in turn has been worked until there is an elasticity to the glutens. It was a rich and savoury paste, and very, very solid. At each end of the table were ornate silver platters covered, in turn, by vast silver domes. This, I was told, was the main event. These platters were why we were here. As we admired the silverware, Khalel told me that, according to Emerati tradition, animals must be slaughtered as close as possible to the time they are eaten. The two lambs under these domes were, he said, slaughtered at six that morning. I am not at all sentimental about these things. I believe that, if you are going to eat meat, you must face up to what that means: the death of a creature. Nevertheless I found it a little disconcerting that I knew exactly when my lunch had died, not least because I also knew there was almost no chance of us finishing any of this. It seemed grossly wasteful, as had so much of this lunch.

When the first silver dome was lifted, I was relieved to see that a Dubai lamb is rather smaller than its British equivalent, just 4 to 5 kilograms (9 to 11 pounds). The lambs – known as *ouzi* in Arabic – had been cooked long and slow over water in a large pot called a *jidar* so they were steamed to a sweet and delicate tenderness. Khalel admitted that the addition of chestnuts to this first lamb dish was one of his little flourishes and not really traditional but he thought it worked. I agreed.

The second lamb recipe – *ouzi laban* – was, however, made exactly the way it had been taught to Khalel by an Emerati who could trace his family back to 1824. I understood: this little lamb had great lineage. It was culinary nobility. The meat, which had been cooked underneath thin sheets of flat bread, was so tender it could be carved with a spoon and was pale, almost white. This, I was told, was mostly due to the sauce of dried yoghurt with which it had been cooked. There are many foodstuffs I have not heard of before let alone tried – novelty is a pleasure of the job – and dried yoghurt was one of them. (When, I wondered, does dried yoghurt become just cheese?) The moment I put the meat in my mouth I knew why I had never tried it. Dried yoghurt is another way of saying milk that has gone off. It is sour and has an edge of bile that catches at the back of the throat. It has that pungent, acrid attack that is developed by a bottle of milk left in the sun for three days. The flavour was so foul, so putrid, I found it hard to swallow.

I felt guilty about this because everybody had gone to so much trouble on my behalf. What's more, this was one of Khalel's specialities and he seemed like such a nice man – but it was horrible. As I ate my way through the few pieces I thought I could get away with before admitting defeat, I was told this dish was completely authentic. I nodded slowly, my mouth closed. Of that I had absolutely no doubt.

The curse of the A-word

Should anybody ever invite you to sample pressed pig's ear, think very carefully before putting it in your mouth. If chewing on something with the texture of raw kneecap and the flavour profile of a vinyl raincoat appeals, then clearly that pressed pig's ear is for you. Don't hold back. Knock yourself out. Otherwise I can't recommend it. I tried it a few years ago at a new restaurant in London's Chinatown called

Ecapital. I now look back at the review I wrote then and blush.

At the time Ecapital was being lauded by its admirers because it specialises in the cuisine of Shanghai, rather than Canton or Beijing as most of Britain's Chinese places tend to. Ecapital, they said, was the real thing: lots of shredded jellyfish and braised pig's knuckle and pressed pig's ear. When it opened, I said the novelty of its menu was a welcome addition to London's dining scene. It's the sort of rubbish desperate restaurant critics reach for when they are too embarrassed to admit they don't like what they've just eaten, because other people have said it's authentic.

Ah, the A-word! Authenticity, the greatest red herring in gastronomy, the best excuse for putting nasty things in your mouth that any chef has ever come up with. What do you mean you don't like pressed pig's ear? It's the real thing. It's authentic. The problem isn't the dish; it's you. Well, I'm a few years older now and much wiser and more stroppy and prepared to say the problem actually is the dish. I don't care if it's what real Chinese peasants eat. I don't care if Shanghai is overrun by earless pigs because it's so popular. It's horrible and I won't eat it ever again.

In many ways the growing cult of authenticity is a function of the burgeoning global restaurant scene. In other words it's our fault. In a saturated market it is no longer good enough to open a Chinese restaurant. Now it has to be a Chinese restaurant specialising in the food of Shanghai or Zhangzhou or the north-eastern suburbs of Dandong just past the gasworks by the second set of traffic lights on the left. It can't be an Indian restaurant. It has to be Gujarati or Keralan or Goan. Italian restaurants have to be Sardinian or

Neapolitan. Forget Polish; what about the luscious cuisine of Gdansk?

This creates two unique pressures. Firstly, if a chef shrinks the geographical catchment area of their menu, naturally they narrow the number of dishes from which they can build that menu. At some point they are bound to alight upon something truly horrible because it happens to be all the rage in, say, downtown Tbilisi. Secondly, if they make such a song and dance about their restaurant being a genuine reflection of the food diners might find on their holidays (if they were unlucky enough to spend two weeks in Tbilisi), they can hardly then start reinterpreting the dishes. They are immediately in thrall to the demands of authenticity. The chef has to do it the 'correct' way.

But here's the real problem: dishes lauded for their authenticity are either created out of necessity – would *ouzi laban* have been prepared with dried yoghurt if fresh yoghurt had been manageable in the desert climate? – or they are those eaten by poor people, and most poor people's food is not pleasant. Why did anybody in Shanghai have the stupid idea of pressing the pig's ear in the first place? Because they like pig's ear? No. Because they were broke and couldn't afford to waste anything, not even the nasty, bristled ears. The wealthy don't eat pig's ear. They eat the expensive bits like loin and leg.

Meanwhile the poor get by on what they have to hand, resulting in some wretched dishes. Take that great Cantonese delicacy of long-braised chicken's feet. There is no meat on a chicken's foot. Just skin, cartilage and bone, but when a chicken is a precious and expensive object, nothing can be thrown away, including the toenails. Or there's my mother's perfectly authentic boiled gefilte fish, which, long before I had been able to think about these things, I knew I hated on principle. The Jews made a serious effort to escape a life of grinding poverty. The last thing I ever intend to do is glamorise the world from which they came by clinging to traditional dishes simply because they have been labelled authentic.

Of course, my resistance to the cult of authenticity is all well and good. It's a perfectly defensible intellectual position, a great subject for debate. But it is of no help whatsoever if you happen to find yourself sitting with a mouth full of baby sheep that has been doused in stinky, soured milk, while you are being watched by a table of eager hosts who have been up since before dawn just to make sure you have the meal of a lifetime. I took a deep breath, swallowed, smiled and said the only thing that came to me: 'What an interesting dish.'

I ran my tongue round my mouth and wondered how long it would take for the taste to subside.

It is the next morning and I am sitting in the City Star Restaurant in the Al Quoiz district of the city. Across the table from me is a Pakistani journalist called Malik. As long as I protect his identity he is happy to show me the hidden Dubai, the one the authorities don't like him writing about. Malik has already done a good job. Last night he took me to the Cyclone Club, a barn of a place draped in fairy lights in the old town where 250 neatly turned-out Chinese hookers stood in lines, trying to attract the attention of anybody with testicles and a wallet.

Dubai

The Dubai authorities enforce strict laws on morality. Mixed couples are not allowed to live together if they are unmarried, and the Internet is fiercely regulated so that access is barred to any site whose contents are deemed 'inconsistent with the religious, cultural, political and moral values of the United Arab Emirates'.

They don't seem to care about the trade in prostitutes. The expatriate men like their services and Dubai needs the expatriate men. The only rule the Cyclone enforces is that the girls prove they are over twenty-one before being allowed into a place where alcohol is served. We strolled around the room, trying to look casual, and as I passed, lines of pretty Chinese women reached out to tug at my sleeve with a call of 'Hey fella, hey fella.'

Malik suggested we talk to a few of them. I shook my head. 'I am so far out of my comfort zone here,' I said, and slugged my beer.

He told me to finish my drink and took me instead to Pancho Villa's, a seedy club in the Astoria Hotel, once a favourite haunt of the international security services who have long liked to hang out in Dubai keeping tabs on each other. In the 1980s Pancho Villa's Dance Club was famed for its Tex-Mex food, which was reputed to be the best on the Arabian Peninsula, though there is no record of how much competition it had. When we arrived, a belly-dancer was entertaining the sweaty crowds, and hookers from West Africa reached out, not to tug at my sleeve but to grab my arse with a raucous, throaty laugh.

'The real Dubai,' Malik said, with a grin. 'It's a crazy place.' He was amused by my discomfort.

As the prostitutes groped me, I told him about the

restaurants I had been eating in, with their mineral-water lists and their tasting menus. Which is why, this morning, he has brought me here to the City Star. It is a noisy, cluttered room of chipped Formica tables and greasy tiled floors. Fans that buzz and clank from years of hard work fight to keep the heat at bay. Outside, on a painted board, the menu makes a virtue of the cheaper cuts. It reads, 'Brain fry, kidney fry,' and, for those with a few extra dirham, 'chicken fry.' Around us, men from across the Indian subcontinent – Pakistan, Bangladesh, Sri Lanka, India – sit hoovering up buttery flatbreads, samosas and milky cups of sugary tea.

At Al Mahara a meal costs 1,000 dirhams (about £130). At the City Star it is about 3 dirhams (or 30p), which suits the economy in this part of town. Malik offers me some of his vegetable samosa and I try to resist. This place really is filthy, and a bout of gastric distress, brought on as much by meeting unfamiliar bugs as toxic ones, would not be helpful. But I realise I can't refuse and chew on the flaky pastry and the soggy filling of potato and peas seasoned with garlic, chilli and turmeric. It's pretty good, even at 7.30 a.m.

Malik has brought me to where the labourers live, in square concrete blocks, ten to a room, thirty to a bathroom; to where the sides of the road are piled with rubbish, and stinking rivulets of water run in what passes for the gutters.

'The glittering Dubai was built on tears, man,' Malik says. He is small and squat, with bloodshot eyes that only emphasise the intensity with which he speaks. He smokes too much and punctuates his conversation with a jab of the burning cigarette invariably caught in his knuckles. 'Most of the workers are trapped. They are forced to stay here because of the loans they have taken out back home to pay travel agents and recruitment agents to get them here in the first place. It's a vicious circle.'

This is not hyperbole. A 2006 report by the pressure group Human Rights Watch into the conditions faced by the 500,000 migrant construction workers employed in the UAE described appalling conditions. It is standard practice for newly arrived workers to have their passports taken away by their employers so they can't abscond, and for wages – on average just $175 a month – to be withheld for months on end, forcing labourers to stay in the hope of finally getting their money. In 2004 the Dubai municipality admitted thirty-four of these men had died building the towers and islands that were putting Dubai on the map; the magazine *Construction Week* had found evidence that closer to 880 had actually perished.

The hours are gruelling, particularly in the fearsome heat – temperatures can reach the high forties – and there is little regard for the damage done to the human body by working in such conditions. In the summer of 2004 it was estimated that 5,000 men had been brought into the Accident and Emergency department of just one Dubai hospital. Critics have called the conditions a return to serfdom and little more than indentured slavery.

The migrant workers, increasingly with nothing to lose, had started to kick back, though. There had been protests as unpaid men poured off the building sites to block the Sheikh Zayed Road, the main highway through Dubai. These protests had led to riots as tensions overflowed and, with the release of the Human Rights Watch report, the government had finally committed itself to cleaning up the industry. More inspectors were being employed, and construction firms were being threatened with having their contracts curtailed if they didn't stop abusing their employees.

There is still no disguising just how grim life remains down here, only a few minutes in the wrong direction from the Sheikh Zayed Road. The air stinks of sewage, and as we drive around we can see down long, cramped concrete canyons between the hastily built accommodation blocks. The world here is entirely male. There are no women, no children. The men will see their families perhaps once a year on trips home.

'It's true money is going back to India, Pakistan and Sri Lanka that wouldn't otherwise be going back,' Malik says, 'but that doesn't mean the system isn't corrupted and twisted.'

I say, 'This place really is terrible.'

He says, 'There's worse.'

We drive to the Jebel Ali district, where gentle hills rise and fall, and the tightly packed accommodation blocks give way to an industrial wasteland of electricity pylons and corrugated sheds on dusty, rutted red earth. We turn on to an unmetalled road leading up a hill and follow a chuntering tanker marked 'Portable water'.

'If anybody stops us, just say you're going to one of the churches,' Malik says. Although Dubai is Muslim, other religions (apart from Judaism) are tolerated. Up here, at the top of the hill, the churches are crammed together. There is a church for the Anglicans, one for the Episcopalians and another for the Evangelicals. A new Greek Orthodox church is also being built. We park around the side of the Catholic church, and Malik points down into the valley. A short distance below us, ringed by high wire fencing, is a tightly packed compound of perhaps 1,000 Portakabins. At least ten workers will live in each of those cabins. There is no drinking water down there, Malik explains, hence the tanker. I ask if we could go in. He shakes his head. The gates are guarded against people like us, he says.

Malik lights up a cigarette and we stand in silence, looking down upon the compound. I realise that a few years ago, in another life, these camps would have been my reason for coming to Dubai, the story I would have covered. The city's restaurants would simply have been the way I rewarded myself for a hard day's work. Now the restaurants *are* the work, and I have come to look at the labour camps not because I want to, not because I need to, but because I feel I should. It is an uncomfortable thought. It leaves a nasty taste in the mouth, one that goes far, far beyond the vicious confection that was lamb in a dried yoghurt sauce. I tell Malik we should go.

I realise now that I am still searching for the quintessential Dubai experience, the one that sums up the place in the way that Pushkin, with its mix of play food, sentimentality and sky-high prices, sums up Moscow; but it is difficult to get a handle on this city. Many of the signs are in Arabic. The spoken language is English. Most people are Indian. The food is from everywhere. The restaurant critic is confused.

I visit Indego, the high-end Indian restaurant at Grosvenor House, where the British-based chef Vineet Bhatia is the consultant. In Moscow, at Indus, where he had the same sort of consultancy deal, his food had been castrated to suit the

Russian palate, and without the aid of anaesthetic. Nothing had been done to mitigate the loss of heat. It was the culinary equivalent of beige. Here, the chillies are back and I recognise the Bhatia dishes that I have loved so much in London: the tandoori-spiced, home-smoked tranche of salmon, the aromatic biryanis and the crisp chocolate and almond samosas. (How could anyone resist a dish that uses the words 'crisp' and 'chocolate' so close together?) I feel comfortable eating this food. Quickly I realise why. As so many of the people I am having contact with in Dubai are Indian – the waiters and the cooks, the doormen, the receptionist and butlers – it feels right to be eating Indian food served by Indian people. Except of course that I am still a bloody long way from India.

I take a trip to the Emirates Towers Hotel for a long, lazy dinner at Al Nafoorah, which is regarded by many people I talk to as the best Lebanese restaurant in Dubai. I am there with Guillaume Rochette, who, as in Moscow, happens to be in town at the same time as me. I take the opportunity to ask him whether Mrs Putin really did have money invested in the restaurant she had suddenly arrived at, the day he had taken me to meet Arkady Novikov.

Rochette, keen not to betray a good client's confidences, purses his lips in a showy display of keeping his silence, but he is a noisy Frenchman, incapable of muting his body language, and he rolls his eyes theatrically as if to say: the naïvety of this boy! Why else would the Russian president's wife spend forty-five minutes touring an unopened restaurant?

We drink a bottle of Château Musar, the soot-black Lebanese red from the Beka Valley that kept being produced throughout that country's civil war in the 1980s, and eat fatoush, a lusciously smooth hummus and great smoky skewers of expertly grilled lamb and chicken. Quickly we begin to imagine that this is the Middle East we are really in, when of course Lebanon and the United Arab Emirates are not the same thing at all.

One morning I am taken by the French executive chef of the Grosvenor House, Patrick Lannes, to meet a seventy-year-old Bostonian who has just arrived in town. The moment we see each other I feel only pity for him. This Bostonian is a 12-pound lobster, dragged out of the chill waters off America's north-east shore only forty-eight hours previously. He is a huge, black-blue thing, with 2-foot long pincers that are misshapen and gnarled from years of growth. He is still alive, but sluggish and heavy of claw.

I point out to Lannes that, at this advanced age, the lobster will make for very poor eating, the meat woody, tough and flavourless.

'Perhaps,' the chef says, staring admiringly at him over the top of his fashionable black-framed glasses, 'but he will make a very impressive centrepiece for the New Year's Eve buffet.' Life in Dubai is a parade, a raucous spectacle and, after surviving for seventy years, this lobster will now die to become a part of it.

That night I go for a dinner with a brassy Mancunian woman called Gail Colclough, who was once the private DJ for the Sultan of Brunei's brother and his harem. 'They wanted a woman because they didn't trust a man around the girls,' Gail says, over Barbie-pink daquiris. 'It was the largest private rig in the world. The lights were so powerful they kept setting fire to the curtains.'

Was she a part of the harem?

'No, love. I just put on the Abba.' She took the job, she says, because she wanted to find out if the richest people in the world were happy. 'In the end it was pity that drove me away. They were all sad. They were the saddest people I'd ever met.'

So she left Brunei and came to Dubai, where she promotes tours by British stand-up comedians and runs package holidays for wealthy women who want a little cosmetic surgery done while they are in town. Cosmetic surgery is booming in Dubai. 'Liposuction is the most popular,' she says. 'After that it's breast enlargements and facelifts.' She arranges a lot of facelifts.

Gail is such a remarkable source of stories, delivered in such a deadpan manner, that she almost manages to distract me from the curious food being served to us at Tang, which is located inside a beach hotel not far from the Jumeirah Palm. The young chef, Stephane Buchholzer, has become enamoured of the cooking of Ferran Adria at El Bulli, even though he has never eaten there. So there is a deconstructed Niçoise salad: raw tuna wrapped in a lettuce leaf, alongside powders of olive, green beans, garlic and tomato, all topped with a foam of smoked egg. I drag the fish through the powders and it almost tastes like a Niçoise, but not quite.

Strands of crab come wrapped in dehydrated mango and sprinkled with liquorice powder, and foie gras is served with tubes of coffee-flavoured gel. The young team is enthusiastic about what they are doing and it seems churlish to point out that I have seen versions of all these dishes at restaurants in London and New York. One thing is certain: theirs will be the only place specialising in this kind of culinary mischief for 1,500 miles in any direction. That is an achievement of sorts, and a mark of the speed with which ideas are now disseminated round the world. If a dish is served in the Catalan hills one week, it will be on a menu on the other side of the world the next.

None of these adventures manage to sum up Dubai for me. No matter. I now know what I have to do. I ask my butler to call up the limo so I can return to the Mall of the Emirates.

I take a table at the St Moritz Café and sit next to the plate-glass window looking into Ski Dubai, where children in salopettes throw snowballs at each other, skid down icy slopes on their bottoms and laugh uproariously. Next to me is a fireplace where logs burn fiercely, casting a warming glow across my table. Except that it is not a real fire, but an image of one on a 60-inch plasma screen fitted into the fireplace. Naturally, I order the fondue.

My wife is half-Swiss. As a result, fondues have been eaten without irony in our house for many years. I know a lot about them. I know about the need to rub the pot with cut garlic to start, and I understand the careful mix of salty Gruyère for flavour and waxy, dull Emmental for bulk, and what temperature to heat the wine to before the melting can begin. Of course, the fondue served here is awful. How could it be otherwise? St Moritz is unlicensed so they cannot use wine, and there is a graininess to the melted cheese that speaks of much too much flour to thicken it, but there is a guttering paraffin burner, a basket of cut bread and a prong with which to introduce it to the cheese.

Outside the Mall of the Emirates, it is 23 degrees Celsius, which only adds to the experience. The televisual logs crackle, the children rub snow into each other's hair, and I eat my fondue and revel in the glorious fakery of it all. I am afloat on the seas of the twenty-first century, enjoying a lunch that only modern technology could gift me. The fondue part of it should be comforting. It should have grounded me. Instead the whole experience is so bizarre, so contrived, I quickly realise I am in the grips of an intense culture shock. I conclude this is no bad thing. I regard it as an initiation, a taste of things to come – because where I'm going next I'll be getting an awful lot of that.

4. Tokyo

My cab driver is lost. This is not a criticism. All Tokyo cab drivers are lost for most of the time, and mine, a tidy middle-aged gentleman in the standard uniform of black jacket, white collar and tie, is no different. Or, to be more precise, he knows where he is but he has no idea how to get me to where I need to go. Few of the city's streets have names and most addresses are merely descriptive – third door along on the left, just past the big tower block opposite the park – which makes the end of many journeys a random event. One might imagine that, after years of having to deal with the problem, the drivers would have devised a cunning strategy to get round it, but they haven't. They have merely made an accommodation with it, submitted to its chaos, and I have been told I should do the same.

Which is why, despite nine time zones of jet lag and a pathological tendency to control freakery, I am not at all bothered when the driver swerves to the side of the road, flings open the door, jumps out and disappears on foot down a shadowed alley in search of my destination, leaving me alone in the cab, its engine idling. If anything, I am pleased. It means the restaurant I am about to visit is the real thing, a place of such refinement and exclusivity that, despite the likely size of the bill and the difficulty of securing a reservation, almost nobody has ever heard of it.

Tokyo's restaurant world has proved a steep learning curve for me. In the other cities I have visited, identifying the top restaurants has been a breeze, hardly demanding the investigative talents of, say, a Bob Woodward or Carl Bernstein. In Las Vegas it had to be the restaurants of Robuchon and Keller. In Moscow it had to be Pushkin and Turandot. In Dubai it had to be Al Mahara, Ramsay and the rest. In Tokyo nothing is obvious. Sure, there are the cloned outposts of the Western chefs, the restaurant of Pierre Gagnaire, say, or – stifle the yawn – Robuchon and Ramsay. What fascinates me about Tokyo is not merely its appetite for non-Japanese food, which is both deep and broad, but its parallel commitment to its own culinary traditions. I had been told stories about tiny high-end places, hidden away in apartment buildings or in the basements of office blocks, serving intricate menus of extraordinary clarity and precision to just four or six people. There were dozens of them. The problem was that I didn't know any of their names, let alone how to book myself a seat.

I called Pim Techamuanvivit, the San Francisco-based Thai woman whose website, Chez Pim, has become one of the most famous food blogs in the world. She used to undertake complicated behavioural research for high-tech companies in Silicon Valley and now spends the cash she made there travelling the world, eating in expensive restaurants and photographing her dinner for her blog. I told her what I was looking for.

She laughed. 'They won't let you in.'

'Why not?'

'You're a round-eye. Plus,' she said, 'you don't speak Japanese.' She told me about a Japanese-American friend of hers who had considered herself reasonably fluent in Japanese, until she was refused bookings at some high-end Tokyo place because her grasp of the language was not considered good enough. I shouldn't feel put out, Pim said. Many of these restaurants are closed to Japanese people too. A lot of them won't grant you entry unless you are recommended by an existing customer; ideally one who is related to you by blood. Then there was the bill to worry about. She told me $1,000 a head wasn't uncommon.

The money thing was frightening. Into my mind came an image of my platinum credit card, that dear sliver of gunmetal-grey plastic that had become such a friend to me on this journey, now suddenly belching smoke, *Mission: Impossible*-style, as it came into contact with the bill. Otherwise I liked what I was hearing. I still appreciated the notion of democracy attached to high-end restaurants – the way the price of dinner might buy you a glimpse of a plutocrat's gilded life – but I liked this Japanese idea of specialness even more. Getting into these restaurants wasn't simply about financial heft; it was about connections, about proving your worth in other ways.

It was, of course, completely undemocratic, grossly elitist and, being rooted in an unspoken anti-Western racism, utterly reprehensible. Even so, I couldn't stop myself imagining that there was a direct and positive correlation between the difficulty in obtaining a booking and the unalloyed deliciousness of the food available. As I pursued these reservations, I became convinced that, simply by landing them, I would mark myself out as some kind of hardcore gastronomic ninja, a seeker after true taste. I would be the Roald Amundsen of the table, the Ernest Shackleton of the sushi bar. High-end Japanese restaurants are like that. They can turn you just a little bit mad.

One day, not long before my trip, I went to see Jean-Luc Naret, the French head of the Michelin restaurant guides, who was in London to launch the new British edition. Though it hadn't yet been announced officially, it was suspected that Michelin was working on a Tokyo guide. I told Naret what I was looking for, that I wanted the names of the really small places, serving only the good stuff, and he promised to help me. As requested, I emailed him. He never replied.

I called Mark Edwards, the London-based executive chef for the Nobu Group worldwide. I asked him for recommendations. He said he could do better than that. He said he could get Nobu to book them for me.

Nobu!

Booking tables!

FOR ME!

I was a made man. Surely every door would open now? Nobu Matsuhisa himself – the man responsible for spreading the doctrine of high-end Japanese food about the world, Robert De Niro's best pal, the one who feeds all those slinky models and actresses who don't eat – he was going to play concierge just for me. He was going to get me dinner dates. Job done.

Except it wasn't. Having offered to perform a task I had never asked of him, Edwards stopped returning my calls and emails until it was far too late. The days until my trip slipped away, the window for making impossible-to-get bookings becoming smaller and smaller. I imagined Nobu rolling his eyes at Edwards's request. Reservations? For a London restaurant critic? Don't be so bloody silly. Now plate up some more of the black cod in miso that the skinny models and actresses like to pick at.

With just a week to go until my trip, I threw myself upon the mercy of Hide Yamamoto, the executive chef of the Mandarin Oriental Hotel, where I would be staying. I gave him a budget of $500 a head per meal. Yamamoto said he would see what he could do.

Which is how, on my very first night in the city, over-travelled and under-slept, scrubbed and suited, Tokyo-dazzled and jet-lag hungry, I find myself standing by my cab, watching the driver walk the pavement peering at street signs and door numbers. Eventually, together, we find the entrance. It is a red lift door in a small, anonymous, six-storey apartment block. It looks like the kind of place where a woman with too many cats might live a life of quiet desperation. I take the lift to the third floor and discover that it is nothing of the sort. There is no old woman. There are no cats.

Instead I find food heaven. It is the restaurant at the end of the universe. It is deliciousness in seventeen courses. I have found my way to Yukimura.

Clearly, in another life this was an apartment and the brightly lit, modest room I enter would have been the lounge. Half the space is filled by a three-sided blond-wood counter, seating nine people, which cuts off one corner. I mutter Hide Yamamoto's name at a young woman in a black trousersuit, the only waiter in the place, and she smiles and nods. They are expecting me. I am shown to seat three on the bar, and the chef, Jun Yukimura, bows to me.

He is a cheerful middle-aged man in white jacket and white triangular cap of the sort worn by burger-flippers in American diners of the 1950s. His cap is set at a jaunty angle and his hair is buzz-cut to a fuzz at the nape. He is accompanied by three young and earnest-looking cooks, who move between the preparation area at the bar and a kitchen in a room behind, talking in whispers. Jun is both chef and host. He jokes with his customers, offers up asides of wisdom and encouragement. Obviously I understand not a single word of this, but he has a mobile and animated face that supplies subtitles of its own. I smile a lot.

It begins. I am presented with a shiny, square, black plate bearing two slices of the sweetest raw scallop I have ever eaten, with some slivers of crisp pickled vegetables, golden grated crumbs of preserved sea cucumber roe and a luscious, white, mayonnaise-like sauce. Next, a pot of a hot custard flavoured with more of the sea cucumber roe, tasting ripely of the sea. Then a small emptied crab shell filled with leg meat and fish roe and a little light sugar syrup. There are slippery, tender slices of raw venison, the colour of a fresh haemorrhage, followed by tiny, white, vinegared fish, and then some pieces of cured mackerel with just-warm rice wrapped in crisp, toasted sheets of seaweed to be eaten by hand. There are small fish I do not recognise, cooked on the hibachi grill in the corner, the sweetness of which is undercut by the sudden, life-affirming bitterness of the guts. I am served some greaseless tempura, a refreshing salad of mushrooms and greens, and a steaming bowl of soup with silky bean curd and the sudden nose-tickling hit of horseradish.

To one side of me, a couple orders a bottle of Chassagne Montrachet. On the other, I am joined by a young man and an older woman, mother and son. Mr Suzuki is in building management and is eager to test out his English. He offers me a glass of the DVX Mumm Cuvée Napa Champenoise that they have brought with them for the occasion.

He says, 'How do you come to be here?'

I explain that the executive chef of my hotel booked me in, that I am a writer investigating the restaurants of Tokyo. He looks impressed. I ask him why.

'I have never seen a foreigner here before. This is a very special place. You have to know about it to eat here.' This last seems a statement of the obvious, but I know what he means. As if to explain himself he says, 'You need to be recommended to come in and it takes a long time to get a reservation.' He tells me he booked in over two months ago, but says that's what you have to do if you want to taste the crab.

As he talks, one of the cooks places a whole pale-pink beast a foot and a half across on to the counter, which, from the ridges on its shell and the long, spindly legs, looks like a species of spider crab. This is why everybody is here. This is what they have come for. The zuwai-gani, fished from the waters north of Kyoto, the city where Yukimura trained before coming to Tokyo in 2000, is only in season for a couple of months and I am fortunate to be here just as that season is ending. I am ashamed that I had no idea about this, that I had simply rocked up in search of dinner.

The crab is sprouting a spume of shiny bubbles from

somewhere around its mouth in a way that suggests it is still alive, but it doesn't stay that way for long. It is cut up with two deft, quartering slices from a machete, dissected further and the pieces placed on the hibachi, where they are cooked until the proteins have only just set. First there is a leg, then another, a claw, then a piece of the body. It is the richest white crabmeat I have ever tasted, with that curious balance of salt and sweet. The amount of meat that I scrape from the shell with chopsticks is slight, but hugely satisfying. At the end of the crab dishes, I am presented with the main shell, filled with a hot and powerful stew of the brown meat, which is so pungent, so savoury, I want to run my finger around the edges to clean it out, though I resist the temptation.

Even then I am not finished. I am given a little more of the sea cucumber roe, which has been barbecued to pump up the flavours of salt, sweet and umami. There is a broth of finely sliced vegetables with ponzu zest (a kind of Japanese lemon), and some soupy rice, and then the sweetest, brightest, lipstick-red strawberries with sake ice cream and finally a lotus-root jelly that tastes calmingly of tea.

At the end, Mr Yukimura and I exchange cards that neither of us can read, and he bows to me and unselfconsciously I bow back. I am presented with a bill for 37,000 yen (around £155) and drop the plastic on to the shiny lacquered plate, convinced I have landed a bargain.

Mr Yukimura accompanies me to the lift and out on to the street, where he bows again to indicate our journey together this evening is over. In one way, it occurs to me, a part of my journey is over too. I may not have slept in thirty hours. I may have no idea where I am. But I have just eaten what may well be a perfect meal.

There are 60,000 restaurants in Tokyo. Or 120,000. Or 300,000. All of these numbers are quoted at me by one guidebook or another during my stay, but none is more revealing than the sight of the restaurants themselves. They are piled on top of each other, like children's building blocks. They are crammed down the narrow side streets between skyscrapers, squeezed in along the major boulevards, secreted away in both the basements and uppermost floors of department stores. They are everywhere. The vast majority, obviously, are Japanese, and most of them offer just one style of cooking: here a tempura shop, there a sushi joint, over there a ramen bar. In the Japanese restaurant business the specialist is venerated over the generalist.

But this is also a city where you can eat the world with only a subway pass. I am told, for example, that there are 20,000 Italian restaurants in Tokyo, from the simplest of pasta places to the Japanese outpost of Enoteca Pinchiorri, the famed Florentine gastro-temple. I come across American burger joints and English-style pubs, Spanish tapas bars and French brasseries. One afternoon I even pass a restaurant that announces on a big sign written in English that it specialises in 'Belarus home-cooking', which doesn't strike me as something worth boasting about.

That the Belarusians should have decided to make a go of it in Tokyo is really no surprise. Since 1965, when the great French chef Paul Bocuse made his first tour of Japan, everybody has been trying to make a go of it here. Big-name European and American chefs have seen Japan as a land of opportunity (for which read 'nice consulting deals'). Long before they had a presence in Las Vegas or Dubai they were in Tokyo, starting with Maxim's of Paris, which opened on the ground floor of the Sony building in the mid-1970s. Maxim's was followed by the Troisgros brothers, and later by ventures bearing the name of Bocuse himself, and many others besides.

Anybody with a passing knowledge of Japanese culture could quite reasonably have assumed that this influx of Western chefs would have left its mark upon Japanese cooking. The adoption of elements of foreign culture into Japanese life – or the concept of *iitoko-dori*, as it is known – has been so important to so much of the country's development that it's hard to imagine it not having an effect on the table. Certainly throughout its history Japan has taken various elements of other culinary traditions – the fermented soya bean and tea from China, the principles of tempura from the Portuguese – and made it their own.

Curiously, though, the impact of the latest culinary invasion has not been on the hosts but on the new arrivals. While Japanese diners might be some of the most adventurous in the world, Japanese cuisine has proved resistant to any further innovation from beyond its own shores; meanwhile Western haute cuisine has filched things left, right and centre, like dodgy guests filling their pockets with the silver spoons while the hosts are out of the room. Some of it has been direct and obvious, like the 'discovery' by Ferran Adria at El Bulli in Spain of seaweed extracts the Japanese had known about for centuries, which could be used for making hot jellies (rather than the cold ones made from animal-bone gelatines that melt above room temperature).

Others were more subtle. Since the early 1990s, when both Thomas Keller's French Laundry opened in California's Napa Valley and El Bulli came to prominence, the convention of the Western multi-course tasting menu has stretched from a mere six or eight courses to a dizzying fifteen, twenty-five or even forty. Keller himself defined a philosophy to go with it – 'With each course we want to strike quick, mean and leave without getting caught,' he wrote, like some Norman Mailer of the stove, in a mission statement for his staff – though in reality these menus simply aped the traditional Japanese meal system.

Joël Robuchon actively acknowledged the influence when he devised the L'Atelier format, which has since spread around the world, with its glossy black counter overlooking an open kitchen. In Europe it was easy to assume the primary influence to be the Spanish tapas bar, not least because a platter of the best hand-cut Iberico ham is always on the menu, but that's simply because Robuchon likes his ham. A trip to L'Atelier in Tokyo's Roppongi Hills quickly reveals the Japanese influence to be much stronger. In a meal pulled back to a succession of small tasting plates there is no space for the complex dishes of the grand old French kitchen, with their eight or ten elements. As with a Japanese dish it becomes about showing each ingredient to its very best: a simple piece of Pyrenean milk-fed lamb, roasted and dressed with a little *jus* and nothing else, for example; a small but perfectly formed langoustine ravioli.

Other, less-skilled chefs have also discovered Japanese food, but only in the way teenagers discover sex: as a new and thrilling pursuit they know nothing about, but with which they are determined to enjoy experimenting. Across

Europe and the Americas there have been unexpected outbreaks of ponzu and daikon, when lemon and radish would have done just fine. Unlikely ingredients have been plonked unceremoniously on top of cushions of rice in the bastardised name of sushi, and perfectly innocent pieces of fish that would have been lovely seared in frothing butter have been left raw to indicate that the chef had either a) discovered a new, Japanese-inspired purity that had helped him to redefine the very essence of his inner being or b) been hanging out after hours down the local sushi bar, trying to grope the waitress.

Most of these gastronomic calamities had the good manners to take place a long way from Japan's shores, but there were some chefs who proved determined to re-import their knock-offs back to Tokyo. The most notable is Wolfgang Puck, whose restaurants, like some multi-drug-resistant strain of tuberculosis, have even spread across the city, knocking out seared hunks of tuna in an ersatz Asiatic style with ill-executed Caesar salads. No matter; there are so many eateries in Tokyo that it is possibly the one place in the world where someone like Puck can safely be ignored.

To a greedy man, the sight of all these restaurants should be encouraging. It should offer endless taste possibilities. Nevertheless, as I explore the unending low-rise concrete forest, I can't escape a nagging fear that, after the joys of Yukimura, I am destined only for disappointment. My warped grasp of statistics tells me this has to be so: even if the proportion of good to grim restaurants is higher in Tokyo than elsewhere, the sheer number of places in the city means there have to be, numerically, many more bad ones than elsewhere. Given what has begun to feel like my talent for finding a bad meal wherever I happen to travel, I am certain to sit down in the wrong place. I am sure it's going to happen.

This nagging fear is not helped by the fact that my next booking is at the restaurant of a man who, up to this point, has only ever disappointed me. His name is Pierre Gagnaire and in Paris his restaurant has three Michelin stars.

This should mean he is good. This should mean he is among the best. But, in this business, I have realised, nothing is guaranteed. For many years I had been intrigued by Gagnaire, a tall, long-limbed man with a bouffant mane of salt-and-pepper hair, a manicured beard and a bright, toothy smile that makes him look like either the forgotten Bee Gee or the life model for the illustrations in the 1970s edition of *The Joy of Sex*. Some people had described Gagnaire to me as a genius, a man who reconfigured the very notion of the meal and who, through his riffs on ingredients, made you look anew at what it was to eat.

Other people I had spoken to thought – and this, after much careful consideration – that he was now a bit of an arse. Increasingly I had come to agree with them. A few months before my trip to Tokyo, Gagnaire was the star turn at a conference of chefs in London that I attended, where he gave a cookery demonstration. However, we were told grandly before he began, he would not be cooking one of his signature dishes. Gagnaire was an artist. Therefore he would cook as the mood took him, according to what appealed from among the ingredients laid out before him on the stage. He would 'create'.

The result was a car crash, relayed to a gawping crowd who had come to worship and quickly found themselves mislaying their faith: here some foie gras, there some scarlet, acidulated jelly, in between a sliver of crisp chicken skin, perhaps a scatter of peanuts. All it was missing was a shot glass of Gaviscon on the side. It was less a dish than a cacophony of stuff clattering across the plate.

A little later I was invited to witness Gagnaire in action again, at a dinner for a few freeloading restaurant critics at his London restaurant, Sketch. I accepted the invitation greedily, eager still to find out what all the fuss was about. On the day, I received a call from his PR woman telling me that once more Pierre was 'going to create'. The great man was going off menu, off piste, quite possibly off his head.

What she didn't mention was that he would also be waiting on us, accompanying every tray to the dining room so he could place the dishes before us. We were reduced to a rumble of artificial purrs and simulated gasps of ecstasy as the man watched us eat. After the event we were sent the menu and it read like serious modern French food, which is to say, as a game of word association: there was 'octopus broth, razor clams, cubes of rock red mullet, anchovy pizza' or 'grey shrimp jelly, mozzarella ice cream, fennel and asparagus heads'. On the plate and in the mouth, however, it was a puff of nothing, bland and unmoving, a set of paintings with ingredients used only for their colour rather than their flavour. Looking later at that menu, not a single taste came back to me. Perhaps he had once been great. Perhaps Gagnaire had been a superstar chef of Bee Gee proportions. But now it seemed to me that he was, like the *Joy of Sex* model by the last page of the book, completely spent.

Tokyo

Being in Tokyo, however, I realised I had an opportunity to give him one last chance. Here, a long way from Paris, there was no way Gagnaire could suddenly go off menu because, of course, he and that menu were separated by thousands of miles. Curiously his absence from the restaurant that bore his name was finally a positive.

Gagnaire's Tokyo restaurant is perched on the top floor of a glass tower above Aoyama, the most expensive district in town. Here, Prada, Gucci and Chanel jostle for space, and most people's underwear costs more than the shoes you have on right now. It is the perfect location for Gagnaire: his ornately tiled circular dining room is more than an equal to the flash and sparkle of the high-class retail joints below.

In Paris Gagnaire made his name by serving five or six different dishes at once for each course. In Paris, I had been told, it could seem contrived as if, like some hyperactive toddler, he was incapable of focusing on one idea. Here, though, surrounded by the kimono-clad ladies who lunch, in a city where everything is about precision, the isolating of these flavours one from another is suddenly appropriate. At the beginning there is a tiny bowl of soft and perfectly executed gnocchi flavoured with pumpkin and Parmesan. The earthiness of that dish is echoed by a smooth velouté of Jerusalem artichokes with a little salted egg yolk, and alongside it, as though the land has slipped quietly away into the sea, a lovely fish soup, rich and intense with a long, peppery end, which is simply the best version of itself that I have ever tried.

The meal is full of wonders: a carpaccio of wagyu beef curled round a jelly of beef consommé. A dish listed simply as 'pork' that breaks the animal down into thin slices of the belly with a compôte of preserved fruits, dense, savoury nuggets of loin and crispy pieces of the skin. It is a dazzling display of virtuosity, full of big, clean flavours and satisfying textures, served with a wry self-confidence. The Japanese waiters know that the parade of warped and twisted crockery upon which all these dishes are served is absurd (for at Gagnaire, very little comes on a mere plate) but they know too that, when you taste the food, it will make sense.

As the meal begins to wind down through a series of riffs on apple, and another on mango, and a third on strawberries, I also begin to relax. In Tokyo, it seems to me, even Gagnaire is good. I immediately decide that this must be the greatest food city in the world. I am happy and in a very profound way, for I now know that it will be impossible to eat badly here.

I am also wrong.

It was when the waiter scooped the lavender ice cream into the green bean soup that I began to have serious doubts. There are lots of good places for lavender; ice cream isn't one of them. Food flavoured with lavender makes me think only of an old lady's underwear drawer. I tried the tepid, overly sweet bean soup, mixed in a little of the loose ice cream and concluded that it was the sort of soft-textured dish that would indeed suit an old lady, especially one with her teeth out.

I was not having a good time.

This was a disappointment. Hiramatsu is the flagship restaurant of legendary Japanese chef Hiroyuki Hiramatsu, who made his name by choosing not to cook Japanese food. Instead he decided to become a French chef. In this he was not unique. The highly regarded Tsuji Culinary Institute in Osaka has been turning out Japanese chefs, trained in the repertoires of France and Italy, since the mid-1960s. Its graduates make up most of the brigades of the Western chefs with restaurants in Tokyo, and a number have gone on to open their own places in the city. Hiramatsu took it a step further. Not only does he have restaurants in Tokyo, he eventually opened a restaurant in Paris, which now holds two Michelin stars.

Today he heads an empire of cafés and brasseries, high-end dining places and partnerships with Paul Bocuse. I had wanted to meet him, but he was out of town opening another business. Instead I was making do with dinner at his first restaurant, which opened in 1982.

It was not a good experience from the start. They had insisted I come at 6 p.m., but when I arrived I was the only customer. I was led through a foyer, hung with glowering oil paintings dominated by their dour, overly ornate frames, to an empty and thickly carpeted bar area on the first floor, where I was abandoned to the stygian gloom with just a menu to hide behind. I'd soon had enough of solitary confinement and stepped out of the room to find two waiters lurking outside the doorway, like pall-bearers anticipating the call. I asked to be taken to my table. I was led upwards to the equally deserted dining room on the floor above, which was little better. It was all silly chandeliers and claw-footed chairs and deathly hush. None of the staff smiled. They seemed determined to avoid eye contact. Then I noticed their outfits, and I began to understand their melancholy. They were wearing tailcoats. I have not seen waiters wearing tailcoats in a big-ticket restaurant since sometime way back in the last century. Yet, here they were, stiff and uneasy in their flapping jackets.

It all felt like a gross and foolish parody of what a grand French restaurant is supposed to be. In his astute and broadly sympathetic book *Inventing Japan*, the journalist and writer Ian Buruma describes how, in the latter part of the nineteenth century, the Japanese establishment responded to the perception that the country was culturally and socially backward by trying to be more Westernised than the West. What he describes as the 'high tide of ostentatious Europeanised posturing' was a ball held in 1885 by the foreign minister to mark the emperor's birthday.

It took place in a pavilion, designed in a mixture of 'high Victorian, French Empire and Italian Renaissance styles' and filled with men in tailcoats and women in huge hooped satin dresses. 'Doing their best to strike the proper European attitudes, gentlemen puffed Havana cigars and played whist,' Buruma writes, 'while others picked at the truffles and pâté and ice-cream sorbets laid out on the buffet tables.'

Here I was, more than 120 years later, and in this room it seemed nothing had changed. There was still a part of Japanese society that was trying to ape the West, and doing so in a clumsy, anachronistic manner. It was not enough, apparently, to be a French restaurant; it had to be grand, stupid French. It had to be all the grand, stupid things about French restaurants that are wrong. If the food had been nice to eat – the delicious, technically precise take on the great French repertoire that I had been told to expect – it might not have mattered, but it wasn't. If anything, after the ill-judged lavender ice cream–bean soup combo, dinner took a turn for the worse.

Once-beautiful langoustines were served tepid under a strange cheesy crust, with strands of orange zest, on top of what was described as a potato tart. It wasn't. It was a tablet of over-set potato mousse, which tasted of potato not at all. After that came a main course of pink lamb sliced so thin and laid so flat on the plate it looked like wet, sweaty ham. It too did not taste of itself, under an armed and violent assault by truffle and reduced meat juices so that the only real flavour was of sticky demi-glace sauce.

All of this was served with the kind of enthusiasm and jollity one might expect of waiters who had heard only that morning that their mothers had died unexpectedly of the plague. I have a curious, perhaps eccentric expectation of expensive restaurants, which is this: the more money I spend, the better time I should have. I am always baffled when all it buys is formality and stiffness, as though what you had actually purchased was entry to a religious ritual, with an emphasis on the finer points of sadomasochism. I don't go out to eat so I can pay homage. If I wanted that, I'd go round my mother's place for dinner. I want what all eaters want: pleasure. Eating at Hiramatsu was not a pleasure.

Some might argue that I was merely experiencing a cultural clash between the Japanese tendency towards politeness and deference on the one hand and the tendency towards exuberant hedonism of the fat Jewish boy on table seven on the other. I don't think so. After all, Jun Yukimura had been the perfect host. No, it wasn't about the manner of Japanese people. It was about *these* people, regardless of their nationality.

Across the room from me were sepia paintings of flowers that looked, beneath their varnish coat, to be rotting, and I experienced a surge of sympathy. I felt like I had been interred alive in my very own fat-cushioned coffin. I resigned myself to my fate, which in this case was dessert. A good rum baba should be sodden with boozy syrup. It should be as wet as a bathtime sponge. This was dry and flaky, a wasted opportunity for indulgence. I ordered coffee and, when it arrived, toyed with the idea of accidentally on purpose tipping it over on to the snowfield of white linen just to see the waiters react.

I resisted the urge. I told myself it was only food, which I understood was what people with a normal relationship to their dinner might think, even about a dinner costing a little over £100 a head including just the one glass of wine.

Still, I couldn't help wondering: back home I would never go to a sushi bar staffed by a bunch of white boys from, say, Wimbledon, because, well . . . you wouldn't, would you? The culture of Japanese food was understood to be too deep, too intense and complex to allow for that sort of casual journeyman approach. Was it outrageous to suppose that the same applied in the opposite direction? Michelin stars or no, had I been foolish to assume a Japanese chef could run a really good French restaurant without tripping up? Or had I started to formulate some unpalatable theory of culinary apartheid, extrapolating unfairly from one dismal experience?

Of one thing I was certain: the next night I was booked

into another high-end Japanese restaurant, courtesy of Hide Yamamoto at the Mandarin Oriental, and that would make everything better.

Wrong again.

I am lost in Ginza. Unlike on my first night, this evening my cab driver simply abandoned me. He brought the car to a halt, activated the automatic back doors that all Tokyo taxis have, told me to give him just 1,000 of the 1,300 yen showing on the meter and drove off. I don't even know whether I am on the right street. Worse, the weather is closing in. A gusty, warm wind is blowing around me, carrying a scatter of raindrops, and I have no umbrella or coat.

I pull my jacket tightly about me and run, head down, into the wind, across to the doorman standing guard on a smart but sombre-looking restaurant across the road. I have with me a computer printout of a map, with the details of my destination, a place called Asami, but the doorman shakes his head and gestures carelessly towards the darkened furthest reaches of the street. I reward him with the one word of Japanese I have – *origato*, for 'thank you' – and carry on, stopping at the next lit doorway: another smart restaurant.

There, the hostess also appears to have no idea where it is, but again waves me away in the same direction. I move on, hopping from what I now realise is one fancy restaurant to another. Do they really not know where one of their neighbours is located, or are they simply refusing to acknowledge the competition? The wind blows. The rain threatens.

Eventually I find it, marked by a stark sliding wooden

door, which leads on to a low-ceilinged room with the now familiar counter, this time seating ten. This, however, is a very different place from Yukimura. Yes, the waitress smiles, and they have clearly gone to some trouble on my behalf; waiting on the lacquered wooden tray where I am to be seated is tonight's menu, translated into English. But the mood here is serious. The chef does not look up or acknowledge me. A late-middle-aged man to one side of me actively looks away when I sit down. At the far end of the bar is an elderly couple with a sour expression as if they have a mouthful of wasps. I bury myself in the ritual of the hot towel that is presented at the beginning of every meal, withdraw my notebook and pen, and study the menu in search of clues.

The first dish is listed as steamed black rice with salt-fermented sea cucumber. The tiny wooden bowl arrives almost immediately and contains something that, even allowing for the lamb in rotting milk that I sampled in Dubai, is one of the nastiest things I have ever eaten. The rice by itself would have been fine, but it is dressed with a sticky, fishy, stinky gunge that makes me retch silently. It tastes like I imagine the slime that gathers on the skin of day-old fish might taste, if one was ever moved to lick it off, and has the consistency of phlegm. I am, however, well dragged up, and I know I must eat it all. I do this quickly, both to get the terrible business over with and to move on to the next dish, which has to be better.

It is, but only just: in a light broth there is a large square of very soft tofu with sea urchin. Usually I love sea urchin, which has a musky, dirty, sexy taste, but I have always eaten it alongside something with a more solid texture, some rice or sheets of toasted seaweed, or both. Here in this bowl are two slippery things, wrestling with each other, and in my mouth they flop about my tongue as if trying to decide whether to slip back out again. That's if I can get them to my mouth. Obviously I have only chopsticks and it's like trying to eat jelly with knitting needles. Scratch the attempt at illuminating analogy. It *is* eating jelly with knitting needles.

On to some clam. That should be fine. I like clam, but tonight everything is a shock. The long, pink, purple and white flap of seafood is tough and rubbery, everything the novice might assume raw mollusc to be. Where the tofu and sea urchin skidded around my mouth, this just bounces, getting caught in one twisted lump in my oesophagus until I swallow hard with a jerk that makes my shoulders rise and fall suddenly. The man on my right stares at me, and I manage a closed-mouth smile. I imagine myself saying a big, satisfied 'Mmmmmmmm' but no sound comes out.

I consider myself a broad and fearless eater. I consider myself an enthusiast. When I was a child, my mother would tell me that I couldn't say I didn't like something unless I had tried it at least once and so, by an early age, I had tried a lot of things that were foreign to my friends. I had eaten those snails and then moved on to frog's legs. I had snaffled offaly bits, and the occasional fiery chilli. This was a matter of pride to me, and I have tried to pass on the message to my kids. Here, in my forty-first year, I realised I had met my match. There was, it seemed, a place where the Japanese culinary repertoire became too challenging for the Western palate. Or at least for this Westerner's palate.

Then a thought came into my mind, one husbanded by too many hours spent in front of kitsch trash television. The thought was this: I am eating Klingon food. All I could think of was Commander Wharf in *Star Trek* attacking a bowl of squelching, squeaking, still-pulsating tentacles and barking, 'Bring me heart of targ and a flagon of blood wine!'

Immediately I felt ashamed. The problem, I told myself, was not the food; it was me. I was not worthy of it. I was not up to the task. Then again, I realised, I was being inconsistent. Did I not always say that authentic was not the same as good? If that applied to Cantonese chicken's feet, should it not also apply to salt-fermented sea cucumber, or raw clam with the texture of rubber? Was I holding the Japanese culinary tradition in higher regard than that of China? Surely I had the confidence to say no, actually this is horrible and I don't want to eat it any more.

I wasn't sure I did, not here in this restaurant, which Mr Yamamoto had gone to such trouble to book me into. For a moment I wondered whether I was the victim of one huge prank. Clearly a foreigner like me, a *gaijin*, was a rarity in this place. Perhaps I was the first foreigner ever to eat at Asami. Maybe they were throwing all the really weird stuff at me that nobody ever eats to see whether I'd be too polite to refuse.

'Look!' I imagined them whispering to each other behind the curtain that led to the back kitchen. 'He's actually putting it in his mouth! Can you believe it! The clam!'

Then I saw that my neighbours were getting many of the same dishes.

I did not have much time to think about this, because I had just read the fourth course, and that was far more troubling.

At the airport in London, just before flying out, my

mother had telephoned me on my mobile, as mothers do.

'Have a lovely time, dear,' she said, 'and you are not to eat any fugu.'

I laughed and told her that my wife had said exactly the same thing; the blowfish, famed for the fatalities caused when it was badly prepared and the violent toxins from its internal organs allowed to infect the flesh, was out of bounds.

Back in London, I had emailed Eric Drache, the professional poker player who had been so fascinated when we dined at Nobu in Las Vegas by the odds on dying from eating fugu. I had asked him whether he would try fugu if he was in my position, but he had not replied by the time I left. (When he did reply, his response had shown him to be less of a gambler than I had imagined. 'I probably would eat the second half of your portion,' he wrote, 'after observing you for thirty minutes or so.')

None of this was of any use to me now, as I awaited the imminent arrival of what the menu told me was a fugu dish: grilled blowfish milt. The word 'milt' was familiar. I recalled reading accounts of high-end Japanese meals as part of my research, flicking back and forth through a dictionary of food terms to orientate myself. Finally it came to me, as it never would come to the blowfish ever again. It was sperm. In front of me was placed a plate holding two white, wobbly pouches of bulging membrane, bearing the slightest grill marks from where they had been cooked. It looked like an awful lot of sperm for a straight guy. Still, like everything else, I couldn't *not* eat it. I remembered my mother's commandment, that I must first try, and piled them into my mouth. It was thick and creamy and ripe and rich and, after the sea cucumber and the tofu and the sea urchin and the clam, still so much more of much too much.

There were occasions as the meal progressed when I felt myself to be advancing on to more solid and reliable ground. There was a tiny tranche of marinated grilled salmon, say, or a piece of impeccably made sushi of sea bream. Then something else would come along and throw me back: a dish of soft-shelled turtle, which looked in the bowl like uncooked entrails and felt like it too in the mouth, or some octopus that was more hard, knotty sucker than soft, yielding tentacle. It didn't help that, in the middle of the meal, the weather delivered on its threat. Torrential rain could be heard battering against the windows of the back kitchen, and the wind howled. I was adrift, caught in a storm of so many kinds, and dreaming of the sanctuary of dessert.

Even that was a challenge: a large bowl of iced water containing huge, fat, clear ribbon noodles made with kuzu root that had the texture of frog spawn, which I was supposed to dredge from the liquid, dunk into another dish of cane syrup and somehow drag to my mouth. I leaned my head down as far as I could in the hope that the faulty mechanics of the chopsticks could be supplemented with a little suction. Somehow I cleared the bowl and when they brought the bill, for north of £200, I paid more with relief than gratitude and still felt guilty about it.

They called me a cab and, when it arrived, asked me to stand just inside the door for a moment while unexplained arrangements were made furtively beyond my line of sight. I could hear the rain lashing down and could see the door shaking in its frame. When they slid the door across, the three chefs were standing in a line on the steps to form an honour guard, umbrellas lifted to protect me from the downpour on the short walk from door of restaurant to cab. I threw myself into the back seat and, as the automatic door closed, turned to look back. Through the rain-drenched window all I could see were the three chefs bowing deeply in unison to my retreating cab.

A couple of days later and I am in the Ryogoku district of town, where the sumo-wrestler stables are located, when I feel an urgent twinge in my guts. I am with Robb Satterwhite, an expatriate American who is the founder of a restaurant-guide website for Tokyo. We have just been for what he called 'ultimate unagi' – eel, Japanese-style – in a tiny restaurant a short distance from the imposing sumo stadium with its oxidised green copper roof.

I have always loved unagi, but have long been disappointed in London's Japanese restaurants that it comes in such meagre portions, usually just a single slice draped across a cushion of sushi rice; a hit of crisply grilled, oily flesh, slicked with intensely savoury sauce, which is gone as quickly as it arrives. Here we had been able to order whole slabs of eel, both white – without sauce – and with sauce, alongside a bowl of candied liver. It had been a quick but delicious meal and now Robb was walking me across to have a look at the blocky, modernist Edo-Tokyo Museum.

Robb is talking about how sushi restaurants sometimes charge Westerners more than locals just to scare them off when there it is again – a sudden straining in my stomach, a bubble of discomfort that rises and subsides only to rise again. I continue the conversation and tell myself I have a case of mere wind, nothing more, but somewhere at the back of my mind, alarm bells are ringing. The discomfort is too insistent, too determined, to be just wind. I have experienced forms of gastric distress while on trips before, in both Toronto and New York. Until now I had thought of these episodes only in terms of inconvenience: of time wasted, meetings cancelled. As we walk, I slip away inside myself to analyse the information my body is giving me, to listen to the breaking news, and it occurs to me that I face a more serious threat. I am in a city I don't know, with a pleasant but reserved man I have only just met, and I need a toilet. Now!

Robb suggests we visit Akihabara, or Electric Town, which is only a short distance away by subway. On any other occasion I would love nothing more. I have always been fascinated by the Japanese obsession with gadgetry. Today, the very thought of a train journey sends sweat gushing down the small of my back. I have no choice. I tell him my needs and to his credit he stays very calm. He says there will be facilities at the train station we are near, but he doesn't know where.

He is walking around asking people, and I am now deeply suspicious that, for the first time in my adult life, I might just be about to do something that is grossly humiliating for a five-year-old, and completely unthinkable for an adult. I am trembling, as though I have become the epicentre of my own coming earthquake. More sweat is breaking out across my brow. I feel like I am on the run, a fugitive in fear of my own body.

Finally he's got directions. He leads me across to a simple block. I am grateful but so desperate I barely have time to thank him. I barge in there, leaving him standing outside. It's a tiny space designed for small Japanese men and I am a large man, even by European standards, but there is a cubicle, which is what I need, except – oh, please! Give me a break! – it contains a traditional bowl-less affair. There are just two footpads and a hole in the floor. I can barely stand, let alone squat. Somehow I work out the necessary gymnastics and it's fine.

Though only for now. I know what's going on, even if I don't know what's caused it. My suspicion is nothing in particular and everything in general: jet lag, travel, meals, life, the shameful business of being me. No matter. I am clear that this episode isn't over yet and that I really need to get back to my hotel room. So I thank Robb and jump in a cab and he's probably delighted to see the back of me. But of course this is Tokyo, a city so obscure the hotel hands out laminated cards with a map of where they are for guests to show to cab drivers. I show the driver mine and he sits staring at it for what feels like minutes but which is probably just a few seconds.

Finally we set off, but slowly, slowly, slowly. We are stopped at every traffic light, every junction. When we get close to the hotel, the driver pulls over to ask a policeman for directions. Now, of course, I really do need the sanctuary of my hotel room, and I have not the subtle nuance of the Japanese language with which to explain this.

At last we get there, but I have to wait for change, because in Tokyo it's terribly impolite to tip (though probably less impolite, it occurs to me, as I tense my buttocks against the leatherette seat, than to crap inside his cab).

I get my change and make for the lift. This hotel has a

curious design. Reception is on the thirty-eighth floor of the tower block, the rooms on the seven floors below. So I must take one lift up and then another down. The lift goes straight from the ground floor to the thirty-eighth, with only a possible stop on the third floor, which has been a rare occurrence during my stay. This time it stops on floor three. A hotel porter holds the door as he stares down the corridor at something he can see but I can't. Then the party arrives: a bride in yards of ivory taffeta, her groom in impeccable tailoring, holding white gloves. Plus the cameraman and the soundman there to record the event. And the make-up lady and a couple of others. All of us crammed tightly into this tiny lift.

It is the bride's big day, the most important day of her life, and pushed back into the corner of the lift is a man with a rebellious bowel. She is sharing the space with a human time bomb. Up we go to thirty-eight and, because I am at the back, I have to wait while they all process out, in a stately fashion for the camera. Finally I can escape, out across the lobby. Into the second lift, down six floors, dodging the hotel staff, who are grinning and bowing at me as they always do, and into my room.

I click the privacy button and I am safe. Sweating, shaking, I throw myself into the bathroom. The emergency is over. It is, however, a reminder of something very important. It doesn't matter how expensive a restaurant is. It doesn't matter how difficult the reservations are to get, or how exquisite the food.

Eventually, it all ends up the same way.

In search of (a) good taste

It is four forty-five in the morning and I am in a brightly lit shed at the Tsukiji Fish Market in central Tokyo watching a man stick a spike into the tail end of a 400-pound tuna. Dozens of fish like this, each at least 5 feet long, are lined up in rows. Men step gingerly between them, shining their torches into the belly cavity, prodding at the silver-black skin to see how taut it is, hoping the few clues they are allowed will tell them ahead of the auction which is the fish worth paying up to $20,000 for and which is not. I watch, fascinated.

Standing here, dry ice curling around my ankles, I am reminded of a London bookshop event about food writing that I once took part in, alongside Anthony Bourdain, author of the abrasive cook's memoir *Kitchen Confidential*. A member of the audience had asked a question about Japanese food and Bourdain, who had pronounced himself a devotee, said that most people misunderstood it. For example, he said, 'Sushi is not about the fish. It's all about the rice.' I nodded sagely when he said this, looking out at the crowd of tattooed, bed-haired, leather-clad maniacs who seem to follow Bourdain wherever he goes. They were hanging on his every word. Disagreeing with him didn't seem like a good idea, not in front of this crowd, so I mumbled, 'All about the rice,' and nodded again.

As I watch this curious ritual, this silent adoration of the tuna, the truth strikes me. Sure, good rice is important. Good rice is vital, but only as a minimum qualifying standard. As far as I can see, it really is all about the fish. Indeed here, in this shed, I feel as if I am seeing the very essence of Japanese food laid bare. It is about what the chef started with, not what appears at the end. If the ingredients aren't good enough, the food won't work. This might seem like a truism, applicable to all culinary traditions, but it isn't. There are whole categories of dishes in French cookery, for example – big stews like coq au vin or daube or cassoulet – specifically designed to make something magical from the most veteran and uninspiring of ingredients: the pensioned-off cockerel; the tough, overworked part of the cow; the saggy, fat-bound belly of the retired pig.

Japanese cookery, on the other hand, is simply about the quality of the fish on the market shed floor. It's about the cult of the ingredient, which is something I always felt I understood. And I felt I understood it because of the vinegar.

I need to explain this, and to do so we will have to go back around six decades, to the period immediately after the Second World War, when a young woman called Denise de Choudens came to Britain from the town of La Chaux-de-Fonds near Neuchâtel in the French-speaking part of Switzerland. She worked as an au pair and, in time, married, had children and became my mother-in-law. It is possible that the latter was not part of the original game plan.

Denise lives now in the West Midlands, where my wife, Pat, grew up, but there has always been a bit of her family's sensibility – involving the stomach, mainly – located in Switzerland. It was by meeting Pat that I came to understand, for example, that a cheese fondue is not just some kitsch cliché from the 1970s. I discovered the joys of *viande des Grisons*, wafer-thin slices of air-dried beef that could put a carpaccio to shame, and of rich cheeses and silky chocolates.

Then there was the vinegar. There is nothing special about Kressi vinegar with fine herbs, which is to say, it is neither rare nor exotic, at least not in Switzerland. Kressi is a mass-market brand. It is on the shelves of every supermarket in the land. But it does have a special taste. Forget about other white wine vinegars with their numbing, metallic acidity which forces you, involuntarily, to expose your gums when you taste it. Kressi has a relatively low acidity (about 5 per cent compared with the standard 6 or 7 per cent). It is salty and has a light, herby lift at the end. There is no better salad dressing than olive oil, a crunch of sea salt and a modest splash of Kressi.

Naturally, my mother-in-law introduced her family to the joys of Kressi for it was as much a part of her landscape as the wildflowers in the meadow above the house. When Pat was growing up, they would visit her mother's family in Switzerland once every two years and, on return, the boot of the car would contain a good few bottles; enough, they always hoped, to see them through until the next trip. But, of course, they would run out for the true number of bottles needed to cover their consumption seemed absurd, and they could never bring themselves to dedicate that much space in the car to the pursuit of the perfect salad.

Thus after a year, or perhaps fifteen months, disaster would strike Pat's childhood home. The Kressi would be finished and they would have to go cold turkey. For this is the tragedy of Kressi: no one in Britain sells it and they would never find a suitable replacement because there was none.

I met Pat in the 1980s, and I was welcomed into her family. This meant I inherited the Kressi obsession. Is it really that good? Yes, I think it is, but then we most of us have a specific taste or flavour that roots us or reminds us of who we are. The British obsession with Heinz tomato ketchup or

Hellmann's mayonnaise is barely the half of it. I know someone who has to have her fridge at a particular temperature, so that the milk is cold enough to remind her of childhood. For others, it is not just English mustard but Colman's English mustard. It must be Bird's custard, McVitie's digestives, a dinky bottle of Tabasco. A store cupboard without one of these small objects of culinary necessity is an empty cupboard. This is how I feel about Kressi. When it runs out, I feel like a bit of my life is missing.

One day a few years ago we finished the last bottle of Kressi, a souvenir from a work trip to Gstaad. This time, however, I was determined to do something about it. I contacted the commercial department of the Swiss Embassy, which confirmed that no, nobody imported Kressi. I telephoned a very good Swiss restaurant in London called St Moritz to see if they had any, but they didn't. I felt like an addict trying to score my next fix.

That didn't stop me. If we couldn't get it brought into the country, we'd just have to make an effort to find a replacement here. Over two weeks we tasted seventeen different white wine vinegars. Some were as rough as a gravel track. Others were passable, but no Kressi. A Chardonnay vinegar made my teeth ache. From a high-class food emporium in Central London I bought a 'vinaigre de vin blanc grand cru' because it sounded smart, but it wasn't. It hurt to taste it. I went to the famed Selfridges Food Hall and bought organic vinegars, and vinegars made with champagne because it sounded classy, and one flavoured with bog myrtle because I was desperate. There was a Muscatel vinegar that was OK and a supermarket's own label that wasn't.

That's when I had the notion. We now live in the age of

budget air travel. How much could a ticket to Geneva cost? Could it be cheap enough to justify a day trip to buy vinegar? I decided it could. The turnaround time on the ground would be only three hours, but that, I was sure, was more than enough time. Taxi to the supermarket, stock up and return. I emptied my sports bag in preparation and imagined myself being stopped at customs with two dozen bottles and having to plead innocence on the grounds of gastronomic imperative.

And maybe I would have been stopped at customs were it not for one small problem. The day I went to Geneva, it was closed. Completely and utterly closed. It was a bank holiday. I had done my research on the Net. For example, I had noted that I shouldn't go in the same week as the G8 Summit because of potential violence in the city. But nowhere – not on the websites I looked at, not in my diary, which usually carries this vital intelligence – did it mention a bank holiday. When Geneva observes a bank holiday, it does so properly. The city was like something out of one of those sci-fi movies where everybody has been struck down by a mystery virus. The only thing that moved in the neat and tidy streets was a hot wind off the lake.

Still I wandered, hoping against hope that I would find one shop that could sell me Kressi. I felt like the least intrepid journalist in the world. For months my colleagues had been risking life and limb covering a desert war in Iraq. And me? What was I doing? Looking for vinegar in a closed city.

'If your plane crashes on the way home,' my wife said, when I telephoned her for moral support, 'no one will say your death was in a good cause.'

I went into a restaurant in the hope that I might be able

to buy their stock, but they had none to sell. There was, however, one supermarket in the city that was open, the maître d' said, at the train station next to the airport. I jumped in a cab and, yes, indeed, there in the station was the supermarket and, yes, it was open – and packed. The entire population of Geneva appeared to be in there, trying to pick up those vital items that the antiquated Swiss commitment to religious holidays had contrived to deny them. I fought my way through the crowds, feverishly checking each aisle for my blessed Kressi until I reached the correct shelf, the vinegar shelf, and discovered . . . they were sold out.

I ended up sitting in the departures lounge of Geneva Airport, at the end of a long, hot day, with an empty sports bag at my feet, cursing my wife because I didn't have the heart to curse myself. If I had never met Pat, if I had never married her. If she had never made me a bloody salad, none of this would ever have happened. It was all her fault. As the time passed, I became more philosophical. Perhaps this was the way it was meant to be. Kressi vinegar had spent the past forty years being elusive. It had always been out of reach and it had decided to remain so.

At the time, of course, I felt foolish. No man who has flown to another country simply to secure a limitless supply of a good taste only to come back empty-handed can feel otherwise. Here, in the Tokyo fish market, however, I begin to feel better about the whole thing. These men with their spikes have been up all night and are standing in a freezing shed eyeing up fish both the size and cost of a small car, all because people like the way it tastes, and they do this every day. By comparison my vinegar trip feels like the effort of a rank amateur, which is exactly what it was.

As dawn broke over Tokyo, the daily auctions began and the tuna sheds filled with the ringing of handbells and the shouts of men bidding against each other. I was there with Jeff Ramsey, a chef from the Mandarin Oriental Hotel. He suggested we follow a fish back from its place on the floor to the purchaser's stand in the main market hall. We chose a huge hunk of sashimi on the bone that the new owner said he had just paid around $10,000 for, and watched as it was heaved on to a wooden trolley and guided away through the clatter and noise of the market at its busiest. We crossed the jammed avenue between the tuna auction sheds and the main covered market, and made our way past stalls of octopus and squid and bubbling tanks with huge penile molluscs of a sort I had never seen before, to a small stand in the centre of the hall.

Three middle-aged Japanese men gathered around the fish, which, in one deft action, they had slipped from trolley to slab. They looked again inside the belly cavity, then fetched a thin 7-foot blade and set to work quartering the animal, one man holding the tail, another the head as if, in this last moment, it might finally try to get away.

'This is the first sight they'll get of the *otoro*,' Ramsey said, referring to the most highly prized fat-marbled belly cut, the quality and quantity of which would justify the money spent. A single long cut had already been made down the middle of one side of the fish, from head to tail. Now, without lifting it out, they turned the blade 90 degrees and moved down towards its underbelly. The hunk of deep purple muscle, shading to pink and then the white and pink stripes of the *otoro*, came away in one piece.

'It's looking good,' Ramsey said, with a slow nod of his head. He was a very happy man, standing here amid these lumps of the world's freshest fish.

Ramsey was a good person to have as my guide. He is half-American, half-Japanese – his mother was born in Hiroshima only a few months after the atom bomb was detonated – and was classically trained as a sushi chef in Washington DC. Later, like so many other young chefs, he became intrigued by the modernist cookery of Ferran Adria at El Bulli. A few nights earlier I had eaten at his restaurant at the Mandarin Oriental Hotel.

At the Tapas Molecular Bar he served me a dish of crispy beetroot shaped like a ball of pink, frizzy wool, and another of clear jelly noodles with the exact flavour profile of Parmesan linguine, and a bowl of gazpacho sprinkled with shards of olive oil flash-frozen in liquid nitrogen. There had been a tiny and delicious fillet of wagyu beef cooked under vacuum for six hours and then shoved in a canister of nitrous gas so that, for reasons that escaped me, it came out fizzing, and a jelly of miso soup on a spoon. It was an entertaining meal and, while not every dish had worked, I admired the effort. Still, this was not what interested me most about the Tapas Molecular Bar or Jeff Ramsey.

While we watched the tuna being quartered, I said to the chef, as casually as I could, 'Tell me about the accusations of plagiarism that were made against you.'

Ramsey looked at me wearily, took a deep breath and said, 'The lawyers tell me I can't talk about that.'

Tokyo

In April 2006 a detailed post about Jeff Ramsey and the Tapas Molecular Bar appeared on egullet.com, arguably the most established and influential of the online food discussion boards, with over 15,000 registered members and more than 1.3 million posts on every aspect of the international food scene, from the latest restaurant openings to the fundamentals of Thai cooking. It is the place for people who think the next most important decision they will make is what to have for lunch. Naturally, I hang out there a lot.

This particular post carried extra weight, as it was made by Steven Shaw, a former lawyer turned food writer who was one of the site's founders back in 2001. Shaw had been contacted by José Andrés, the El Bulli-trained chef at a restaurant called Minibar in Washington DC, where Jeff Ramsey had worked for over a year before moving to Tokyo. At Minibar, two sittings of six diners at a time eat at a counter and enjoy a multi-course tasting menu of modernist fancies. Andrés had come across a blogger's account of their meal at the Tapas Molecular Bar in Tokyo and had been struck by the similarities: two sittings, seven diners at a time, all at a counter and with a list of dishes that looked familiar.

'All told,' wrote Steven Shaw, having reviewed the menus of the restaurants side by side, 'fifteen courses of the Tapas Molecular Bar menu turn out to be near-exact copies of Minibar dishes. Some have minor plating variations, but they are fundamentally copies.' Andrés served 'beet tumbleweed'. Ramsey served those 'crispy beets'. Andrés served 'pineapple and salmon ravioli'. So did Ramsey. Andrés served 'hot and cold foie gras soup'. Ramsey served 'foie gras soup – *chaud froid*'. The similarities went beyond names. Shaw also posted photographs of dishes from both restaurants and, as he said, it was hard to distinguish between them. Andrés was so furious that he consulted lawyers, who in turn approached the Mandarin Oriental Hotel Group, demanding they pay him to license his dishes.

Though Ramsey had been ordered not to discuss the issue, friends of his said he was distraught about the controversy. They pointed out that he had been allowed just three weeks in which to launch the Tapas Molecular Bar and said that, understandably, he had fallen back on dishes he already knew. Ramsey also told friends that he had openly announced to diners that some of the dishes on his menu had come from Minibar but that this had gone unreported.

The charges levelled at the Tapas Molecular Bar were not isolated. Another egullet.com member called Sam Mason, the pastry chef at the highly regarded avant-garde New York restaurant WD-50, noted similarities between dishes being served there and those at another restaurant called Interlude, 10,000 miles away in Melbourne, Australia. For example, WD-50 served a dish of 'pasta' made with minced prawns, reconstituted using transglutaminase, an enzyme that works like an adhesive on proteins. Interlude served exactly the same dish. Other dishes at Interlude appeared to have been lifted both from Minibar and from Alinea in Chicago, which had just been named 'Best Restaurant in America' by *Gourmet* magazine. Interlude's chef, Robin Wickens, had worked unpaid at Alinea for a week.

Wickens responded to accusations of plagiarism by arguing on egullet.com that he had never said the dishes were his own, and that he was simply picking up ideas he had come across elsewhere and evolving them.

'The evolution part might be where you are coming up short,' responded Mason sharply.

Apart from being the kind of intense, bruising, fetishistic row that the food world loves, it also points up an intriguing development in haute gastronomy. For most of the twentieth century, Europe's great chefs had not competed against each other to create new dishes, but to produce the best possible versions of old ones. The great French chef Auguste Escoffier had established the repertoire at the beginning of the twentieth century and everybody who came after was intent only on keeping it alive. It was about who could cook the best sole Véronique or tournedos Rossini.

Places like El Bulli and those that followed have changed all of that. These restaurants want to confound your expectations, an increasingly difficult trick to pull off, as diners specifically go there to have their expectations confounded. Customers want to be shocked, or amused or disconcerted. They want foamed palate-cleansers 'cooked' in liquid nitrogen that disappear into a cloud of ice-cold vapour as they hit the tongue, or a dish of caviar that turns out to be tiny beads of a porcini-flavoured jelly. Nobody goes to these places looking for better versions of the same. They don't want comfort food. They want *discomfort* food.

The result is a huge market in innovation, and one that certain chefs are determined to protect. They see their creations not merely as things that might be nice to eat, but as both their unique selling point and as independent revenue streams that could secure their pension. Homaro Cantu, the award-winning chef at Moto in Chicago, has devised a piece of edible paper bearing the image of candyfloss that tastes of candyfloss. The paper also carries the following message

'Confidential Property of and © H. Cantu. Patent Pending. No further use or disclosure is permitted without prior approval of H. Cantu.' As the journalist Pete Wells pointed out in *Food and Wine* magazine, this meant that Cantu was claiming ownership of the food you had paid for even as you were eating it. (God knows what he would do if you were unfortunate enough to later throw up; might this not be regarded as the unauthorised release of commercially sensitive information?) The chef is apparently attempting to copyright or patent more than a dozen of his food ideas even though patent attorneys are divided over whether it's possible to do so.

To meet this feverish market, a new kind of customer has developed, aided by new technologies. In the old days the committed eater would visit a grand restaurant and perhaps bring back a copy of the menu. If they were really fanatical, they might hang that menu on the living-room wall and then bore the tits off anybody stupid enough to ask them whether they'd enjoyed their dinner there.

A printed menu is no longer enough. Now brigades of diners go out armed with digital cameras, determined to collect their experiences, much like butterfly collectors with their nets and killing jars. They photograph each plate of food as it arrives and within an hour of returning home can post on the Web a fully illustrated account of their evening out. Any chef who once thought they could get away with copying a few dishes because they happen to be thousands of miles from the restaurant that created them is now mistaken. It doesn't matter whether you are in Melbourne or Tokyo, and it certainly doesn't matter whether nobody else in Tokyo has ever cooked crispy beets before or shoved beef in a tube with nitrous oxide. If somebody else somewhere else has already done the same thing, the butterfly collectors will spot it.

It seemed to me that being a young chef trying to forge a reputation – being a Jeff Ramsey – had become a very tricky business indeed. Later he took me for breakfast at one of the steamy cafés that ring the market and tried as best he could to answer my questions about Japanese culinary culture, but it was clear that, by raising the plagiarism row, I had trampled on to delicate territory. I felt sorry for ever having mentioned it. All I wanted to do was resume my search for the perfect dinner.

It was when I saw the dining room that I realised I was about to experience something special. I had asked Hide Yamamoto to make sure that one of my bookings was in a sushi restaurant, and expected him to tell me that he had secured a seat at one of the big-name joints – Kyubei, perhaps, or Mizutani or Jiro. Instead he booked me into somewhere called Okei-Sushi and I became increasingly suspicious he had sent me for white-boys' sushi. The restaurant boasted a website, for God's sake, on which was proclaimed, 'We are really happy when customers are amazed by our unique ways of preparing sushi and go, "Wow, it is delicious!!" ' Those two exclamation marks worried me.

But now I was here and everything was fine. It was better than fine. It was as good as it could be. When I knocked on the door, a young man dressed in white had stuck his head out, grinned and nodded while intoning the name of my hotel. When I nodded back, he pointed me to the next building. There was a sliding door, which, like something in *Alice in Wonderland* after she had swallowed the cake marked 'Eat Me' and begun to grow, was only two-thirds of my height. I bent over to get inside and found myself in a small, coir-matted anteroom, where another young man was waiting for me, kneeling down, his back perfectly straight. Beside him was a pair of slippers and I understood I should remove my shoes. Obviously he wanted me to put on the slippers, but we could both see they would barely fit over my big toes, so we ignored them. Instead he led me in stockinged feet to the dining room, where there was a beautiful blond-wood counter. The floor stood at roughly the same level as the counter, save for just in front of it, where there was a rectangular well into which I was to fit my legs.

I could see that normally this counter had space for five or six people. Not tonight. There were no other diners. Instead, tonight, it was set for just one, and that one person was me. I had found my way to the smallest and most exclusive high-end restaurant in the world.

Standing behind the counter was sushi master Masashi Suzuki, a stocky, round-headed middle-aged man with gently bulging eyes who looked a little like a Japanese Peter Lorre. He had on a white, short-sleeved jacket and round his completely shaved head he wore a red coil of material called a *hachimaki*. He bowed deeply to me and I bowed back. He indicated that I should sit, and I crammed myself into the space, dead centre of the counter.

Neither of us spoke each other's language, save for a little shared food vocabulary. I could say '*uni*' for 'sea urchin' and '*otoro*' for 'belly tuna'; bar the odd catchphrase he could say only 'mackerel' and 'cuttlefish' (or almost, for the *l* sound really does present the Japanese with problems). None of this mattered. Here, in this restaurant for one, there were always ways that we could make ourselves understood, even if occasionally we had to resort to the infantile gesture of belly-rubbing to indicate pleasure. In any case not that much was required of me. My job was to eat what I was given and coo when what I had been given was lovely to eat, which demanded no acting on my part, as it had when Robuchon watched me eat his food in Las Vegas. Save for one noxious dish of sliced sea cucumber – which felt like it had been thrown in to remind me how fabulous Asami hadn't been and how marvellous this was – the food here was extraordinary.

When I looked later at my notebook, I counted thirty-two different stages to the meal and noticed that relatively few had been traditional nigiri or maki sushi. There was sashimi of red snapper, sprinkled with lime juice, and pieces of marinated cuttlefish, which I was instructed to eat with cold sake sipped from a tiny glazed saucer. Mr Suzuki made a bowl of bright-orange salmon eggs mixed with wasabi and more sweetened sake, which was dense and intense. He gave me the crisp roasted bones of tiny fish to chew on, which were crunchy and savoury, and made a simple salad of pickled sliced onion and the sweetest of tomatoes.

Like a children's entertainer, he pulled from underneath the counter his box of tricks, an open cabinet filled with perfect cuts of raw fish. One corner was taken up with sea urchin. There was bream and octopus and a sizeable chunk of *otoro*. He took this from the box, sliced it up and pressed the pieces on to a hibachi grill for a few seconds. He indicated that I should eat them immediately and I did as I was told. The layers of fat had just begun to melt and my mouth filled with an outrageously rich and perfumed fresh fishiness.

He took some pieces of clam from the box and threw them down on to the counter as hard as he could, to watch them curl back on themselves, which I understood to be his way of proving their freshness. He seemed satisfied with the degree of curl and put the pieces in a bowl with a little soy, ponzu and pepper. These too went on to the hibachi for a moment to seal them. This time the clam didn't get stuck in my throat as it had done at Asami. Instead it was gone from my mouth too soon.

He tipped the box towards me and invited me to choose, so I had some sea urchin, which he shaped on to a lozenge of rice without the aid of the seaweed collar usually used to keep it in place. I had some freshwater prawn and then a tartare of the *otoro* mixed with wasabi. Next he pulled out a long banana leaf and began to form pieces of nigiri sushi, each one a delicate little sculpture. He painted them with a slick of soy – heaven forfend I should dredge them clumsily through a bowl of sauce myself – and when I lifted my chopsticks to begin eating he raised his hand to stop me.

He wanted to show me how sushi should be eaten: the way each piece should be rolled on to its back by the middle finger, and then picked up between thumb and index finger. Now I am told to tip my head back and place the sushi on my tongue, fish side down. Of course at first I got it wrong. I tried to do the roll with my index finger and my digits ended up in an uncomfortable muddle, a confusing game of

Twister. But the second time I got it right and I felt the warm glow of Mr Suzuki's approval. He was the master and I was his student. He made more and more nigiri, eager now to see me eat, working his knife with ever more delicate strokes through the bream and the eel and the mackerel.

We had become friends and to prove it he performed party tricks. He took a length of cucumber and, lying it flat on the counter, flicked his blade across it so fast it disappeared into a blur of shiny metal.

'Showtime!' he whispered, as the cucumber fell apart into delicate fronds. He made a maki roll with the pieces and then slapped one down on the counter so it stood upright, the lengths of cucumber sticking up high above the rice. 'Tokyo Tower!' he said with a big grin, referencing the city's landmark telecommunications array that can be seen from almost anywhere in the capital.

At the end he gave me the sweetest of marinated cherries, which was the size of a plum, and then a little bitter jelly of grapefruit. Finally, to secure our fellowship, he produced from under the counter a large glass flagon of clear liquor with, coiled round the bottom, a slender 3-foot snake, its jaws wide open so I could see its fangs. He poured two glasses and we toasted each other and drained them in one, so that I was left only with the heat and the burn of raw alcohol, which I took to be the snake's revenge.

The young man who had overseen the removal of my shoes now appeared at my side with a slip of paper upon which was written a number. That number was 50,000. Any attempt to calculate the value of this meal in terms of the ingredients used was, I knew, deeply silly. I had been given nearly three hours of the sushi master's time and that was what I was being asked to pay £210 for, the most I had ever paid for a single meal, though in my state of rapture, it seemed irrelevant. This was what I had come for. This was what Tokyo had been all about. I threw down my credit card and waved it on its way.

After Tokyo I would be going to New York, which I regard as one of the most exciting food cities in the world. After that I would be spending time back in London, examining the flavours of home for clues about my own history, before heading off for what felt like an inevitable engagement with the grand food opera of Paris. But it seemed to me, as I eyed the jug of hooch and felt the alcoholic burn work its way down my insides, that wherever I now went, wherever next I ate, a part of me would always remain here in this Spartan room with the sushi and the snake and the force of nature that is Mr Suzuki.

5. New York

Morning in Manhattan. I stumble from my bed on the thirty-sixth floor of the London Hotel. My room looks north over the Upper West Side, with just a glimpse of Central Park between the shadow-locked buildings, and today, beneath an early summer sun, the view is magnificent. Or at least it would be if I could be bothered to look at it. I have been here a couple of days and already I am bored with the view. In any case I have more important things to do today. I slump down at the desk, spark up my laptop, launch the Internet browser and go straight to a food discussion board called Opinionated About.

The thread I want, the one I have been waiting for these past twenty-four hours, is finally there. It's located exactly where it should be: in the 'Formal Dining' part of the website, under 'New York' in the 'US and North America' section. The first post had gone up about an hour before and is by a man called Steve Plotnicki. There are a couple of dozen photographs, all of them of plated food: an egg in an eggcup with a turban of cream piled high with shiny black caviar; slices of fish, fanned across the plate and drizzled with a sauce in a funky shade of yellow. There is a duck dish and a foie gras dish, and a whole bunch of other things besides. Plotnicki has invited the members of this site to identify where the meal that these dishes were a part of was served. He is giving no clues.

The first response, from a woman in London who goes by the online name SamanthaF – short for Samantha Friar – had been posted just twenty-four minutes after the original.

Her message says simply, 'Per Se,' naming Thomas Keller's place, which is inside the Time Warner Center, just a few blocks from where I am sitting. Per Se is one of only five restaurants in the city to have four stars from the *New York Times*, and one of only three to have three Michelin stars – for what that accolade is worth to New Yorkers, which isn't very much. I note that Samantha hasn't bothered with a question mark. She is certain she is right.

She is. 'That was one of the places we ate at,' Plotnicki replies.

A few minutes later someone called Ian chips in, 'Eleven Madison Park and WD-50.' Both have three stars from the *New York Times*. Again no question mark. Ian is telling, not asking.

'That makes three,' Plotnicki says. 'Two to go.'

Ian is on a roll. 'Jean-Georges,' he says, naming the flagship restaurant of Alsatian chef Jean-Georges Vongerichten. Again, four *New York Times* stars, and three from Michelin. From my window I can just about see the ludicrous golden building on the south-west corner of the park that Jean-Georges calls home.

'You're a clever lad,' Plotnicki says. 'One left.'

Now the first note of disbelief creeps in, from a poster called Scotty. 'Five dinners in one night? Respect.' Just for good measure he adds an emoticon of a smiley face. The Opinionated About crew are clearly enjoying this.

One woman tries to identify the remaining restaurant from the type of placemats pictured. Another user recognises a particular plating of desserts but is confused because, he says, the pastry chef responsible cooks in Chicago. A few minutes and some feverish Internet searching later, he's back to say that he now understands the pastry chef concerned is cooking in New York, not Chicago, which would explain it.

'Did you have reservations at these places, or did you just show up?' asks one.

'How does one logistically eat that many meals @ dinner?' asks another. 'Or does this include lunch too?'

'Some serious eating there, chaps,' says a third. 'I applaud your bravery and your gluttony.'

Finally Plotnicki explains that these dishes were part of a restaurant crawl taking in five of the very best restaurants in the city – no more than two or three small, tasting-menu-sized courses in each place – that it was pre-arranged and that the two diners involved weren't always served the same dish at each course, which explains the large number of dishes he had to photograph. Not that any of this is news to me. I know all the details. I know all the dishes. As he has already said, Plotnicki was not alone on this adventure. He had an accomplice. That accomplice was me.

I had eaten at Jean-Georges only once before, and what I remembered most from that day was the man in the corner attached to the oxygen tank. The lunch, back in November 2005, was hosted by the publishers of the *Michelin Guide*, to celebrate the release of the first star ratings for New York. I should have been absorbed by the pasta with its blizzard of white truffle shavings. I should have been swooning over the sashimi of Nantucket scallops on the vivid red cranberry jelly. Instead I couldn't take my eyes off the elderly Japanese couple, seated at a table by the door, and the delicate transparent tubes that ran from a tank on the floor, over both of the gentleman's impeccably tailored shoulders only to disappear up his nostrils.

I was impressed. The man's life was ebbing away. His vital organs could barely keep him going without support. And yet here he was in one of the city's best restaurants, enjoying a good lunch. The high-ceilinged room was flooded with light that day from the tall windows and this, combined with the sight of the intubated man, only added to the sense that we were eating at altitude.

There is nobody on any kind of life-support machine this evening as we arrive for the first leg of our dinner, but there is a notable mood of excitement. Or perhaps that's just what happens when you accompany wealthy men out to restaurants. Perhaps Steve Plotnicki is always received like this, with huge snowfield grins of recognition and bold, vigorous handshakes. I may be paying the bill but he's the sugar daddy, the one everybody is interested in. Bizarrely this makes me the arm candy.

Certainly it convinces me I am with the right guy. I want to see New York through the eyes of the high-end food bloggers, the butterfly collectors, the ones who photograph their dinner, and Steve Plotnicki has done an awful lot of that. He has eaten everything from one side of America to the other side of Europe and digitally photographed almost all of it. He has both his own blog, Opinionated About Dining, and the discussion forum, Opinionated About, which is known to its members as OA. I have been one of those members since it launched in 2003.

The son of a Brooklyn kosher butcher, Plotnicki, who is approaching his mid-fifties, made his original fortune in the music business and later from his ownership of *Robot Wars*, a hugely successful television show, versions of which aired in a number of international territories. And then there were the lawsuits, from which he also made serious money. Plotnicki was famously litigious, which stroppiness he attributed to being the child of a survivor of the Holocaust who had been forced to hide from the Nazis in the forests of Poland.

'I think because my dad was a Holocaust survivor, I'm fiercely protective of what's mine,' Plotnicki said. 'Perhaps overly protective.'

His revenge for his father's experiences was to live well. After all, what better contrast was there with the privations of the old man than to turn a matter of survival – food – into a hobby? Now he had made his money, he was determined to pursue his hobby with as much seriousness as possible.

My idea was that I should live well with him, if only for one evening. I proposed that he choose his perfect location for a meal. We would eat, he would blog it and I would pick up the bill.

'Can we do a crawl?' he said.

We started talking restaurants. He made some ambitious, completely unachievable suggestions. I told him to see if he could make it work. I didn't for a moment think it would come off.

Of course, I was wrong, meaning that tonight I am back at Jean-Georges playing arm candy.

Everybody here seems to know what we are up to this evening. They appear genuinely pumped up to be the first leg. It is just after 6.30 p.m., as we are shown to a table in the middle of the outside wall with a perfect view of the room, which is already full.

'This is the table that Tim Zagat always sits at,' Plotnicki says in a stage whisper, naming the publisher of the hugely influential Zagat guides, whose reviews are compiled from those of diners across New York.

The Asian waiter who is in charge of us for our Jean-Georges hour approaches the table. 'And so,' says Jin, 'to get you started we have a little champagne.'

He pours us a glass and announces it as a Tattinger 1996. I shudder. Plotnicki has told me not to worry about money, that he's happy to chip in; he would prefer to eat well and pay for everyone than be denied the chance of a good night out. Still, I want to pay my way. Then again, a Tattinger 1996! That's not a loose-change champagne. That's a remortgage-the-house champagne. That's a sell-the-kids-into-slavery champagne. Mentally I rehearse an explanation for my long-suffering wife as to why we'll be feeding the children on the supermarket's 'value' range for the foreseeable future.

The first dishes arrive and I shudder again: there is the famed Jean-Georges egg, a mixture of warm, loosely scrambled yolk and white, beneath the cool cream punched up with vodka, and on the top a huge, tottering pile of caviar from farmed Californian sturgeon – a bigger serving than any I could ever recall seeing before. That's for Plotnicki. I receive a different dish: two thinly cut and toasted slices of brioche sandwiching a soft egg yolk, the whole piled with another heap of caviar the size of a baby's fist.

I say quietly, 'That's a lot of caviar.'

As if reading my mind, Plotnicki says, 'Perhaps they'll comp us.' He removes his tiny digital camera from his pocket and starts taking pictures. These dishes are not simply for eating. They must be recorded too, fixed for future discussion.

I eat. The combination of yolk and black eggs, bursting on the roof of my mouth, with the crunch of the toast is both luxuriously adult and a trip to the nursery. It is both comforting and filthy rude. Next, for me, massive sea urchins – twice the size of anything I ate in Japan – laid on slices of black bread spread with cold salted butter and decorated with discs of jalapeño pepper. Plotnicki has a wheat intolerance, a reaction to antibiotics taken for pneumonia many years ago, so he gets slices of hamachi, dressed with a bright-yellow purée of Meyer lemons – the most vibrant, lemony lemons I have ever tasted – and sprinkled with Iranian rose petals.

It was at this point that I realised I had turned into a true food nerd. The room had disappeared. All that remained were me and the plates and the delicious things on them. And if you think it's going to get any better than this, if you think I might maintain even the slightest grip on reality, dream on. Food bloggers are true obsessives and tonight so am I. I am one of them.

Perhaps you find this all too rich for your blood, too exhausting, simply too bloody much. I understand. You're welcome to flick ahead seven pages to a whole new passage on power-eating in New York, and why my first ever restaurant meal in the city was also one of the most disappointing. Feel free to do so. Go ahead. Flick. It's good stuff. Of course, I'll be disappointed if you do. This, after all, is what we came for. This is what *I* came for.

We were supposed to get only two courses at Jean-Georges. We were also supposed to have been served the same thing, but they have decided to have some fun with us here tonight and so they throw out an extra dish: tuna sashimi in a vibrant, spicy but light soy broth spiked with ginger for Plotnicki, and for me a riff on sea trout, involving sashimi, roe and crisped skin. Jin fills our glasses. To our right, society ladies in sunglasses the size of hubcaps, the social X-rays of Tom Wolfe's *Bonfire of the Vanities*, air-kiss each other like the 1980s never ended.

We ask for the bill. Jin spreads his arms wide. 'There is no charge tonight, gentlemen. It is our pleasure to be a part of this great experiment.' They behave as if they are genuinely grateful that we should have included them in our night out.

'Told you,' Plotnicki says, as we stride down the steps. He is purring now. Setting this up was a struggle and the fact that he is getting it for free has cheered him hugely.

We turn and walk the short distance to the Time Warner Center, the building with the highest number of Michelin stars in the world: situated inside this high-end shopping centre, this gilded food court, is Café Grey, with one star; the hyper-expensive Japanese restaurant Masa, with two; and the place we are going to, Per Se, with three. The restaurant is designed in greys and blacks and chrome, reminiscent of the ballroom of an ocean liner.

This time we are not to eat in the dining room. Instead we will sit at a low coffee table in the bar area, but it suits the purpose perfectly. We are a restaurant hit squad now: in and out, light on our feet, grabbing dishes as we go. For us, it is a night of overtures, of culinary foreplay. None of these meals will be consummated in and of themselves and that suits us fine. Personally I love beginnings and endings far more than middles. Tonight there should be no saggy middles.

It is dusk, and laid out before us is Central Park, turning an emerald green in the falling light. We sip our champagne, which is a non-vintage something or other, and take this demotion from the heights of Tattinger 1996 across the road manfully. Now they present us with Thomas Keller's trademark savoury cornets: for me, a tartare of salmon with a little red onion; for my sugar daddy, a cornet made from a curl of crisp potato topped with a tartare of wagyu beef, seasoned with chives and horseradish.

Here, though, we have come for one dish in particular, and Plotnicki already has his camera out on the table ready for it: Keller's oysters and pearls. Later, when he comes to write an account of our meal on his blog, Plotnicki will describe this solemnly as 'the first dish created by an American-born chef that can compete with the best of what Europe has created'. The oysters are poached and are sweet rather than salty. They sit in a chive-flavoured sabayon, at the bottom of which is a little tapioca. On the top is a spoonful of caviar. (More caviar? Oh, well, if I must.) The dish is, as it was the first time I tried it; a fearsomely good combination of flavours and textures, the tapioca and the caviar playing tag with each other in the mouth. There is a lobster dish each after that – something light and soupy with artichokes and lemon verbena for him; for me, a combination of apple-wood-smoked bacon and tomato, so that it has the flavour profile of a bacon, lettuce and tomato sandwich.

We are led into the kitchen to meet the monkish head chef, Jonathan Benno. In the kitchen of Per Se nobody shouts. Nobody hectors. It is calm, quiet, industrious. At Keller's restaurants there aren't brigades of chefs; there is a brotherhood. Benno has his shaven head bowed over the pass.

He looks up and, misremembering the title of the book that Plotnicki has told the restaurant I am writing, says, 'You must be the man who ate everything.' I give a goofy gee-shucks kind of shrug and thank him for the food.

Benno turns to Plotnicki. 'And you must be the man who *complains* about everything.' Plotnicki loves the abuse. It proves they know him here and that's what matters.

We ask for the bill and again we are told there isn't one. Plotnicki grins. He has spent a lot of money at Per Se since it opened in 2004. It's nice to get something for nothing. It would, he says, be 'inappropriate' to argue. So I don't.

Downtown we head in a cab, bouncing through the neon shimmer of Times Square, towards Bouley in TriBeCa, on the Lower West Side. There is one other top joint in town, Le Bernardin – four *New York Times* stars, three from Michelin – but Plotnicki says he had a dismal meal there a few weeks ago and he refuses to return. So we're making do with a mere Michelin two-star, though one which, Plotnicki says, is responsible for some of New York's best fish cookery.

The change in status is notable the moment we walk through the door. We had come from the very top end of New York eating where everybody knew why we were there. In the homely vaulted dining room at Bouley, the dinner service is in full swing, and only one guy seems to know about the arrangement. Our waiter keeps trying to offer us cocktails and menus, and wants to recite the specials as if we're bedding in for the evening.

'Here, they'll charge us,' Plotnicki says simply, once we've got rid of him.

Still, the kitchen knows what's going on and sends out two plates of pearly Chatham cod in a light broth flavoured with *dashi* – a Japanese stock made from a reduction of kelp and shavings of dried, fermented and smoked tuna – with artichokes, salsify and bok choy. Though our stay at Bouley feels rushed, hesitant, a distraction from the restaurant's usual business (which is what it is), Plotnicki will eventually declare this his dish of the night. I can see what he means. It has a clarity and a simplicity that allows the quality of the fish to shine through. For me, though, it has to be the sea urchins at Jean-Georges, on their bed of dark bread and cold, salty butter.

We are served a plate of seared foie gras, with a purée of this and a little of that, but, courtesy of the champagne and the glasses of Nuits-Saint-Georges, my attention is wandering. I pay the $170 bill – Plotnicki was right – and grab another cab.

Just two restaurants left. First, Eleven Madison Park, a big, busy, urban bistro in a grand high-ceilinged landmark dining room run by the Union Square Hospitality Group. There, we are served far too much crispy skinned duck from a whole roasted bird presented to us at the table first, bunches of lavender sticking out of its bum. After that there is a plate of suckling pig. We also hit what Plotnicki calls our 'first bump in the road', two mediocre little mid-courses: for him, a shot glass of dull asparagus mousse with morels and a quail's egg; for me, something described as a strawberry gazpacho. It tastes of under-powered gazpacho. It doesn't taste of strawberries. I can't work out whether this is a good or bad thing.

I can't work out much any more because I am very, very full. It should have been fine. It should have been easy. After all, the plan was to do a standard high-end tasting menu – twelve to fourteen courses, perhaps – just in a bunch of different places. The time taken to get to each restaurant would also help. The problem is, firstly, that these damned chefs have insisted on sending out extras. We are beginning to feel besieged by food, chastised by it. Secondly, Eleven Madison doesn't really do the itsy-bitsy-teeny-weeny-plates thing. Its food is accomplished but it is also robust. For God's sake, they showed us the whole damn duck. We do our best to clear our plates, pretty certain now that we won't be charged here either (we aren't), but we're clearly flagging. Plotnicki appears to be making more effort to shoot pictures than eat, as if the recording of the meal, the knowledge of it, has now taken precedence over its consumption. He needs to turn this dinner into content, so that his readers can also consume it. I push slices of duck around the plate and wonder whether I can get away with eating just the fantastic skin. Plotnicki does exactly that.

I fear we have reached the saggy middle. The issue may be the whole premise upon which the evening is built. Plotnicki is trying to establish whether it is possible for a perfect restaurant experience to be constructed from a set of mini restaurant experiences. Certainly it is one evening out, with its own dynamic of highs and lows, but I can't yet decide whether it really is amounting to a single meal. It strikes me that my search for the perfect dinner has now become a little desperate.

No matter: dessert is on the way. Arriving at WD-50, we feel like athletes scrambling across the finishing line, though of course we are nothing of the sort. We are two middle-aged men attempting to conquer the city in the only way we know how: with our stomachs. WD-50 is an interesting choice. It is as far from the understated luxury of Jean-Georges as you can get. This is industrial chic, all moody lighting, concrete and rough-hewn wood. Then there is the food, prepared by chef Wylie Dufresne, who has long, lank, reddish hair to the jawline, killer sideburns and steel-framed glasses. He looks like a cross between an Alabama backwoods man limbering up to shout, 'Squeal, little piggy,' and a computer nerd. His food has a touch of the nerd about it too. He is pretty much the only chef in New York experimenting on the outer shores of El Bulli-esque gastronomy.

It is late now, close to 11 p.m., and there is a wired, kinetic, school's-out feel about the place. Dufresne comes out to greet us and insists on a blow-by-blow account of our evening.

Plotnicki says, 'It's all gone smoothly. The food hasn't jarred at all.'

'That's my job,' Dufresne says. 'To throw everything out of kilter, to make everything uneven. To screw everything up.' He attempts to do so by announcing that before dessert he plans to give us a couple of savoury dishes – a tiny piece of fish, a small serving of beef short rib – and I groan.

'It's small,' he says, sounding wounded. Not wanting to offend him, we accept. The fish, seasoned with musky nigella seeds, is odd rather than pleasant. The short rib, cooked under vacuum for hours and served with a witty take on one of those mass-produced cheese-whip sauces, is much better.

Dufresne asks us what we would like from the dessert menu and Plotnicki, after a moment's thought, says, 'Bring everything.'

My cholesterol-basted heart drops. 'Steve! For God's sake!' I sense that he's bought into the giddy mood here.

He looks at me as though I'm a lightweight. 'We don't have to eat it all.'

'But if they serve it . . .'

He pulls the menu towards him and swiftly narrows it down to just five desserts and shortly afterwards it begins, the table filling up with parades of little plates: a guava-flavoured parfait with a liquid centre and a crush of peanuts that makes the dish taste like a peanut butter and jam sandwich; something with white chocolate, black sesame seeds and the strange vegetal sweetness of carrot; a mousse of coconut with cashew nuts, cucumber and the tang of coriander.

These and the others that follow are all good, but none is as diverting as what happens next. There is a shout from the front of the restaurant. Apparently some drunk Wall Street bankers, who had been sent out gently into the night by the sommelier a few minutes before, are now trying to restart the argument. A barman has sounded the alarm and the entire brigade of cooks has come running out of the kitchen led by

Dufresne, his long hair trailing behind him. The sheer weight of numbers frightens off the bankers, who retreat, and the cooks saunter back to their kitchen, towels shoved in their apron strings, to make our last desserts and clean down.

It is nearly 12.30 a.m. We have been eating for six hours. It occurs to me that in one night in New York I had managed to experience as much of this city's restaurant scene as I had in a week in all the other places I had visited. This, it seemed to me, was down to the nature of the trade here. It was adversarial, a battle of wills. Clearly, once Plotnicki had got Jean-Georges and Per Se on board, the others had felt duty-bound to play ball. And then, with the enthusiasm of New Yorkers, they had all bought into it fully, accepted it more as a happening than dinner.

Steve Plotnicki, king of the food bloggers, had turned eating out into a competitive sport. Our only opponent had been ordinariness, and it seemed to me that we had won.

In the spring of 1978 the journal of the American Political Science Association published a short paper that proposed what the author called a whole new 'subfield for political science'. The grandly titled John Whiteclay Chambers II, a professor at Columbia University, suggested that social scientists had focused too much on what politicians thought when, instead, they should be looking at what they ate. 'The possibilities are tantalising,' he wrote. 'Is there a correlation between gastronomical and political style and success? Does digestion determine decision-making? What, in fact, is the connection between a politician's head and stomach?'

The paper, which went on to survey the late-1970s New York dining scene, reads like a restaurant guide for members of the APSA, whose annual conference was to take place in Manhattan that year. And yet, even three decades later, it still makes an intriguing point. Every major city has a few restaurants that are favoured by figures in public life: the politicians and media big wheels, the singers, actors, hookers and hangers-on who give everybody else something to look at.

As Chambers described it, New York's restaurant industry was different. There weren't just a few of these joints. There were dozens of them. They were not just restaurants people visited for reasons of status or even, heaven forfend, dinner. They were gladiatorial arenas in which a whole strata of public life was acted out. They were debating chambers or offices, only ones with nice napery, shiny glassware and a good line in fettuccini.

According to Chambers, the Kennedy clan could be found in the grand French restaurants of the East Side, places like Lutèce on East 50th, or La Goulue on East 70th. Ed Koch, then the city's mayor, usually had lunch at Charley O's Bar and Grill on West 48th or the United States Steakhouse, also in midtown. Moving up (or down) the political food chain, the disgraced former vice-president Spiro Agnew liked to eat at Frank Sinatra's favourite Neapolitan restaurant, Patsy's, while his former boss Richard Nixon – and just about everyone else – went to Le Cirque, where the infamous Sirio Maccioni presided over the highest-scoring A-list in the city. It was said that Richard Nixon and Henry Kissinger had enjoyed their reconciliation lunch at Le Cirque, and that Brian Mulroney, after stepping down as Canadian prime minister, even had his post delivered there for want of anywhere else.

It was around the time of Chambers's publication that I first became aware of New York – though not like most kids my age would, as a place with a bunch of tall buildings; more as an eating opportunity. I read an interview with Woody Allen in which he said that he never ate at home, but instead went to restaurants every night. As a twelve-year-old, with an enthusiastic appetite, this sounded impossibly glamorous. Considering the cost of this lifestyle, it also suggested that there might well be profit in being a smart-arse Jewish boy.

It took me another decade to get to New York, though it was not for dinner. It was to find out stuff about famous people that they didn't want anybody to know, or to flatter myself that I might be capable of doing so. I was twenty-two years old and the gossip columnist for a now-defunct London supplement of the *Observer*. I had been sent to America to write a column to mark the inauguration of George Herbert Bush as president, though obviously I was in entirely the wrong city. I should have been in Washington DC, snuffling out truffles of delicious political intrigue, but my editor took pity on me and my meagre journalistic experience. He sent me instead to Manhattan, where only an idiot could fail to find a story. On my first night at the Algonquin Hotel I ordered room service – a perfect hamburger made from crudely ground beef that, unexpectedly, tasted of something – and plotted my assault on the city's glitterati.

I never did find out anything that anybody wanted kept secret, though I did have fun. At a warehouse party on the

Lower East Side I met Quentin Crisp, the self-styled 'stately homo' of old England, then in his eighty-first year, who had made a fine life for himself in New York. Later, I gate-crashed a crew-only party for a rarely remembered movie called *Tap*, and watched Gregory Hines, Savion Glover and Sammy Davis Junior dance off against each other.

And, of course, I ate. I hummed Supertramp's most famous song to myself over breakfasts of pancakes, crisp bacon, maple syrup and butter. I ate caramelised nuts from the shiny chrome food wagons that seemed to occupy every block corner and filled the streets with the smell of hot sugar. I fell in love with the honey-roasted spare ribs at Ollie's, a cavernous Chinese place just off Times Square. It was noisy and bustling and just the spot for a young man a long way from home who was looking to disappear into the crowd.

I had just the one proper restaurant experience, and it was a disappointment. I was invited to lunch by the late Jack Kroll, the highly regarded film critic of *Newsweek*, who was a friend of my parents. He told me he would take me to a media hangout for our lunch, and I imagined a corner table at one of those restaurants you could be on first-name terms with – Elaine's, perhaps, or Michael's – where smart men *talked in italics* and women drank martinis and wore dresses cut on the bias. In the lift down from his office Jack told me the restaurant we were to visit was a cause of much excitement because nothing like it had opened in New York before.

When I got there, I found out why: it was an Indian restaurant, complete with flock wallpaper, the pluck of sitars on the sound system and a menu of chicken tikka masala and pilau rice. Indian food was literally the one thing New York had never, and still does not, do well. London does it well.

London is possibly the best place for Indian food outside India. I had travelled 3,500 miles to be fed the only meal I could be certain of getting back home. I picked morosely at my seekh kebab, as Jack entertained me with stories of the old days in movies before *Jaws* and *Star Wars*.

I returned to New York many times after that, to cover many different kinds of stories, but somehow all of them managed to lead me to food. In the early 1990s, for example, I went to Brooklyn to write a long report about the Crown Heights Riots between the African-American and Hasidic communities and, in a small bakery off Eastern Parkway, discovered the best bagels it had ever been my pleasure to eat. On another occasion I ate huge muffins with the enormously fat porn baron Al Goldstein, while we discussed his battle with the TV companies who wanted to stop him filling public-access television with hardcore porn. Later, on the same trip, I went to hear Woody Allen play clarinet to a half-deserted room, for a $40 cover charge, and marvelled at how poor the food was at the midtown bar he had chosen for his residency. He might eat out every night, I concluded, but the man had no taste.

The odd lacklustre meal aside, I came to realise the one thing about New York that everybody else had already clocked: it regards itself as the greatest city in the world. Not just one of them. Not merely in the premier league. The greatest. And New Yorkers don't mind saying this out loud. In my room at the London Hotel I would watch television adverts for a bond issue to raise money for investment in New York's government. They finished with a voiceover imploring residents to help keep it 'the greatest city in the world'.

Further, I realised, New Yorkers regard its restaurants as an expression of that self-confidence. The city's residents would not have been at all surprised that some academic had been able to create a map of power in Manhattan simply through its eating houses. Where else would important people go when they needed to be seen?

It has never mattered that Paris might lay claim to the greatest number of great gastro-palaces. From the opening of Le Pavillon on East 55th Street in 1941, seen as the city's first formal luxury restaurant, through the arrival of Lutèce in 1961, to the transplanting of Le Bernardin from Paris to West 51st in 1986 and the opening in 2004 of Thomas Keller's Per Se at the Time Warner Center, New Yorkers have happily convinced themselves that they have restaurants that can compete with anything anywhere. It was summed up for me by an article in the magazine *Vanity Fair* in spring 2007. It was about the global spread of sushi and discussed the Japanese restaurant Masa, where the tasting menu could cost $450 a head depending on the available ingredients, before tax and service. The writer described it, quite reasonably, as the best sushi restaurant 'in America' and then added, quite unreasonably, that it was possibly 'the best in the world'. Only a New York-based magazine could have the arrogance to suggest that the best sushi restaurant in the world might be in their city rather than in Japan.

Naturally, I found the pugnacious certainty of most New Yorkers – both professional critics and eaters alike – that their city was better than any other deeply annoying. After all, I lived in London, a world city in its own right, and one that also had a bunch of really good restaurants, thank you very much. But there was, if I'm honest, one thing in particular that bugged me about the way these people talked up New York, the way they shamelessly called it the greatest city on earth: I suspected they were right.

I am standing outside an Italian restaurant opposite the Time Warner Center and I am having a John Whiteclay Chambers moment. Parked up alongside the kerb in front of Gabriel's are a dozen shiny black limos. One of them has the numberplate NY05.

'That's someone seriously high up at City Hall,' says Tim Zagat, publisher of the guides that carry his name, who wants me to check out this restaurant that the politicians clearly love. 'If it was NY01, it would mean the mayor was in there.'

Zagat and his wife, Nina, two former lawyers now in their sixties, have invited me on a tour of Manhattan restaurants. It is something Tim Zagat does regularly: he hires a limo and sets off with a pocketful of Zagat product to cast an eye over a section of the city's eateries. He says there are months when he does it every other night, and that people have bid up to $20,000 at charity auctions to join him on the tour. There is no sense of wonder in his voice when he tells me this. He makes it sound entirely reasonable that people should value his company so highly. Zagat is a large, jowly man, as befits a guy who eats out eight times a week, and he appears less to wear clothes than to have made an accommodation with them. His shirt-tails keep escaping from his waistband and by the end of the night his suit jacket will look as though it is trying to get off his shoulders and back into the closet unaided.

The Man Who Ate The World

I have asked if I might join the two of them on a tour to gain an insight into the New York restaurant scene. For me, it is a great opportunity, but I can't for the life of me work out why Tim Zagat bothers. It's not as if the Zagats actually review restaurants. They simply publish the guides, which started nearly thirty years ago as a restaurant tip sheet circulated among their friends. People were asked to score restaurants out of thirty on food, service and ambience. By the third year of the exercise over 500 people were providing information on more than 300 restaurants and 10,000 copies were circulating for free. As Tim Zagat once put it, their hobby 'had blossomed into a ten-thousand-dollar after-tax expense'.

It was in 1982 that they turned it into a business. More than twenty years and many dinners later the New York guide sells over 600,000 copies a year and the law career is a distant memory. There are editions covering more than forty US cities, as well as London, Paris and Tokyo, all using information supplied by over 100,000 individual restaurant surveyors. There is now zagat.com, a website providing information on restaurants worldwide, and Zagat for the Palm Pilot.

In the Zagat guide for New York, Gabriel's has a solid score of twenty-two out of thirty for its modern Tuscan food, though, as Tim says, it is more famous for the famous people who eat there than what they eat. As we walk through the door, the small, stocky maître d' falls on Zagat like he were a long-lost son. It is 8.30 p.m. and the room, which is lined with curved booths, is full. The NY05 limo, we are told in a whisper, belongs to the New York City director of finance.

Paul Wolfowitz, who had only just resigned in disgrace

from the presidency of the World Bank, had been and gone, as had the billionaire Herb Allen. Towards the back is a CNN reporter and *Vanity Fair* writer called Jeffrey Toobin, having dinner with his wife, who used to work for Zagat. So we stop by the table for a dose of chat so small you would need a microscope to spot it. This is the shape the evening will take: we will walk into a restaurant, look at people eating, exchange words with someone senior in front of house and maybe stop by a table of Zagat's friends.

I quickly note that Nina is staying out of it. She remains in the limo or slumps down on a sofa by the door with a magazine until we are done, as though she is merely tolerating her husband's need to tour the tables.

We move on to the Time Warner Center. He wants to show me Porterhouse, which he says is a great new steakhouse, but really he wants me to meet Michael Lomonaco, the head chef. Lomonaco was head chef at Windows on the World at the top of the North Tower of the World Trade Center. He only survived 9/11 because he went to ground level to get his glasses fixed. Almost his entire staff died. Now he is back, with a big, butch American steakhouse, and Zagat clearly regards the man's return to the stove as a sign of renewal in the city. Lomonaco comes out of the kitchen to glad-hand Zagat, as if he has nothing better to do right in the middle of the dinner rush.

Ten minutes – a long stay by Zagat standards – and we're done. Now he wants me to see Café Grey, a New York take on a Parisian brasserie, which he tells me is flawed 'because the menu never changes'. Still, he says, the interior is pretty with all its glossy wood and shiny metal bits, and he's right. The open kitchen is by the windows and looks out over the starfield of Manhattan. Zagat tells me I must have a look at the private dining room.

'Aren't there people eating in there?' I ask.

'Sure, but it's not like we're going to sit down with them. We're just going to look.'

That's what we do. We walk into someone's private party, look at people eating who look back at us, startled, as if we're the scary drunks from the bar, and then we leave. I clench my buttocks in embarrassment.

It only gets worse. He insists we go across the way to Masa. People in this Japanese restaurant are paying at least $500 a head for dinner. They are having a once-in-a-lifetime experience, and Zagat wants to look at them having it. As we approach the door, carved from a single piece of 2,000-year-old wood, he announces theatrically that we should be quiet, but then he strides in, stands at the end of the beautiful blond-wood bar and hails the chef, Masayoshi Takayama, with a big, hearty, country-club wave.

The small, bald Japanese man comes over to see him. It strikes me that no chef would refuse to talk to Zagat, but this one looks awkward and is clearly eager to get back to his customers. Zagat seems oblivious. He wants to know about a kind of stone that has been used for the décor so that he can get his architect to buy some for his house. Masa shifts from foot to foot and glances back over his shoulder at his $500-a-head diners. Eventually Zagat lets the chef go back to feeding his customers.

We climb into the limo and barrel on down to the Meatpacking District, where, Zagat says, 2,000 new restaurant seats recently opened on a single city block. 'The expansion of the business is at such a rate right now that it's even got this optimist thinking it can't last.' We wander through pan-Asian brasseries and Mexican places and faux-French joints, carved into old funky warehouse spaces, with bare brick walls and polished concrete floors and the ripple of heavy sub-base in the air. Every table is occupied, every chair filled.

Zagat does not appear to be recognised everywhere we go. Occasionally he is challenged by a glossy young person at the door holding the reservation book. He says, 'We're just taking a tour,' like people do that every night in New York's restaurants, wandering around, sticking their heads into private dining rooms or standing between tables as waiters thunder by with plates of food. They all let him pass. Sometimes he stops at a table and offers the diners a Zagat guide, a map or a card with a code that will give them a free subscription to zagat.com.

'It's not a business card,' he says, 'so don't throw it away. It's worth thirty dollars.' Some people are baffled by this tousled man. Others appear genuinely grateful. This element of the tour – personal hand-to-hand marketing by Zagat himself – makes a kind of sense. But it still seems a lot of effort from a guy who runs such a huge company. It's certainly not necessary to the business. If it were, somebody would be doing the same in London, and I know for a fact they aren't.

'I like restaurants,' he says, when I ask him why he is doing this. 'I like being in them. I like watching people. This is my version of being a politician.' In launching the Zagat guides – by harnessing the critical faculties of all diners – he says he has created 'a new form of democracy'. This point is unarguable. The Zagat guides predicted the era of online democracy, when the Web would allow every consumer a critical voice, and did so long before the Web had even been thought of, let alone provided an easy mechanism by which to achieve it.

He also says that wandering around restaurants gives him a sense of how the business is doing. 'I can tell just by looking at the tables, by seeing who's here and what they're ordering, how healthy the restaurant is.'

'Really?'

'Oh, sure. It's important to see the age of diners.' Not that he appears entirely comfortable with what he finds. We stand in the middle of Morimoto, a slick, buzzy Japanese restaurant, designed in shades of white, and he mutters, as if to himself, 'Look at them, they're all so young. They're all so damn young.' In another place he reacts with surprise at the sight of four women eating together. 'It's good that they have the confidence to do that.'

I suggest gently that this might be a generational thing, that in the twenty-first century young women eating together is not exactly worthy of a stop on a sightseeing tour.

'That's what I'm saying,' he replies. 'It's good to see.'

In Mario Batali's Italian place Del Posto, he relaxes. 'Look!' he says, pointing. 'Look! People with grey hair.'

He leads me into a pan-Asian restaurant called Buddakan, which is exactly how I imagine hell would look if the Devil went into catering. It is a grotesquely large restaurant of bare brick walls and over-inflated chandeliers, made up of interlocking echoey chambers reached by huge staircases, and I can't help but think that somewhere is a final staircase that leads to a fiery pit, full of hornèd beasts, serving only 'Belarus home-cooking'.

We shuffle through the crowd. 'A girl could get pregnant on the way to the bar here,' Zagat barks into my ear, above the noise. Young people wolf down plates of chilli rock shrimp and spiced tuna tartare as though their lives depend upon it, and my ears consider haemorrhaging in time to the music.

Suddenly Zagat spots some friends at a corner table. He introduces me to 'everyone's favourite old-time cop', a late-middle-aged man with stubble over his fat-pleated chin. Bo Dietl, a former New York policeman, is reputed to have arrested more felons during his career than any other, and is now a private investigator. His suit, with its Stars and Stripes lapel pin, shines under the light, and his receding hair is slicked back. With him is a media-friendly Harvard law professor who shares his name with the playwright Arthur Miller, and a silver-haired class action lawyer called Mel Weiss, who is under investigation by the Federal government for allegedly paying plaintiffs to bring lawsuits.

They shout questions about restaurants and food at Zagat, who shouts back. Dietl makes apologetic noises about their choice of restaurant that night.

Zagat waves them away. 'You're not here for haute cuisine,' he says to Dietl.

The former cop grins up at him. 'No. We're here for pussy.'

Zagat, startled, rocks back on his heels. 'Oh, yeah,' he says awkwardly.

I can't help but look down the table at the two young women, wearing shiny dresses in primary colours with plunging necklines, who are sitting with these old men.

It is while we are escaping this festering live action movie by Hieronymus Bosch that an unexpected thought occurs to me: I am hungry. It is nearly 11 p.m. and I have just spent the past three hours wandering New York's top restaurants, watching other people eat. I have seen plates loaded with magnificent steaks, and platters of pristine sushi. There have been roast chickens, and complex Asian curries, and huge, crisp salads of a size that only Americans would consider reasonable. I have not been able to touch any of it. I would say I had been like a eunuch in a harem, except that a eunuch is supposed to have no urges, and I was now one huge, trembling heap of urge. I couldn't remember when I had last been this hungry. I was sure it was sometime before the onset of puberty.

This, I realised now, was a genuinely rare occurrence. While eating in restaurants obviously fulfils a basic need, I generally don't go to them because I'm feeling dizzy through lack of food. I go for the experience, for the taste, for the pleasure. Nutrition comes a distant second. That was all the more true on these eating trips of mine. The issue was not about getting enough. It was always about more, about fitting everything in. I didn't do the workouts merely to keep off the fat; I did them to build up an appetite.

Now I have one, a serious one, and it is an uncommon pleasure. After much debate, and a few calls to various restaurants to discover the kitchens are closed, we head for the Pearl Oyster Bar, a New England-style seafood restaurant in the heart of Greenwich Village. Nina raves about it en route and reads me the review from zagat.com on her Palm Pilot. Tim falls silent for the first time as we approach the narrow street where Pearl is located and at last I begin to understand at least one reason why he might undertake these tours. At the end there is always the promise of a well-earned meal, which is the best kind of meal there is.

That night we eat deep-fried oysters in a crisp overcoat of batter with coarse tartare sauce. We eat meaty steamer clams, dipped in pulled butter, and then I have a lobster roll, the most promiscuous use of a luxury ingredient I have ever come across, created purely out of abundance: the prime meat of an entire pound lobster, bound in a mayonnaise sauce on a sweet, soft-grilled hot-dog bun. It isn't pretty. It isn't subtle. But it is definitely dinner.

It was in New York that I first began to worry about my Internet gastro-porn habit. I feared it was out of control. My morning could not begin unless, perched naked at the hotel-room desk, my back arched to avoid it touching the cold plastic of the chair, I had checked the food discussion boards. There were now so many of them: egullet.com, obviously, which was the online equivalent of a noisy conference centre. There was Opinionated About, for a more select discussion, plus Mouthfuls, a break away from both egullet.com and OA, set up by people who resented the latter's exclusive invitation-only policy. And then there was the secretive NIAC, a tiny site with just a few dozen members that didn't think the OA membership policy was anything like exclusive enough. ('First rule of NIAC: do not talk about NIAC.') Nobody knew what NIAC stood for, save the founders, and they weren't telling. It merely added to the cliquey, college-society feel of the site.

I belonged to all of these, and I was left with a terrible

sense of incompleteness, of tasks undone, if I had not logged on to all of them first thing to get the latest news from New York. In London seeking news on foreign restaurants like this almost made sense; now that I was here, continuing to do so was bizarre. It made the similarities between Internet gastro-porn and the below-the-belt variety unavoidable. It was about doing vicariously at my desk what I should have been doing for real.

Back in London I had wasted hours reading accounts of other people's meals at Jean-Georges or Per Se. Because I earn my living as a restaurant critic, I had been able to tell my wife that this was vital research. Sadly, she's not stupid. Every time she caught me salivating over pictures of someone else's lunch she observed me as if I had been found with my trousers about my ankles. It got to the point where I wished she'd catch me looking at something genuinely made of naked human flesh, rather than the roasted-animal variety. It would, I concluded, have been slightly less embarrassing.

Here, in New York, I felt that self-disgust all the more keenly. Only sad people look at pictures of other people's food on the Internet. The main issue, I realised, was the yawning chasm that could open up between the business of looking and the business of doing. This had been brought home to me on my first night in the city when I went to dinner with friends at Peter Luger's, the legendary Brooklyn steakhouse just over the Williamsburg Bridge from Manhattan, which was established in 1887. For years I had read about the steaks at Luger's and dreamed about going there to try one for myself. Britain does not do good steak. We have the cows, but not the will. British restaurants are never prepared to cut the beef thick enough or to serve it in large enough slabs. The British steak is a thin and insubstantial thing, an insult to the animal.

Digital pictures of Luger's steaks suggested a different dish altogether: a crisp, blackened char on the outside, cut to reveal innards of pink or purple that leaked their juices across the plate. People wrote about these dry-aged steaks as if they were wines that had been allowed to develop a fine 'mineral' taste, with a rich, meaty 'end'. They discussed the smoky fat and the virtuous interplay of meat, salt and fire. When Michelin gave Luger's a star in their first New York guide – a remarkable award for a restaurant that had no fancy linen and refused to accept anything other than cash – I decided that one day I would go there.

It looked as I had imagined, all rough-hewn wood and bare floorboards. The waiters, with their barrel chests, thick forearms and sharp backchat, also fitted the script. I liked the side dish of fried potatoes, and I loved the thick-cut dry-cured bacon. But the steak itself was a huge let-down. It was dull, insipid, just so much blood-sodden meat on a platter. Eating it was relentless.

I knew that Steve Plotnicki was a regular at Luger's. He was a regular everywhere. I described to him how my steak had been nothing compared with the ones I had read about online. He nodded sadly. 'My dad, the kosher butcher, used to say you can't crawl inside the meat.'

I frowned. 'By which he meant?'

Plotnicki shrugged. 'Every animal is different. You can't really tell whether the steak is going to be any good until you start chewing.'

Perhaps, but at $250 for a three-person steak dinner I had the right to expect a reasonable quality threshold. I returned to reading other people's online accounts of heroic meals at Luger's, like a newly deflowered virgin staring at something X-rated and wondering, baffled, why my first time hadn't been quite like that.

The only comfort I took in my online habit was that it was not unique to me. In London the online food community was small enough that we could get most of us round one table. (We had once done so. A few years ago I went out with fifteen of them to eat a whole pig at St John in Clerkenwell, and I quickly realised that almost all the people I had ever corresponded with were there.)

By comparison New York's online world is gargantuan. It isn't just the discussion forums. It is also the blogs, with their instant reviews. For years New York's restaurateurs had been used to worrying only about the *New York Times* critic, who could be relied upon to come at least three times and as many as five. A bad review from the *New York Times*, usually written with all the wit and energy of a church sermon, might be devastating for business, but at least the chefs and owners knew it was properly researched. Nobody could or would say the same about the bloggers.

'They play to a different set of rules,' I was told one morning by Danny Meyer, the owner of Manhattan landmark restaurants like the Union Square Café, the Gramercy Tavern and Eleven Madison Park. 'They don't have to check their facts. They can do it anonymously. Speed is the name of the game. That drives me nuts.'

Mario Batali, the celebrity chef and restaurateur, felt the same way: 'Many of the anonymous authors who vent on blogs rant their snarky vituperatives from behind the smoky curtain of the Web,' he wrote online, in summer 2007. 'This allows them a peculiar and nasty vocabulary that seems to be taken as truth by virtue of the fact that it has been printed somewhere. Unfortunately, this also allows untruths, lies and malicious and personally driven dreck to be quoted as fact.'

Batali's diatribe appeared on eater.com, a commercially run blog about New York restaurants, which makes its money from advertising. There is also Grub Street, the blog of *New York Magazine*, which competes with eater.com to be the first with gossip from the city's food business, and Diner's Journal, the *New York Times*'s food blog, where Frank Bruni, the newspaper's critic, posts stuff he can't fit into his column. Now, any chef trying to open in the city has to have one eye on the plate and one on the computer screen.

No one knows this better than Gordon Ramsay, whose restaurant at the London Hotel, where I was staying, had received a kicking since its opening in November 2006. Some of the criticism had come from the old media. A major profile in the *New Yorker* magazine had portrayed a shambolic operation with a gifted, ambitious but troubled chef desperately trying to play catch-up. The review in the *New York Times* had been mediocre. 'For all his brimstone and bravado,' Frank Bruni wrote of Ramsay, 'his strategy for taking Manhattan turns out to be a conventional one, built on familiar French ideas and techniques that have been executed with more flair, more consistency and better judgment in restaurants with less-vaunted pedigrees.'

What had really damaged the place, what had really put it on the back foot, was a constant stream of bad stories on the blogs. First, there was Bruni announcing that, when he booked, he had been told he could only have his table for two hours. He was also informed that he had to wear a shirt and jacket. 'Glad to have that spelled out,' Bruni responded. 'Like many a New York diner, I often enter restaurants bare-chested.'

Then eater.com revealed that the place was threatened by an all-out strike by non-unionised European staff who had discovered they were going to be cut out of the tip pool. Neighbours also moaned to the blogs about smells from the extraction units. It was OK when they were cooking bacon, they said, lousy when it was duck. Naturally, I read every single one of these stories, hungering for any snippet of gossip I could find, for I liked to live the life of the virtual restaurant-goer.

The restaurant's spokespeople tried to claim these were just normal teething problems – that the two-hour limit was a mistake by an over-zealous reservation clerk, that the union-tips issue was just a little local labour difficulty – but the sense that the restaurant was in trouble was unavoidable, not least because Ramsay quickly sacked his head chef, Neil Ferguson, and replaced him with a New Zealander called Josh Emett.

Ramsay's restaurants now felt to me like embassies for Britain's culinary efforts, their chefs the ambassadors who I called upon as a matter of courtesy if I happened to be in town. I had eaten at his place in Dubai and interviewed his chef there, Jason Whitelock. In Tokyo I had met up with Andy Cook, Ramsay's head chef at the Conrad Tokyo. Now I was in the kitchen at the London sipping coffee with Emett.

'I find it all mind-blowing,' Emett told me. 'There's just so much information out there, and we're constantly trying to work out where it's coming from. You just don't get that sort of thing in London.'

I asked him if he read everything. 'Jean-Baptiste [the maître d'] reads everything and he tells me what to read and what not to read.' For a while he brooded on the fact that they had been ridiculed for not knowing the precise definition of a Nantucket scallop when they put the term on the menu. 'I was concentrating on other things, not geography, so we came a cropper on the whole Nantucket-scallops thing.' He looked around at his huge brigade of chefs busily preparing for the lunch service. 'You only have to look at how much effort is going into this to know how serious we are about it.' And then, almost desperately, 'We did this exactly the same as any opening. We didn't do anything differently.' He was at a loss as to why they had received so much negative publicity.

I thought I knew why. A couple of nights before we met, I had eaten at Gordon Ramsay at the London Hotel, in the subdued melancholia of the dining room with its mother-of-pearl-style walls and its gloomy elegance. If this room had been a person, it would have been an elderly lady in an expensive cashmere two-piece, hair just so, ankles crossed tidily under the table: attractive, but hardly exciting. That night I had eaten, well, I had eaten . . . food. There was a scallop dish. There was a duck dish. There was something with sweetbreads and an apple tarte tatin. It was all expertly prepared. It was all assured and confident. No one should ever attempt to deny the glossy professionalism of the Ramsay operation.

It was also completely unmemorable. What did stay with me was the clientele. Just as Ramsay's in Dubai had been, it was full of English people: a couple of braying posh boys in rugby shirts; some girls in footballers'-wives dresses with bottle-blonde hair; a few mousy English couples, fidgeting in their seats. Dubai had been Guildford. This was suburban London, a little further into town but not by much.

That night, after dinner, I went to my hotel room, thirty-five floors above, fired up the laptop and went looking for other people's thoughts on Gordon Ramsay's attempt to take Manhattan. I read reviews on both egullet.com and OA, many of which agreed with me, some of which did not. I browsed pictures of platefuls of neo-classical dishes – seared protein, reduced sauce, turned baby vegetables – and grew tired. It was when I started looking for reviews on Mouthfuls that I decided I had had enough. I was done with this restaurant. I didn't need other people to confirm for me that my money had bought me a boring experience. I logged off, closed the laptop and went to bed. I decided I could stop worrying about my Internet gastro-porn habit. I was clearly making progress.

There was one hot place in town that didn't appear much on the discussion boards. It was called the Waverly Inn and it didn't appear much because few people on the discussion boards could get into it. The Waverly, an old-style pub in the West Village with low ceilings, black beams and saggy red banquettes, was now part-owned by Graydon Carter, editor of *Vanity Fair*, who had styled it as a clubhouse not for the people who read his magazine, but for those who appeared in it. In the few months since it had reopened after a makeover in autumn 2006, it had become a regular haunt for the likes of Sean Penn, Gwyneth Paltrow, Tim Robbins,

Robert De Niro and Bono. Getting a table was not simply a matter of phoning up the restaurant.

For months, if you did call the number, you would hear a voice (on a machine that didn't take messages) saying it wasn't yet officially open. Notionally it was in a try-out period, but this went on for week after week, and its dining rooms were always full. It was open but not open. If you were so presumptuous as to want to eat there, you had to call the only real reservation clerk, who was one of Graydon Carter's assistants in the Condé Nast building on Times Square. Assuming you knew either Carter or his assistant.

If John Whiteclay Chambers were mapping New York's power restaurants now, he would, of course, include the Waverly, and naturally I thought I should eat there too. I had heard that, while it was a scene – the presence of so many movie stars turned it into a movie set – the food was rather good. I had just one possible route by which to get a booking. As a sometime contributor to *Gourmet*, itself a Condé Nast publication, I would simply have to debase myself by shamelessly begging the office of *Gourmet*'s editor to make a call on my behalf to Graydon Carter's office.

I received an email suggesting I had about as much chance of getting a seat as joining the kickline of the Rockettes at Radio City Music Hall but that they would see what they could do. Then came the startling news that, by some miracle, through some unexpected rupture in the fabric of time and space, they had found a table for me.

And so, on a Friday night, I went to the Waverly. As I stood in the bar with my friend Greg, a senior editor on another magazine, I scanned the room for faces that I recognised. I was looking for Gwyneth, Sean or Bobby. I didn't see anyone. Later we were led into the dining room, with its dimly lit corner tables and its mural of all the famous New York faces by Edward Sorel – the likes of Norman Mailer, Jackson Pollock, Andy Warhol and Marlon Brando. I saw all those faces on the wall, but only in passing because we were led into the dining room – and straight back out again into what is widely regarded as the Siberia of the garden room. There had been nobody famous at the tables in the dining room and there was nobody famous out here either.

I ordered a bowl of chilli to start, and then a veal chop. Greg had a chicken pot pie, under a dome of golden puff pastry. It was comfort food, very good comfort food as it happens, but comfort food all the same.

'You realise,' Greg said to me over his pie, 'that you are the only person here I have ever heard of.'

Half cut on the cheapest bottle of wine on the list, I took him seriously. 'I'm not famous,' I said, puffing myself up at the thought that my writing had finally given me a profile in New York.

'Er, no, you're not. That's my point. I've only heard of you because you're a friend of mine. Everybody else here is a complete non-entity, just like you.' Then he slumped back in his seat, struck by a thought. 'Of course! It's a Friday night. Everybody worth seeing has been helicoptered off to their place in the Hamptons.' I had debased myself to get into the hottest restaurant in town on one of the few nights when it was as hot as Alaska in February.

We looked around the room. It was full of boys in bandanas, and the girls who love them. Greg told me most of them would have been personal assistants to media big wheels, taking the place of the big wheels themselves. I had no reason to doubt him. Conversations were shrieked, air kisses puckered out like so many rounds of automatic gunfire. The room was filled with the smell of lip gloss and highly flammable hair gel. I wished I had a cattle prod to hand. These were people I could never have tired of hurting.

It all seemed a terrible waste of a perfectly nice restaurant, with nice food at a not unreasonable price. Suddenly I found myself thinking back over my restaurant experiences: to the bottle-blondes at Ramsay's and the social X-rays at Jean-Georges, to the braying Russians in the gilded restaurants of Dubai, and the big-ticket Americans in their red braces, clanking their fiercely expensive bottles of wine into ice buckets at Pushkin in Moscow. Now an image came to me, a clear and unappetising picture of the kind of people who occupy the dining rooms I so often review in London, and that in turn led me to an unavoidable truth . . .

Hell is other people

If you want to see what skilled professionals can do with very sharp knives to expensive pieces of meat, you could do worse than visit one of the top restaurants in New York, London, Paris, Moscow or Dubai. You'll find enough facelifts in those dining rooms to make a whole new party of six from the off-cuts. You know the sort: shoes by Manolo Blahnik, scarf by Hermès, permanent look of surprise by the hottest surgeon in town – and that's only the men.

Or maybe you don't know the sort, but I do. This has been the true horror of my job as a restaurant critic. Yes, I get to sit in opulent dining rooms, eating extraordinary food and having Dom Perignon squeezed into my mouth from a

South Seas sponge, and all on somebody else's dime. But I also have to do this surrounded by the sort of trussed and lacquered, gold-encrusted, preening, lobotomised, bigoted, tasteless, self-satisfied, self-abusing arguments for involuntary euthanasia – won't somebody put these bloody people out of my misery? – that, even in this post-Soviet era, could make a strong argument for Bolshevik revolution.

From such long, selfless service watching them clank their jewellery on the tableware and from listening to their inbred caterwauling over their *amuse-gueules*, I had reached a profound conclusion: expensive restaurant experiences are generally wasted on the very people who can afford them.

Let me give you an example, possibly *the* example. In July 2001 the international press thrilled to the news that a party of bankers had run up a bill of £44,007 for a single dinner at the London restaurant Petrus. The restaurant is named after arguably the greatest red wine in the world, and certainly the most expensive. During the meal the boys ordered three bottles of it: a 1945 at £11,600, a 1946 at £9,400 and a 1947 – regarded as the greatest vintage of them all – at £12,300. There was also a £1,400 Montrachet and a £9,300 Château d'Yquem. (Two bottles of Kronenbourg beer accounted for the extra £7.)

While the rest of the world was thrilled by this remarkable exercise in pure, unadulterated bling, the wine world was quietly singing a different song. These men were obviously scalp-hunters who simply wanted to chalk up the trio of sequential vintages for no other reason than because they could. The truth is that, while the 1945 and the 1947 genuinely are two of the most important wines of the last century, the 1946 is regarded as a non-starter. It just happens to be old. If these people had really cared, they would have ordered a couple of bottles of the two other vintages and ignored the 1946 altogether.

More to the point, if drinking these wines had genuinely meant something to them – beyond the opportunity for cock-waving – they wouldn't have gone to Petrus in the first place. They would have gone to an auction house and bought them there because in July 2001 even the 1947 was going under the hammer for a little over £4,000. In short, these great, totemic wines were drunk by people who were not worthy of them.

This is not petty snobbery. Or, at least, it's not *just* petty snobbery. It's important. The enduring taste-bypass exhibited by the moneyed classes at Petrus goes a very long way to explaining why, for so many decades, food in Britain has had such a stunted culture compared with somewhere like France. In France the food culture is a bottom-up affair, with high gastronomy only being its ultimate expression. The notion of *le terroir* to which every Frenchman cleaves – that there is a specific piece of land from which their identity comes – may well encourage gastronomic conservatism, but it does at least lend the whole business a certain democracy.

In Britain food is, and always has been, from the top down. From the moment the Industrial Revolution herded the peasantry off the land into the cities so they could spin wool and send their children up chimneys, the link with the land was broken. It left the way open for the British aristocracy to reinvent food as a status symbol. Off they went on their grand tours. They travelled Europe, ate interesting food and hired the people who cooked it. The first of these culinary scalps, Antonin Carême, who came to

Britain in the early nineteenth century to cook for the prince regent, was also the most typical.

Food historians like to describe Carême as the father of haute cuisine, but for the prince, the Elvis Presley of his day (in the deep-fried peanut-butter sandwich stage), Carême was just a means by which to make an ostentatious display of his wealth. The chef would create menus of 100 dishes and set the table with food carvings made from pastry, spun sugar and lard. What better symbol of the British failure to understand the importance of food is there than the way the prince and his court would celebrate the arrival at table of a scale model of the ruins of Antioch made entirely from carved animal fats?

A century later Auguste Escoffier landed at London's Savoy Hotel and again served the same purpose to the aristocracy, and it continued on down the decades, until relatively recently. Today the Roux brothers, Albert and Michel, are known in London as the founders of Britain's first restaurant to win three Michelin stars – Le Gavroche – but when they arrived in the 1960s it was as chefs to the aristocracy. I once asked Albert Roux the gastronomic difference between France and Britain. 'In France,' he said solemnly, 'every taxi driver would know the price of black truffles and would save up to eat them at the Tour d'Argent.' By contrast in Britain, he said, every taxi driver would know the price of a box of Black Magic chocolates and would save up for a bag of chips. That made me very sad indeed.

What now troubled me, as I sat at the Waverly in New York surrounded by nightmarish people, was that I had come to assume that this situation was entirely unique to Britain, that it was purely a function of my country's peculiar historical circumstance. Up to a point I was sure that was the case, but if my journey round the world had taught me anything, it was this: every night in the great food cities of the new millennium there were terrific restaurants filled with horrible people who were there because they could afford them or, through status, gain access to them, and who were having a much nicer time than they could possibly ever deserve.

I decided the time had come to pay another call on Mario Batali, not least because it was his fault that I had embarked on this journey in the first place. I had wanted to test his claim that three Michelin stars had merely become a guarantee for rich people that they could eat the same food wherever they happened to be in the world.

We met again at Otto, his pizzeria at the southern end of Fifth Avenue. It was too early for food. He had no pieces of ham to wave at me this time to emphasise his points. Instead we perched our large arses on his tiny bar stools, sipped coffee and talked about the business. When last we met, Batali had been a New York chef with New York restaurants, but the lure of the famous sweetheart deals had proved irresistible.

'We've now got two restaurants in Vegas,' he said, with an air of inevitability. 'At the Venetian.' One was a high-end Italian, like Babbo, the other a version of Otto.

I was surprised. Batali had always been so big on using local ingredients. There aren't any ingredients in Las Vegas. He shrugged. 'I just pretend the restaurants are on the coast in California because that's where all the ingredients come from. We drive it overland for four hours from the farmers' markets in Santa Monica.' And then, with a slow shake of his huge head, 'Vegas! It's a weird place.'

Had he eaten well there?

'Oh, yeah, I had a great meal at Robuchon. It was every bit as good as the meal I had in 1987 at Robuchon's restaurant in Paris, right down to the menu items.' He said this with a wry smile. 'The question you have to ask these multi-starred chefs is how important is place and how important is innovation. Take Ramsay. He thought he could simply wow people here with showmanship. Ramsay's guys didn't know anything about ingredients here. They didn't realise how important ingredients are here.'

Shortly after it opened in New York, Batali went to eat at Ramsay's. 'But nothing's changed with his food since his second year at Aubergine,' he said, referencing the restaurant in London's Chelsea where the chef first made his name.

I pointed out that Ramsay was at Aubergine way back in the mid-1990s.

'Yeah,' Batali said, 'I know.'

What about the bloggers, which I had heard he so disliked? He was on such a roll that asking the obviously provocative questions was irresistible.

Now he spat out the words. 'It's just people who hate things. But you know what? If they don't like my beef-cheek ravioli and the rock 'n' roll we play on the sound system at Babbo, they can suck my dick. I don't care.'

I barely needed to ask the next question. I already knew the answer, but I asked it anyway. Had he at all revised his view that Michelin stars were just a symbol of a certain kind of consistency for rich people?

No, he said, he hadn't. 'All Michelin does is reward luxury ingredients. It's the only way these high-end restaurants can justify charging four hundred dollars a head, because you can't charge that for spaghetti and clams or a salad.'

The last time he had said this, or a version of this, I had been resistant to the idea. I had wanted to believe that a high price tag generally meant a good experience. I now looked back upon myself as almost sweetly naïve. Sure, I had eaten very well at times – at Robuchon in Vegas and Al Mahara in Dubai, at Yukimura and Okei Sushi in Tokyo and at all the places on our restaurant crawl here in New York City – but I had also travelled too far and eaten far too many mediocre meals for far too much money to mount a serious defence to Batali's argument.

I had one last request. 'Where should I go,' I asked him, 'for the quintessential New York restaurant experience?'

Batali didn't hesitate. A big grin came across his face. 'You should go to Katz's Deli on Houston Street and order a pastrami sandwich. But be warned. If you're doing dinner tonight, don't eat the whole thing.'

I did as I was told. I got on the subway and went to Katz's, a landmark famed for its menu of New York Jewish classics, like its Reuben sandwich, its salt beef and its pickles. Katz's is the place where Meg Ryan faked her orgasm in *When Harry Met Sally*, and the spot where the scene was filmed is marked by a sign hanging from the ceiling, which reads, 'Hope you had what she had.' The place is a barn, a cluttered, scuffed, old-time cafeteria that smells indecently of food, its walls hung with fading photographs of New York celebrities that meant nothing to me, and the occasional piece of neon signage. There must have been 300 people in there and it was still only half full. I fell in love with it immediately.

The counter runs the entire length of one wall and, while there is waiter service, it was clear to me that I should order directly from the guys with the knives and the big forearms on sandwich-making duty. My man fetched a lump of soft, fibrous pastrami from the boiler and brought it back to his chopping board. He took off three slices and threw them on to a plate on the counter for me to try while he went to work. This, I could see, was a Katz's tradition. All of the slicers were doing it. So I stood there and ate the meat while he sliced up another pound of the stuff and piled it between two slices of rye bread, like he was trying to hide a rhino in a jewellery box.

It didn't matter what Batali had said. The idea that I should leave any of this sandwich uneaten was ludicrous. The meat was too rich, too savoury, just too damn good to be abandoned to the plate. It occurred to me that this food had its roots in all the Russian menus that had so disturbed me while I had been in Moscow. But this, I decided, was Eastern European food as cooked by people who had been blessed with the gumption to get the hell out of there. It was émigré's food and all the better for it.

I realised I was profoundly happy here in this room with this sandwich. In a very neurotic, needy and, yes, Jewish way, that bothered me. When I had set out on this journey, determined to map what was going on at the top end of the restaurant world, it hadn't for a moment occurred to me that what I would eat would make me sad or angry. I had only envisaged various degrees of happiness. Instead, a lot of it had made me very angry indeed. It troubled me that my emotional responses were so governed by what I ate. I wondered what sort of person I was, what sort of eater I had become that I could be influenced in such a way by the plate in front of me.

Of course, there was only one place where I was likely to find the answers to questions like that: home.

6. London

Most Christmases when I was growing up, my mother made chopped liver in the Jewish Ashkenazi style, to be eaten on shards of crisp matzo before the roast-turkey lunch. This outbreak of ecumenical feasting made a lot of sense. Almost all the people in our house on Christmas Day were Jewish, and the terrine of rich, grey chicken livers scattered with crumbled hard-boiled egg gave us a shared, if unconscious, reference point. It provided a necessary culinary grounding before my mother, Claire, assaulted us with the roast bird. And the sausages. And the bacon. And the potatoes. And the pickled red cabbage. And the Brussels sprouts mined with chestnut shrapnel. And the bread sauce and the gravy and the Christmas pudding and the jelly and the fruit salad and the cream. If anybody pointed out that chopped liver followed by Christmas roast turkey was a culinary non-sequitur, we would always roll out the same lame joke: Jesus was a nice Jewish boy and what better way to mark his birthday?

Our Christmases were never for extended family. My father was an only child, my mother's siblings lived in

Canada or the US, and she had long ago broken off all contact with her own parents after a miserable childhood she was determined not to revisit. The only relatives were my father's parents, and my mother disliked them intensely. Later, Claire told me that the enormous Christmases she threw – one year twenty-eight of us sat down to be fed from a turkey the size of a small horse – were designed specifically to hide her mother-in-law away in a crowd. This, I understood. I didn't much like my paternal grandmother either.

But it was also, I think, a function of my mother's habit of collecting people. She had a fascination for those who, unconnected by blood, nevertheless created networks that mimicked family just as she had done when she was a nurse, hence many of the Jews who joined us for lunch were also either gay men or actors. Or gay Jewish actors.

They were all keen to be collected. By the mid-1970s Claire was famous as one of Britain's leading agony aunts. She had a weekly problem page in Britain's biggest-selling daily newspaper and a slot answering viewers' queries on a BBC daytime television programme, among other things. She had made her name offering up no-nonsense advice on health worries and sexual dysfunction by insisting that there was no problem, however personal, that could not be discussed, and many of her friends took her at her word.

I remember during one of those long Christmas lunches, my mother telling the story of Larry, a neurotic New Yorker who telephoned after midnight in much anguish. 'Claire,' he said, 'one of my testicles is missing,' as if she was so blessed with wisdom she might instinctively know where to lay her hand upon it. She sighed deeply, told him she was sure it would be back in place come the morning – it was – and went back to sleep.

Looking back, I see now that, however random it might have appeared at the time, there was nothing happenstance about the cast list at these Christmas lunches; like my family, the guests were all regulars of a particular London restaurant, merely relocated to the suburbs for the one day of the year when it was closed. The restaurant was called Joe Allen, and it was where I fell in love with eating out.

There had been other places of course: the *Alice in Wonderland*-themed Mad Hatter, not far from where we lived, where I always ordered the croque-monsieur and wondered at the swirly, glittery bits in the liquid soap dispensed in the toilets; the Great Gatsby, a US-style burger joint in Mayfair, which served an ice-cream sundae that could harden an artery at twenty paces; and Stone's Chop House, where I ate frog's legs for the first time.

Joe Allen was in a different league. It opened in January 1977, on the sort of grim, narrow lane just back from London's Strand that you might visit if you specifically hankered after being mugged, and was marked by its ostentatious lack of ostentation. The doorway, in a street with no other shops or restaurants, was indicated only by a small brass plaque. You had to know it was there to know it was there, and even some of London's cabbies didn't. It also demanded insider knowledge once you sat down. Newcomers were easily spotted. They were the ones asking the white-aproned waiters – usually unemployed dancers – for a menu, before being directed to the blackboards hung high on the walls above the half-open kitchen (a standard feature of gastropub Britain today, a revelation back then).

Then there was the Joe Allen burger, one of the best in the city. It was never listed on the menu, but regulars knew it was available if wanted. In short, Joe Allen had all the qualities of a members-only club but without the fee.

Like the original in New York, which opened not long before its British sibling, the London Joe Allen had quickly become a favourite with theatre people. The bare brick walls were hung with framed theatre posters from both sides of the Atlantic, and late at night, after the curtains had come down across the West End, it was common to see the very people given star billing in those posters sitting beneath them eating supper and pretending to be nobody. Everybody from Elizabeth Taylor to Al Pacino, Laurence Olivier, Elaine Stritch and Princess Margaret had eaten there over the years, and it was soon regarded as the place for celebrity-spotting, though the restaurant had a way to make sure its starry clientele went unmolested. The space was divided in two by an arched wall. If you were a regular or a face (or both), you got to sit on the left-hand side, nearest the kitchen. Everybody else went to the right and had to gawp through the arches.

My mother's notoriety, and my parents' regular custom, guaranteed our family a table on the left-hand side, plus a welcome from pianist Jimmy Hardwick, who had been hired simply to play the live music necessary to secure a late drink licence, but who had become a feature of the restaurant. He had a talent for segueing seamlessly from whatever he was playing at the time to the big number for whichever musical star had just walked through the door or, in my mother's case, 'Clair' by Gilbert O'Sullivan. My parents table-hopped or else we were joined for coffee by the perma-tanned stars of daytime television that my mother had met on the celebrity circuit. It was glamorous, cheesy and very, very camp.

As an eleven-year-old boy, I loved it all.

More than anything else, I loved the menu of American bistro food: the buffalo chicken wings, with their cayenne-boosted spicy marinade that made my lips tingle alongside a cooling wave of sour cream; the spare ribs with the cornbread, rice and black-eyed beans; the garlicky Caesar salad dressed with freshly grated Parmesan rather than the dusty old ground stuff that tasted of vomit, which was what passed for Parmesan in the rest of Britain at the time.

I liked this food too much and eventually it was my undoing. My parents took us to Joe Allen so regularly that, by the time I was sixteen, I felt relaxed enough to go without them. I liked the fact that there was a restaurant in the centre of London where I could phone up and get a precious, hard-to-land table at short notice; that, when I walked in, I would be recognised by the maître d' and the piano player. I must have been a truly repulsive adolescent. Certainly, I was convinced that if I were to take girls there, they would be so impressed by my uncommon maturity and sophistication they would immediately want to snog me.

Perhaps they would have done, were it not for the fact that appetite would then take over. I would do the bit with the maître d' and the hearty hellos with the piano player. Then I would sit down and order the spare ribs, and when they arrived would grab them with both hands until sauce was smeared across my fat cheeks and dripping off my ears so that no girl, however desperate or impressed, was going to shake my hand let alone kiss me. My wife later told me that, in my early twenties, I did exactly the same with her.

'But by then I'd already snogged you, so it wasn't such an issue. Luckily for you.'

Joe Allen remained a regular haunt into adulthood, but fashion moved on and so did I. There were other places to eat now, other places to be seen, in a city which was often better at doing restaurants designed for being seen in than for eating in. Jeremy King, who had worked front-of-house at Joe Allen from the late 1970s, left in the early 1980s to open Le Caprice with his business partner, Chris Corbin, and did the same as Joe Allen – the smart American bistro food, the zippy service, the all-important buzz – only they did it better. Much of the celebrity clientele followed, and stayed with them as they oversaw the Ivy, J. Sheekey and, later, the Wolseley. Those were the places stalked by the London paparazzi now.

Joe Allen has endured. It is now into its fourth decade, a serious achievement in the capricious restaurant business. Still, it has been forced to face up to its fading status by flagging up its entrance with a striped awning so that passing trade might find it, much like a middle-aged hooker hitching her skirt just a little higher above the knee. The blackboards have also gone to be replaced by standard menus (though the hamburger remains unlisted).

In time I became a professional eater, and worked my way about the tables of my home town with the enthusiasm of an experienced lover, grateful to the woman who took my virginity but with no incentive to visit her again. Why would I eat at Joe Allen now? What would be the point of that when I could secure a booking at any number of other places?

Now it made sense that I should go back. If I really did want to understand why being at a table in a restaurant – or even just the prospect of being at a table in a restaurant – should make me feel more content, so very much more myself, I had to return. In undertaking this journey, I had a secret weapon: my elder son, Eddie. He had eaten with me in Michelin-starred restaurants, could tell good Chinese food from bad and liked his steak rare. He was a mini-me, if you discounted the blond hair, the perfect whip-thin physique and his absolute refusal to take either himself or his parents too seriously. His birthday was coming and that presented the opportunity. Perhaps I could get to see what the restaurant looked like through the eyes of the child I had once been. And so, on the day he turned eight, my wife and I took Eddie to Joe Allen for dinner.

This was a mistake, as attempts to revisit the past invariably are. For a start he was not the child I had once been, thank God. He was also with me, rather than with my mother. Thus the reception we received, while friendly enough, was hardly Louis Armstrong and Barbra Streisand in *Hello, Dolly!* No marching bands, no dancing waiters and nipple-tassels, not even a tune on the piano, which rested silently beneath its canvas cover, our reservation having been so early in the evening that Jimmy had not yet arrived. Many of the tables were also empty, though I had come to understand that this was often how it was at Joe Allen these days. There were no famous faces to look at, and the only person we knew was a friend of my parents called Mike, a suburban solicitor with an interest in the theatre. He had been eating at Joe's in the late 1970s and was doing so still – which was one long dinner. A very nice chap, but low wattage when it came to the flash of glamour, as even he would have agreed. Seeing him here just made me feel old. God knows how old it made him feel.

No matter. There was the food. Though there wasn't, not in the way there once had been, because there never is. Flavours are embedded into the fabric of the time and space they occupy – as Einstein would doubtless have pointed out if he'd been a big eater – and cannot simply be wrenched from them.

Eddie ordered the fillet steak – 'Rare, please' – but it came smeared in a gloopy-looking Béarnaise sauce that he hadn't expected and his bottom lip twitched with disappointment. He swapped it with his mother's duck breast, which was cooked to a shameful shade of brown, beneath a dense, fruity sauce. Eddie tackled this with muted enthusiasm, and though I tried to tempt him with one of my spare ribs – with a taste of my youth – he wisely declined. Even the Caesar salad was a disappointment. It was dusty and underdressed. There was a moment, when the lights dimmed and the chatter at the tables seemed to increase, that I thought I caught an echo of the old Joe's, of the buzz that had so intoxicated me. Then it was gone and we were in the present, many miles from the past.

We looked at Eddie, his long hair hanging loose over his eyes, his shoulders sagging. He had been up since six that morning opening presents and playing with them and now he was so exhausted that he couldn't even be enticed to try the chocolate brownie with ice cream and hot fudge sauce, a refusal that on any other day might have warranted a trip to the doctor.

I said, 'What do you think of this restaurant?'

Eddie looked around and, eager not to sound ungrateful, said, 'It's good . . . but I've been to some that are better.'

He was right. He had, and so had I. It was time to visit one of those instead.

Another glossy international hotel room, complete with thirty-two channels of cable television, the gentle whirr of air-conditioning and an 'intelligent' minibar that knows when I've been at the over-priced pistachios. This, I find sinister. I don't like it when machines watch my snack habits.

Give or take a few lushly carpeted square metres and the deplorable lack of a butler, this hotel room at the London Intercontinental is exactly the same as all the other hotel rooms I have occupied on my journey save in one important regard: there is a woman here too. She is lying on the bed in her hotel-issue towelling dressing gown, punching her way from one television channel to the next on the remote, while muttering, 'Crap . . . crap . . . crap . . . crap . . . It's all bloody crap,' under her breath. My wife has never been convinced of the value of cable television, and the selection here is only reinforcing her opinions.

It's true that Eddie, through no fault of his own, was less useful than I had hoped in my voyage of self-discovery, but I am convinced that Pat will do the business. Although I have been slow to admit it, even to myself, I have finally recognised that my pursuit of the perfect meal was doomed to failure because I had been conducting it in entirely the wrong company, which is to say, my own. I was never going to have a perfect meal, or frankly even a good one, unless I was with the woman who knew me best, and who somehow still liked me in spite of that.

So the kids have been sent to stay for the night with their beloved aunt and uncle, and we have booked into a hotel at Hyde Park Corner, only a couple of miles from our South London home. We have played tourist in our own city for the afternoon and now we are going out to dinner at the Square, a highly regarded restaurant in Mayfair with two Michelin stars, one of only five in the city. It has a reputation for serving delicious but unpretentious high-class food, and to lots of people at the same time. The Square isn't some small boutique restaurant. It's big and glossy, with seating for 100 or more, the high walls hung with huge gashes of vibrant modern art. I have eaten there only once before, but I remember that meal fondly for its light, modern way with French classicism. I am sure Pat will love it. The truth is, I am desperate for her to do so. Because I only will if she does.

There is just one problem. There's no doubt Pat likes eating out. She loves well-prepared food and good ingredients. I have seen her genuine, satisfied smile when friends have congratulated her on having lucked out as a restaurant critic's moll: all the food without the bore of having to write anything about it. How good is that?

But she doesn't like all of it, and what she likes least of all is the flummery and corporate frottage of the kind of big-ticket restaurant that we are sitting in right now. I know that if she never has to eat another *amuse-bouche*, it will be too soon, and when the junior sommelier attempts some blatant upselling by trying to get us to order glasses of the ferociously expensive vintage champagne, by not mentioning there is a cheaper house option, she sighs and rolls her eyes.

I know how she feels about all this stuff. I have known about it for a very long time, and yet for some perverse, twisted reason I keep trying to convert her, like a desperate missionary convinced he can get the godless to see the light.

Pat settles down behind the menu, which is of a size small children could bivouac under in a storm, and I watch as she picks at the canapés. I am so keen for her to like the food here that right now I am not even paying attention to whether I do as well. I note the way she scoffs a tiny cornet of foie gras parfait, and her gentle nod at the goat's cheese sable, which she says is interesting. But there is also my disappointment when she dispatches a tiny stuffed mushroom and asks, quite reasonably, what the point of it is. Who bothers to stuff a mushroom?

She orders a langoustine dish to start, and then the lamb. This is no surprise. Pat almost always orders the lamb.

We settle back to wait and I ask her what she thinks of the room.

She looks around, at the plate-glass windows on to the black London night, at the tasteful lighting, and the dark suits, and the glint and flash from delicately handled cutlery. 'This will never do it for me,' she says. 'It's hermetically sealed. No contact with the world. I would rather eat at that place in Soho which does the really good cassoulet. That's part of its environment. Here, you could be anywhere in the world.'

I ask her if she thinks I am strange for being so interested.

'I don't think you're strange, but I also don't understand what you're hoping to get out of it. The first time you try high-end food it's astounding, but after that you are just grading your experiences against themselves.'

'I'm still interested to see what comes out of the kitchen.'

'Why? It's not going to surprise you.'

'Maybe it will,' I say sullenly.

While we are talking, we have been served an *amuse-bouche*: a little watercress jelly, some salmon rillettes, scrambled eggs, potato foam and chives in a tiny glass.

Against all expectation, I watch Pat clean the bowl down to the last smear. She lays down her spoon. 'If this was the first time I had tried something like that, you could have peeled me off the ceiling. But now . . .' She shrugs and looks around the room again. 'Can you see a single person you want to know? Does anyone look interesting? Do we look interesting? We probably look as boring as the rest of them.'

Oh, God. There was I arguing that expensive restaurants were wasted on the people who could afford them, and now my own wife is telling me that I am one of those people.

Thankfully, our starters arrive and, praise be, they are terrific. I have a bowl of silky-soft puréed potato, in the Robuchon style, with rich, pungent Monk's Beard cheese, snails, sautéed wild mushrooms and doll's-house beignet of frog's legs. I nibble on the tiny frog's legs and then dig down with my spoon to get a little of the mushroom duxelle at the bottom and then some of the potato and a snail and a whole mushroom. It is all rich and luscious, and the complete opposite of food designed to be looked at. This is food to be eaten. Pat's huge roast langoustines with Parmesan gnocchi and a potato and black-truffle emulsion also has her saying positive things. I feel we are making progress. This meal is going my way. We have eaten good food in a nice place, and Pat may just be forced to admit she is having a good time.

Perhaps she would have done if the fire alarms had gone

off, or somebody had phoned in a bomb threat, or the River Thames had fortuitously broken its banks in magnificent fashion and swept us all away so that we had not been able to eat another thing. For after that the meal was a disaster.

'You see! That's what happens,' Pat says, as she works her way through her main course of lamb with a herb crust. I can see that she is bored of chewing, that the dish has become a trial. I know what she means because my veal – a little sweetbread here, a bit of the rump there, some celeriac purée – is exactly the same. It is just so much protein on a plate, food as sedative.

'They build you up and they bring you down,' Pat says, as she lays down her cutlery, much of the dish uneaten. The service is distracted, disinterested. Nobody asks why food has been left behind, as if it might be intruding into private grief, and when we complain about unequal measures of highly priced wines by the glass, the sommelier suggests that we are making a fuss about nothing.

At dessert, things only get worse. I am served a slice of cheesecake with a rhubarb sorbet. I take a tiny spoonful of the sorbet and, startled, insist that Pat tastes it. She is so cross now that it does not surprise me when she doesn't bother with cutlery, choosing instead to scoop some up carelessly with her fingers. She recoils, with a look of disgust on her face.

'It's mouldy.'

I nod sadly. 'Well, technically it's not the sorbet that's mouldy, it's the rhubarb from which the sorbet was made, but . . .'

She shakes her head at me. Before her is a plate of chocolate fondant that she has barely touched.

'Why did you make me have dessert? I didn't want dessert. I could have been back at the hotel having another cocktail.'

We ask for the bill, pay it as quickly as we can and leave without saying anything to the chef, Phil Howard, a nice man whom I have interviewed on a couple of occasions and whom normally I would have wanted to meet. We just want to leave. He calls me a few days later.

He says, 'You couldn't wait to get out of there, could you?' To his credit, he wants to know what went wrong, wants to know about everything: the upselling by the sommelier, the bored waiters, the mouldy sorbet, and I tell him. He asks me to come back again, as his guest. I thank him for the offer.

It makes little difference. The meal had cost £222. True, I had spent more on some meals during my travels and on occasion eaten just as badly, if not worse. I had simply shrugged them off and put them down to experience, perhaps even revelled in the opportunity I had to take my revenge in print. This was different. With those poor dinners abroad I had excuses. I was a stranger in a strange town, and in those circumstances a good restaurant can never be guaranteed.

London was my town. I was on home turf and I had no excuse for eating badly. My job was to know these restaurants inside out, and if even I couldn't make sure that I had a good time, what hope was there for anyone else? I was furious about the expense of £222 for such a truly dismal, disappointing, depressing experience. For days afterwards I wandered about, angry and irritable. I was brooding. I was meant to have eaten a great meal. Instead I was allowing the bill for that meal to eat away at me.

Curiously, my wife didn't seem at all troubled by this turn of events. Pat was in a very jolly mood indeed.

I knew who to blame for my bad night out. It was the same people who were responsible for every bad meal I had ever eaten in London – though, to be fair, they were responsible for many of the good ones too. It was those titans of British gastronomy Margaret Thatcher and Rupert Murdoch.

This requires the long view, so let's step back a few decades to the Second World War, when, in an act of national survival, Churchill's government industrialised food production in Britain and introduced rationing in a bid to guarantee that the population remained fed. Any link between the land and its inhabitants that had survived the Industrial Revolution was now firmly broken. That, combined with an essentially Protestant culture that tended towards stoicism and self-denial, led to a completely moribund and drab food offering. It would eventually make Britain the laughing stock of Europe, and certainly the last place you would think of popping to for lunch.

In the latter decades of the twentieth century the derision came not only from beyond the country's shores but from within them too, as Britain's well-travelled middle classes happily bored their friends with the revelation that French food culture had an uncommon depth and lusciousness compared with that found at home. While undoubtedly true, it always seemed to me that these critics were failing to recognise the basic reason for this gulf: food culture had endured in France because, when the Germans invaded, the entire French nation suddenly remembered they had something in the oven that needed looking at and quickly surrendered so they could go back to tilling the land and cooking up all those delicious daubes and coq au vins. The British, meanwhile, fought on alone and saw food as merely another part of the war effort.

The thrust of the foodie's complaint, however – that eating out in Britain was a dismal experience, akin to root-canal surgery only without the anaesthetic – was undoubtedly true: overcooked meat, over-boiled vegetables, sauces like wallpaper paste with none of the flavour profile. Both the war and, even more importantly, the nine gruelling years of rationing that followed had left the country with a collective sense that to spend proper money on sustenance was somehow indecent and that the flamboyance and display associated with the 'Continental' restaurant – all that setting fire to things! All that stuffing of one bird into another! – was a gross self-indulgence and certainly not the done thing in Britain.

Of course, there were always those with an interest in eating well. Elizabeth David's elegant food writing, in books like *French Country Cooking* and *An Omelette and a Glass of Wine*, let people know there was another way. There were also stalwart restaurants, George Perry-Smith's Hole in the Wall in Bath, for example, or Sharrow Bay at Ullswater in the Lake District, which fed people well. But the pickings were still meagre, and in most parts of the country you were more likely to starve than get a good dinner. Even in London food of ambition was generally to be found only at prohibitive prices in the dining rooms of grand hotels, like the Connaught, and there was very little of that.

The Man Who Ate The World

Margaret Thatcher's personal contribution to food culture in Britain is hardly glorious: as a young research chemist, before she entered politics, she was part of the team that devised the method for pumping huge amounts of air into sweetened milk solids to produce Mr Whippy supersoft ice cream. However, her political philosophies had a major impact on the restaurant business. Put most simply, Thatcherism made it OK both to have money and to spend it on stuff. A series of tax-cutting budgets and economic measures that favoured the moneyed over those on low incomes encouraged a consumer boom which eventually washed into the catering trade.

After all, once the fat-walleted city boys had bought their houses and their cars and their box-shouldered suits, what the hell else were they supposed to spend their money on? Restaurants presented the opportunity for some all-too-literal conspicuous consumption. It is no coincidence that, when commentators look for the first shoots of Britain's so-called restaurant revolution, they point to once-famed London restaurants like Hilaire, Alastair Little and Clarke's, all three of which opened in either 1983 or 1984, the early years of Thatcher's second boom-time government.

The key year, though, was 1987, which saw the arrival of Bibendum, the River Café and Kensington Place. Most importantly, in January of that year, Harvey's opened in London's Wandsworth, just south of the Thames. In the kitchen at Harvey's was a young, beautiful, gifted and scrappy chef called Marco Pierre White, who liked to shout at his cooks and his customers in between cooking what was reputed to be some of the best food ever seen in the British capital: tagliatelle of oysters with caviar, roast Bresse pigeon with a fumet of truffles, savarin of raspberries.

Marco Pierre White, a motherless working-class boy from Yorkshire with a serious mouth on him, became Britain's first rock-star chef, with all the bad behaviour that title suggests. There are many chefs working today who cite Marco as an inspiration, and it has been argued that the credit for all this fame and adoration should go to a former rock-band manager and restaurant inspector called Alan Crompton-Batt, who became his PR man.

It is true that Crompton-Batt built up the young chef as some mysterious, mercurial figure of the stove, and in doing so invented the profession of restaurant PR. Before Crompton-Batt new restaurants merely opened their doors and hoped that customers would find them. Crompton-Batt, a gregarious, entertaining but troubled alcoholic who would die young as a result, changed all that by targeting journalists and shaping his clients to fit the stories the newspaper wanted to write. He was a vital part of Marco's success.

That said, he was only able to do his job because the British media was itself suddenly interested, and the media was only suddenly interested because of technical innovations introduced by newspaper proprietor Rupert Murdoch.

For decades the newspaper industry in Britain had been held to ransom by the print unions, who could – and would – take a title off the streets if they had a dispute with the management. The result was an industry sentenced to decades of chronic unprofitably. Murdoch, inspired by advances in technology, was determined to tackle the problem. After all, as owner of the *Sun*, the *News of the World*, *The Times* and the *Sunday Times*, he had much to gain, not least by a massive reduction in the number of staff needed to print his papers. One night in 1986, after negotiations had collapsed, Murdoch secretly moved his entire newspaper production to a new site across London in the Docklands and sacked all 6,000 of the printers. It resulted in months of violent picketing outside Murdoch's Wapping headquarters. Eventually the protests collapsed and soon almost all of Britain's national newspapers were making plans to introduce the new technology themselves.

This short lesson in British newspaper history is important because of the impact the new technology had on the structure of the newspapers themselves. Before Wapping, a British newspaper was just one section with perhaps a colour magazine for the high-end Sundays. Suddenly it was possible to print endless supplements and new sections at greatly reduced cost. The problem was, what to fill them with? Taking their cue from successful early 1980s lifestyle magazines like *The Face* and *Blitz*, newspaper editors across the capital decided the future lay in leisure time.

Food and drink fitted the bill perfectly, not least because it was innovative. It's true that some of Britain's glossy monthly magazines had previously run restaurant columns. The model for the British restaurant review, which talked as much about the room and the ghastly people in it as the food, was pioneered by a journeyman writer called Quentin Crewe in the society magazine *Queen* in the 1960s. Crewe, who had muscular dystrophy, had been consigned to a wheelchair since his twenties and the column, with impressive bad taste, was called Meals on Wheels. In the early 1980s the novelist Julian Barnes was employed by Tina Brown to write a similar restaurant column for *Tatler*, under a pseudonym, and the

London *Evening Standard* ran a column, written first by Quentin Crewe and then, from 1972, by Fay Maschler (who continues to this day).

Regular restaurant columns were not a feature of Britain's national press until the mid-1980s, when Paul Levy – one of those credited with coining the term 'foodie' – started reviewing a couple a month in the *Observer*. Then, in 1986, *The Times* appointed Jonathan Meades and the weekly restaurant review was born. Very soon all the (then) broadsheet papers had their own columnists, whose writing fed back to encourage the restaurant sector, which in turn only encouraged the food writers further. The writers were now competing against each other to write the sharpest, most vibrant copy, fully aware that, if the reader found their restaurant writing dull, there was always another guy working down the street.

It is this furious competition that distinguishes British restaurant writing from that in America. In the US few cities have more than one or two newspapers and not all of those employ critics. The restaurant critic therefore has the place to themselves and, in an often extravagantly profitable business, will have the luxury to visit a restaurant three, four or five times before handing down judgement, usually in measured tones. Their British counterparts – and there are around a dozen of them – will go once and then, eager to find a readership, tell it as they find it. No US critic ever alludes in their restaurant reviews to, say, bodily fluids, sado-masochism or the merciless Mongol hordes sweeping across Asia; a British restaurant critic will feel they have failed if they haven't mentioned at least one of those, if not all three. It led the *New York Times* to announce, in 2003, that the profession in London was pursued by a bunch of 'sometimes hilarious, astonishingly brutal restaurant critics who in the last few years have turned English food writing into a blood sport'. I had never been so proud.

And all of this thanks to Murdoch and Thatcher, without whom I would not be able to make a living as a food writer – simply because such a living would not exist, much like many of the restaurants I visit. Still, that doesn't mean it isn't also worth acknowledging the deforming influence their involvement has had on the business. A restaurant sector like that in London, which was encouraged, for the most part, by the availability of the money to pay for the experiences it was selling rather than out of some profound interest in food, is bound to give birth to some God-awful monsters. Likewise, the feverish interest of lifestyle journalists, with an insatiable hunger for the next big thing, cannot help but tempt restaurateurs to pursue ever more contrived unique selling points. Over the years in London, I have eaten in a restaurant that championed the unique fusion of Italian and Japanese food (risotto eaten with chopsticks, anyone?), another that offered tiny, overwrought French dishes, to be plucked from a sushi conveyor belt, where they had all inevitably cooled to an Arctic chill, and a third that made a feature of the hole in the wall beneath the shared sink between the toilets which enabled the women to watch the men pee. Assuming they wanted to.

The most corrosive impact of the forces that shaped London's restaurant sector, particularly at the top end, was a by-the-numbers approach, which insisted that certain things be done not because they might be, say, fun or even merely pleasant, but because it was a 'fine-dining' restaurant, and that's what a joint with that title demanded. With little embedded restaurant tradition to pull upon, there was no real culture of professionalism and precious little skills base in the UK. All the new breed of restaurateur could do was ape what they had seen in France or the US – and all too often they were about as convincing as a six-year-old girl in Mummy's shoes.

I discovered all of this for myself in the early 1990s when I was robbed at a Central London hotel. What I had thought I was doing was having dinner at Marco Pierre White's relocated restaurant at the Hyde Park Hotel, where he had finally won his third Michelin star. Instead it felt like the sort of incident that really ought to have been settled in the courts, or at least by a punch-up.

White was the first British-born chef and the youngest anywhere in the world to win that precious third star. Legend had it that, every morning, he was roasting thirty-six chickens not for the meat, but just to make the best *jus* possible. Once squeezed, the chickens were thrown away. This, of course, was a disgrace and an obscenity and beneath contempt. Naturally, I found it intriguing.

In those days I was consuming restaurant reviews rather than writing them, and had read breathless accounts of his food, describing meals which were, according to these writers, the best they had ever eaten.

I wanted to know what the best tasted like.

I wanted to know what three stars meant.

I *needed* to know.

Sure, it would cost. White was charging £75 a head for three courses, a price tag it would take Gordon Ramsay another ten years to reach, even at his flagship restaurant in Chelsea. But I was an optimist. I assumed it would be worth it.

You can see where this is going. The room was gloomy and shrouded in a morbid silence that was broken only by the half-hearted scrape of silver on porcelain. The food – pretty little scribbles of this and that across the plate – was, as far as I can recall, dull and soulless. It speaks volumes that while it was at the time (and in real terms, remains) the most expensive meal I had ever paid for, I can only access my emotional responses. Of what we ate I remember almost nothing. All Pat could talk about afterwards was the young waitress with the cold, expressionless face whose one job appeared to be showing women to the toilet and back again, and who can blame her for being a little on the dour side with that gig? There had been no attempt to help us towards having a good time, either in the service or on the plate, and it had left me in a depression for a week, at the end of which I swore I would never allow a bad restaurant experience to upset me like that ever again.

Obviously it was a promise to myself that I had failed to keep. That was what made me so cross about our dinner at the Square. It had been more than a dozen years since that meal at Marco Pierre White's restaurant – or the scene of the crime as I now like to call it – and yet visiting the Square had made me feel exactly the same way. I had begun to suspect that I really should get out less.

London

The attention of London restaurant critics can make chefs behave in strange ways. In 2003 a chef called Marcus Wareing suddenly began behaving very strangely indeed. That year Wareing, who is a protégé of Gordon Ramsay, moved his one-Michelin-star restaurant, Petrus, from a site in St James's to a space in Kensington's Berkeley Hotel. I had very much liked Petrus when it was in St James's and, like many others, had been surprised when it had not been awarded its second Michelin star. Wareing was a gifted and unashamedly bourgeois chef who was not scared of big flavours. I still held intense memories of his dishes there: of seared scallops in a lobster bisque tasting ripely of the sea, or his sweet, glazed round of pork belly. There were many who believed he was laying down a serious challenge to his mentor.

The move to the Berkeley was supposed to provide him with the platform from which to achieve that second star, and there was no doubting the money that had been spent. The old Petrus had been a coffin-like chamber of silt-coloured walls and gloomy down-lighters. It always felt as if there was a table of constipated bishops eating somewhere in its depths. In tribute to the grand wine from which it took its name, the new Petrus had fabric-covered walls the rich colour of claret, uplifted by twiddly chrome and silver bits. There were highly polished trolleys that glided about the room dispensing champagne, cheese and sweeties, and a wine list heavy not merely with some of the greatest bottles known to man, but some serious bargains as well to attract the big-ticket-restaurant virgins.

But mostly there was the new menu, which was – and this is a highly refined and very technical restaurant-reviewing term – completely tonto. It is, for example, a curious fish dish that encourages a maître d', on hearing you order it, to announce, 'I am Belgian and in Belgium this is not how we cook turbot.'

Good grief, I thought to myself at the time, this is not how they cook turbot anywhere.

The menu description said, 'Braised turbot with Welshrarebit glaze, smoked cod roe with aubergine caviar and sautéed baby gem lettuce, lemongrass velouté.' The maître d' described the dish to me, just as it was written. He said something like, 'I wanted you to know how complex it is,' and wandered away.

Pat was eating with me. She watched him go and said, 'That sounded like he was trying to dissuade you from ordering it.'

Perhaps so. Certainly I wasn't ordering it because I wanted to eat it. I was ordering it because it read like a car crash, and I can rubber-neck with the best of them. It tasted as it read – a grossly over-seasoned cacophony of flavours. It was certainly a terrible thing to do to an innocent piece of fish. In my review I said so.

A few weeks after it was published, while on a family holiday abroad, I received a message on my mobile from a senior member of the egullet.com team, an auditor for a British telecoms company with ambitions to become a professional food writer. He believed he had a scoop, told me on my voicemail that he was preparing to publish his story but that he wanted my response first. It turned out that I was not the first critic to have ordered the turbot dish. Almost every one of us had done so. Wareing, who had spotted me in the dining room, had become so enraged, so frustrated when I had done so, that he decided to completely change the dish on service. Out went the Welsh rarebit crust to be replaced with a herb crust. Out went the lemongrass velouté to be replaced by a cep sauce. The gastronomic scoop of the century was that, apparently, I hadn't noticed, and Wareing was telling anyone who would listen.

I was intrigued. Looking back at my review, I saw that, while I had been clear that the dish was a mess of flavours and too salty, I genuinely hadn't identified what those flavours were. Perhaps there was something interesting to be said about the connection between what we are told we are eating and what we therefore taste. It struck me that it couldn't have been much of a cep sauce or I would have jumped up and shouted, 'Who put all the mushrooms in the lemongrass velouté?'

What intrigued me most was the lengths to which a British chef might be prepared to go when confronted by a British restaurant critic. There had been a deliberate attempt at deception, which would have been bizarre in any restaurant, let alone one at this level. Then again, it seemed Wareing was going through a curious period of his life. Asked in a newspaper questionnaire around that time how he wanted to be remembered, he said, without a hint of irony, 'As a gastronomic legend,' as if the little voice inside his head that was getting him through the long and brutal working days had somehow escaped his mouth.

Many of the reviews of the new Petrus were negative and it did not achieve its second Michelin star, not that year or for the two that followed. Finally, however, in 2007 Michelin decided the restaurant was right. In January it was awarded its second star. I had not eaten there since the turbot incident, though I had bumped into Wareing on the tight, intimate London restaurant circuit and he had told me that much of his menu had changed. He said he had returned to many of the virtues of the old Petrus.

Certainly, if I was looking for a great meal, for an experience that would right the wrongs of the Square and place my world back on its rightful axis, it had to be one of the restaurants I should visit. I told Pat she had to come too. She sighed deeply and dragged her shiny heels back out of the wardrobe again.

The sleek Belgian maître d', Jean-Philippe Susilovic, was still in place, though he was a little more recognisable now. He had played the role of maître d' for Gordon Ramsay on both the British and the US versions of the reality-TV cooking show *Hell's Kitchen*, which essentially meant being abused by Ramsay for a month at a time. Jean-Philippe said that, after each shoot, returning to the challenges of his restaurant, where the occasional customer might get cross but nobody told him to cut off his own testicles and eat them, as Ramsay once did, was a pleasure. He handed us the menus and, as we opened them, said, 'Are you looking for the turbot with Welsh rarebit? It's not there.'

'You remember?'

'This, we don't forget. You don't mess with turbot. I told him this, but you have to learn from your mistakes.'

The turbot really wasn't there, but lots of other good things were. There was a simple and clean-tasting salad of lobster with pickled vegetables and powerful black-pepper jelly, which reminded me of the best of Jean-Georges in New York. We ate a dish of the freshest crab and langoustines with tiny brown shrimps from Wareing's home town of Southport in Lancashire. There was a faultless fillet of Angus beef with truffles, and a plate of sweet suckling pig – loin, cutlets, crackling – whose infancy at slaughter didn't bear thinking about. We were served extras of scallops with an orange foam and foie gras with precisely acidulated rhubarb, and at the end a parfait of peanuts with an intense chocolate mousse, salt caramel jelly and a raspberry crème. It was a dessert of the sort created by someone who understands the imperative of sweet, and not simply because he knows there has to be something sugared to end with.

But mostly there was just the gentle hum of things done right. Pat attempted to whine – 'At the end all that will remain is the memory of good food in a red room surrounded by people I don't like the look of' – but I could tell her heart really wasn't in it, that she was having too good a time. As we sipped our coffee, Wareing appeared at our table and thanked us for coming. None of the critics had returned, he said. Then, unbidden, he said, 'I got it wrong at the beginning. I went from driving an old banger to a Ferrari and lost control.'

Emboldened by Wareing's declaration, Pat began talking about her problem with the sort of people who came to this sort of restaurant.

Wareing looked baffled. Of course there were customers for whom money was no object, he said. There were always a few of those. But no business like his could survive on that trade alone. 'An awful lot of the people who come here have saved up to do so.'

Pat nodded slowly and said, 'Oh!' I knew what she was thinking, because it was what I was thinking: it was in the nature of what I did for a living that we really hadn't had to save up at all. We both felt foolish and humbled.

We went out into the night with boxes of Petrus chocolates and a signed copy of Wareing's new cookbook, and the gently giddy feeling of an evening well spent.

A couple of weeks later, at the end of a long day, I walked into the bedroom. I had been rereading the Petrus menu, not to remind myself of what I had eaten – those dishes I could still taste – but to remind myself of what I had not eaten, of all the things that were still there to be tried: the breast of quail with the onion fondue and fresh almonds, say, or the Cumbrian lamb roasted with saffron and cumin. It was my version of window-shopping.

Pat was already in bed, reading a novel. I said, 'Did you have a nice time at Petrus?'

She looked up at me and grinned as if suddenly surprised by the memory. 'Yes,' she said. 'I did. It was lovely. Really, really good.'

'What did you have to eat?'

There was silence in the room. She blinked, pursed her lips and said, 'Nope. Can't remember. No idea. Not a thing.' And then, as if she felt she might be insulting me personally, said, 'Sorry.' She shrugged, and returned to reading her book.

In 1976 my mother was invited to present a new cookery programme for national British television. That was the year family mealtimes became unreliable. The thirty-minute show went out on ITV, one of only three channels then available to British viewers, and was called *Kitchen Garden*. In the first half a gardener gave the viewers tips on how to grow that week's chosen vegetables. In the second half Claire demonstrated how to cook them.

It must have been curious for the great British public to witness my mother's sudden reinvention as a celebrity chef. Of course, she was already famous by then, but more for her tips on sexual health than great ideas for dinner. Now, in addition, she was going to be supplying Britain with handy recipes for ratatouille.

I turned ten that year and at the time none of this seemed particularly odd. My two older siblings and I were used to our mother taking on new challenges. She had started her career as a nurse in the 1940s, an escape from that miserable childhood, and risen to the level of sister before trying her hand at freelance print journalism while on maternity leave to have my sister. She never went back to nursing. One-off articles led to offers of health columns. She became a consultant to a BBC television medical drama, *Emergency Ward 10*, and then a pundit on television in her own right. Contracts for non-fiction books about health and motherhood led to the suggestion that she try her hand at fiction and she eventually became a best-selling novelist too, in Britain, the US and elsewhere.

Now she was going to be a TV chef. I well remember coming into the kitchen one weekday afternoon, in our house in the cherry-blossom suburbs of north-west London, to find her standing over a cardboard box full of vegetables, peering at its contents suspiciously. It was not particularly odd to find her at home. Although she was a working mother, one of the first of her breed, almost all her work could be done at the old, clacking typewriter that was located in her narrow office just off the front hall, which she shared with the family gerbil. To find her here in the kitchen at such an early hour, however, was peculiar. The only other times I had seen her cooking during the day were on Christmas Eve or, in the years when we still observed it, just before Passover, when she would be preparing to feed a houseful.

She told me distractedly that she was experimenting, which sounded improbably exciting. What I didn't realise was that I too would be part of the experiment, for she needed people on whom to test her recipes – and who better than her husband and kids? Looking back, I see now that this was just the way things worked in our house. My mother's career was the family business, and we were all employees in it. In 1972, after the success of one of her novels, my father, Des, resigned his post as a PR man in the womenswear business and combined his flourishing career as an artist with the job of agent and manager for my mother.

There were jobs for the children too. Claire received around a thousand letters a week from her readers, a damburst of angst flooding into the house from the four corners of the nation, and she ran a team of secretaries to help her reply to them all. Occasionally, if she received a lot of enquiries about the same problem, she wrote a leaflet covering the subject and then offered that on her newspaper problem page. The response was often enormous and for pocket money we were employed to stuff envelopes – and there could be 15,000 or more – with my mother's pre-printed advice. It was, of course, a fantastic education. At an early age I was an expert on the symptoms of the menopause, could rattle off tips for long-married couples who wanted to rekindle their lovemaking and knew a use for live natural yoghurt that should never be described in a book dedicated to the enjoyment of food.

The new task would eventually seem more onerous than any of that – not least because it was unpaid, save for the dishes laid before us. My mother, it should be said, was a very good, if instinctive cook. To accommodate her working life she had developed a strong line in casseroles, mostly involving chicken or lamb, which could be put together in the morning and then slow-cooked for dinner that evening. She made terrific creamy soups with dumplings, and on winter afternoons there was tea in front of the fire, with crumpets and slices of sticky malt loaf with a generous smear of butter.

Now, with the contract to present *Kitchen Garden*, we were in the land of the vegetable and there our satisfaction at the table was far less certain; dinners became a time of nervous anticipation, and praise quickly given, whatever we thought, for we did not wish to damage her self-confidence. She was the one putting food on the table, if at times all too literally. 'There weren't food economists on the show,' she told me, when we finally discussed it. 'It was only me.' One day that box of vegetables simply turned up at the door. 'And they said, "Cook these." There was kohlrabi and salsify in there, things I had never seen before. I had to guess what to do with it. And for the first time I had to do weights and measures. Up to then I used to do a handful of this or a handful of that.'

There were three series of *Kitchen Garden* altogether, out

of which came three short books, eventually combined into one longer volume. On the cover of the latter my mother, today in her mid-seventies, is wearing a floral apron and is obviously just a few years older than I am now. With her is the gardener, a jobbing TV presenter called Keith Fordyce who made his name on the seminal BBC show *Ready Steady Go!* Part of the idea behind the programme was that it should be presented by people not normally associated with either cooking or gardening and so here they are, in an orchard, positioned around a barrowful of fruit and vegetables. My mother has a tense grin on her face, which, to me, says, 'What the hell do you expect me to do with all of this?'

Browsing through that compilation now is to revisit those days when my mother was experimenting on the wilder shores of vegetarian cookery, a relatively unexplored territory. I remember fondly her peppery cabbage soup made with milk, and less happily a Chinese cabbage chop suey with a sauce that was thickened with cornflour. There was that lush, satisfying ratatouille, which, because of its amenity to slow cooking, had long been a part of the family repertoire, and courgettes hollowed out and stuffed with an irresistible mixture of breadcrumbs, anchovy fillets and olives.

There are some dishes I don't recall at all, among them a lasagne in which slices of aubergine and endive were substituted for the pasta, and a vegetable cassoulet flavoured with Worcestershire sauce, which now sounds distinctly worrying. Then there are the dishes I wish I had forgotten but can't: there was that venerable beetroot soup borscht, a reminder of my family's Ashkenazi roots, which my mother quickly pressed into service and which I still hate to this day. There was a claggy, grey vegetable pâté, made with white beans and mushrooms. But worst of all there was the spaghetti marrow. That, I regarded as nothing less than a culinary betrayal.

In the late 1950s a leading BBC news programme screened a film about the success of that year's spaghetti harvest in Switzerland, which showed teams of Swiss peasants collecting strands of spaghetti from the trees on which they grew. Many viewers were taken in by what was, of course, an elaborate April Fool's joke and phoned the BBC to ask how they might grow their own spaghetti trees. My mother had always loved the gag and, when she was presented by the television production team with a spaghetti marrow, she was entranced by the notion that she might demonstrate how the stuff really did grow on trees, or at least on a ground-crawling bush. 'I just thought it was a hoot,' she told me.

The spaghetti marrow is a pale colour – from off-white to yellow – hard to the touch and can grow to just under a foot long. It is a less than sensitive ingredient that requires a serious boiling for at least forty-five minutes before it might be considered ready to eat by those who like this sort of thing, which I don't. Let it cool for a few minutes, slice it in half and spoon out the seeds. After that, if you scrape at the flesh with a fork, it will come away in long fibres that lend the marrow its name. There, however, the similarity to spaghetti ends. This marrow tastes like, well, a marrow: the fibres are crisp and not un-reminiscent of cucumber. Anybody with a particular love for cucumber might find this beguiling. Anybody who, like me when I was a kid, is told it is a vegetable version of pasta cannot fail but to be disappointed.

My mother made a very good tomato sauce to go with it, one that would have gone exceptionally well with, say, actual pasta, and then gave us cheese to layer on top. I cannot recall how the family responded to this dish the first time it was served for dinner, but I imagine we were as enthusiastic as always. Perhaps we were too encouraging, for the spaghetti marrow quickly entered the domestic repertoire. Some dishes she cooked only for the show. Others turned up at dinner parties. But the spaghetti marrow was served regularly for the family. Or at least that's how I remember it. I recall prowling the kitchen to see what was for the table that night and how, catching sight of its bleached-out skin, my heart would drop.

In adulthood I told my mother how much I had disliked it.

'But you always ate it.'

'You brought me up to be polite.'

'That wasn't it. You were just greedy. You wouldn't let yourself go hungry.'

A few months after she began working on the series, my mother decided to get serious and marked out an area at the back of our small garden as a vegetable patch. There were runner beans and strawberry plants, tomatoes and, of course, an area set aside for spaghetti marrow. That summer was the hottest since records began and, beneath an unrelenting sun, the plants thrived, yielding first their curling yellow flowers and soon bringing forth the marrow themselves, which my mother doted upon every day. Now I would not be able to escape them. The damn things were practically family.

London

Sometime in 1977, during the production of the second series of *Kitchen Garden*, my family moved house. The vegetable patch did not come with us, but for a while the spaghetti marrow retained its place at the dinner table. Eventually, though, it began to recede, to be replaced by other curiosities. Because of my mother's medical background, she was always keen to experiment with the latest innovations in diet, and we became one of the first households in Britain to use low-cholesterol butter substitutes. Olive oil as a cooking medium arrived early. And long before *The F-Plan Diet* was published, my mother came up with a weight-loss regime based on fibre for one of the weekly women's magazines for which she wrote. Each morning she drank orange juice with a bran tablet dissolved in it, which turned the liquid sludge-grey. For a while she even suggested we all do the same and told us how good it would make us feel, but we were wise to her by then. We had been guinea pigs for long enough. We knew where a willingness to please might get us. We all said no.

I had been surprised by my mother's use of the G-word. She had called me greedy. I accepted that I was a man of appetites. That much was obvious, but I was hoping for a more exotic diagnosis, something that combined sensuality, my cultural heritage and a finely honed nose for quality. I had wanted to be told I had a rare disease. Instead I had been informed I had the common cold.

This demanded further investigation and so, thirty years after the summer of the spaghetti marrow, I invited my parents to lunch. A few years ago we would have booked a table at Rules, the oldest restaurant in London, which first opened in Covent Garden in 1798 and which specialises in game. It is a fantasy of dark mahogany wood, velvet banquette and shiny brass rail. Years ago my mother wrote a series of twelve London novels, following two families from the 1780s until the Second World War, and each one had contained a scene set at Rules, for it was one of the few constants in a changing city. Every now and then my siblings and I would each go there alone with just our mother, for a little time pretending to be an only child. I would watch her eat oysters when they were in season or roast pheasant, and I would order jugged hare.

But Claire wasn't convinced that Rules was what it had once been. I didn't think this was fair. I had visited more recently than she had and been amazed by how the place had managed not to become a hostage to its history. It was still a great game restaurant. The truth is, it was my mother who wasn't what she once was. In 2003 she had fallen desperately ill and spent three weeks in intensive care with multi-organ failure, pneumonia and septic shock. Before, like all of us, she had been a large person, but no one spends that long hooked up to the wall in intensive care without losing something, and in her case it was seven dress sizes. With it had gone her appetite, which, to a Rayner, was like mislaying a much-needed limb.

So we didn't go to Rules, where even the starters would have proved too much, and instead booked a table at a classic French bistro on Baker Street called Galvin. It was run by two brothers from Essex who had both cooked at Michelin-starred places in London but who had tired of the demands that sort of food made upon them, their customers and their ingredients. Together they had put together something much more simple and, I couldn't deny, much more appealing. It was a place for all those great French classics I loved so much, and I watched with huge pleasure as, unprompted, Des ordered the snails in their shells with hot, bubbling garlic butter.

Suddenly it occurred to me that I could learn a lot of what I really needed to know about myself from my father. Where had that little boy frying his bread over the burner in the gloomy Swiss hotel come from? Why, from just across the table. Here is the old man with his spring-loaded tongs and his sharp pick tugging out the chewy punctuation marks, dipping the debris of a shattered baguette into the hot, garlicky fat, and enjoying himself immensely. Witness myself when old.

I ordered oysters. My mother ordered steak tartare. We were happy.

I asked them whether I had always been a child of appetites and, to prove the point, Claire retold the story of my birth, the repetition of these tales being her prerogative: she reminded me that I was a huge baby, a little over 10 pounds, who had been born at 4 p.m., which was just in time for tea. But this, we all agreed, was merely family anecdotage, attached to a fat child after the fact because it fitted so comfortably. She also insisted that there must be a genetic element to the way we piled on the weight, that we were a breed of 'winter survivors'.

'I remember seeing photographs of relatives I had never met,' she said, 'and there was always a sprinkling of large arses.'

Naturally, I found this comforting, but again it felt like a justification rather than an explanation. I tried another tack. I knew my parents had endured deprived childhoods, that theirs had not been a life of plenty like mine. Perhaps they had overcompensated as parents to make sure that we never went without.

My mother agreed there might be something in it. 'My memory of the war is not of the bombs or the Blitz but the constant feeling of hunger. When we were evacuated, the people who took us in were given a budget to feed us with, but they rarely spent it. We learned from the local kids what we could eat from the countryside around us.' She developed a taste for sorrel this way, plucked from the hedgerows, and for hawthorn tips, and if there was a boy among them who had a knife they would pull up a swede from the farmer's field and cut it to the core where the good stuff was.

'It's rather pleasant, raw swede,' my mother said, as they took away her steak tartare and prepared the table for her chargrilled liver with girolles. My father was having duck confit. I was having sautéed calves' brains with capers and beurre noisette.

'And so, when your own kids come along, you want to make sure they eat well,' Claire said. It made sense. We recalled that, at many meals, the food wasn't plated; it was in dishes in the middle of the table to which we could help ourselves, and we did, with pathological enthusiasm.

But there were other stories, which belonged only to us children. When I was six or seven, my elder brother had somehow convinced me to go downstairs, while our parents were sleeping on a Saturday morning, to cook him breakfast: bacon seared to crisp, fried eggs, maybe a sausage or two. I did this week after week, usually standing completely naked in the kitchen. My parents told me they never smelled it because the effort of raising three children exhausted them and on Saturday mornings they were dead to the world. They only discovered what had been going on when I spilled a pan full of boiling fat all over my hand, suffering massive burns that demanded hospital treatment. My mother had feared I would be scarred for life, though, fortunately I was young enough and fleshy enough to heal quickly. I was always more than fleshy enough.

'Some things I got wrong,' Claire said. 'As you piled on the weight when you were a teenager, I banned sweets and chocolates. Of course, all I did was turn them into a form of contraband.' My father, who has a sweet tooth, was famous for hiding behind doors to eat his beloved chocolate so he wouldn't be seen by the kids. 'The fact is, love, you've always been a foodie. I remember for your fifth birthday you were insistent on having frog's legs. So you did. And when you had finished them you made the meatless bones dance up and down the table.'

'Are you really telling me I'm just greedy?'

My mother nodded slowly. 'Yes, dear, that you have a certain instinct to greed.'

They cleared our main courses and brought the dessert menu, which was full of crèmes brûlées, rum babas and hazelnut parfaits. My parents said they had eaten enough.

'How about a little melon and mint sorbet?' I said to Claire. 'And two spoons?'

Claire smiled indulgently. 'Why not, darling,' she said. 'I'm sure I could manage a little sorbet.' She was often good to me like that, my mother.

I couldn't argue with Claire's diagnosis. A few years ago I had found myself at JFK Airport in New York, waiting for a flight home with a member of one of the Internet food boards to which I belonged. Our flights were delayed so we pulled up to the bar and ordered some of their spare ribs. The moment they arrived we could see they were awful: gloopy sauce, meat of indeterminate species let alone vintage, all of it pre-cooked and heated through. Together we shared out the ribs and went to work.

'Do you ever think,' asked my friend, between bites, 'that really you don't have any standards at all? It's just that you're willing to spend money to get the good stuff?'

My mouth was full of spare rib so I nodded my agreement. Sometimes, in my hungriest moments, I felt I wasn't really a connoisseur at all, just a greedy man with an expense account.

Still, at least I understood myself a little better. But what of other people? Why did they go to high-end restaurants? My argument that the restaurants enabled those on average incomes to buy a wealthy person's lifestyle for the few hours they were at the table worked, but only up to a point. What if you actually *were* a wealthy person? What then?

I knew just the man to ask. His name was Marlon Abela, he was thirty-two years old and he was worth somewhere in the region of $400 million. He didn't just eat in restaurants all the time. He owned them as well: in New York he owned an Italian called Avoce and another, just outside the city, called Gaia. In London he had three businesses including a hyper-expensive Japanese kaiseki restaurant called Umu.

London

Abela and I had fallen out over Umu. Not long before, the press announced breathlessly that three restaurants in London were now so expensive that average bills per head had passed the £100 mark. I had written an article for my newspaper in defence of the costly dinner, but had pointed out that the experience had to be worth it. Umu was one of those in the £100 club and, I said, it was not worth it. The quality of the fish might be great, the dishes well thought out, but if dinner was going to cost that much, eating there had to be one of the most memorable experiences of your life and Umu hadn't been that for me.

Abela was not pleased. He got his people to call me and organise a lunch there, to prove I was wrong, but he kept postponing the date until I said we should just leave it. The next day there was a knock on my door. Outside was a motorcycle dispatch rider with four bamboo boxes.

'Compliments of Mr Abela,' he said, and handed them over.

I opened them up. Each one contained an immaculate selection of what I recognised to be some of the best sushi available in London: shiny sweet prawn and sea bream, *otoro* and uni and unagi. I liked sushi. Hell, I loved sushi, but there was no way I could eat all of this by myself. I was reduced to wandering my street, trying to foist high-grade sushi on my fellow home-working neighbours. (One, responding with delight, said she would put it in the fridge and have it for her supper that evening. She looked a little bewildered when I told her ferociously that, if she really was going to do that, she couldn't have it; it had to be eaten NOW!)

Abela and I hadn't spoken since he had sent me London's

most expensive takeaway, but he eagerly agreed to meet for dinner and suggested we go to the Greenhouse, the modern French restaurant in Mayfair that he had purchased a few years before. Under Abela its already substantial wine list had expanded to 3,100 bins, certainly the largest in Britain, if not Europe. If it was made from grape juice and in a bottle, it was on the list. The Greenhouse had a Michelin star and had been marked by the guide as the potential recipient of a second. The modern dining room was panelled in expensive glossy wood and looked like the kind of place in which self-confident men sipped dribbles of Burgundy from bucket-sized glasses and casually took decisions that would plunge millions of people into poverty.

Abela was waiting for me at his table, to one side of the room. We had met once before, when I had profiled him for *Gourmet* and then, as now, I had been impressed by the ease with which he occupied his portion of the world. He had inherited his money from his Lebanese catering-mogul father and had grown up for the most part in France, spending his entire life around restaurants. When I asked him to name his first Michelin-three-star experience, he laughed and said, 'Maxim's. Paris. My father always liked to spend New Year's Eve there. I must have been five or six.'

Abela was now famed for eating in his own restaurants night after night, for ordering most of the menu as a method of quality control and then for finishing it all. He favoured a uniform of crisp jeans, open-necked shirts and blazers, and was a dispiritingly normal size for a man who consumed so much. If I hadn't liked him, I concluded, I would have hated him.

'So,' he said, 'shall we have some fun? Shall we open a few wines?'

I told him I was in his hands. He rattled off the names of bottles I didn't recognise and engaged in a long discussion with his sommelier about what was good right now and what was not. I asked him what we were eating.

'No idea,' he said. 'But it will be fine.'

The menus were brought. 'Really,' I said, 'I would be honoured if you would order.' This was partly politeness on my part, but also a calculated ruse: I wanted to see what he would do given complete freedom in his own joint. It struck me that I could be on for something very special, the notion of specialness now being my quarry. I was chasing special, hungry for special, though I worried that special was now destined to remain for ever out of reach.

Abela grinned and opened his menu. 'Let's do this,' he said, like a man mounting the highest diving board. He turned to the silver-haired French maître d' who was standing by the table, leaning in as if fearing he might mislay a word. 'Bring us a couple of the langoustine and one of the foie gras for the table. One of the summer truffle and one of the egg. Bring the egg and the summer truffle after the langoustine. How's the Dover sole today? Is it good? It's good. Great. Bring us the Dover sole. And one of the veal, but the veal at the end. Oh, and I forgot the roasted snail. Bring that with the langoustine.' We had already been told there was a special tonight of a whole guinea fowl – a *pintade* in French – stuffed with ricotta, spinach and truffles, served, like the Dover sole, for two. 'And bring us the *pintade* as well.'

I looked at him. 'Did you just order the whole bird on top of everything else?'

He lifted his hands, palms forward to reassure me. 'It will be fine. It's a small bird.' It wasn't.

Next the wines. Something sweet and crisp and Austrian to start, which was listed at a mere £80 a bottle. After that a 1996 Montrachet, costing £595, but Abela didn't like it. 'It's gone. Too old. Can you smell the sulphur at the end?' I said I could, to be polite and to sound sophisticated, though I couldn't.

'We'll get another,' he said, and he chose a 1997 Montrachet worth £325. That one he liked. 'It's good, isn't it?' he said. 'It will go well with . . .' and he waved towards the dishes that even now were arriving: giant langoustine tails, with a slippery purée of peas and mint, dotted with cubes of a mint-infused jelly; a slab of an absurdly rich foie gras terrine buried beneath a leaf-fall of summer truffle shavings alongside pebbles of a clear, bitter jelly flavoured with cocoa; something fiendishly clever involving a shell of poached whipped egg white infused with fresh herbs, surrounding a centre of liquid yolk; a dish of roasted snails on top of confit pork ribs; a platter of soft polenta dressed with an intense veal reduction and another shrubbery of truffle shavings. Most of the food had to be dug out from under (mostly tasteless) truffle shavings before they could be eaten. I commented on the volume.

'They're probably being a little more generous because it's us,' he said, knowing how ludicrous this statement was. Of course it was because it was us.

I asked him what he thought was the purpose of restaurants like this.

He thought for a moment. 'Imagine if they didn't exist. That there was nowhere for that special moment. It's not something you want to do every day, of course, but you want it to be there.'

'*You* do it every day.'

'It's my job. It's my passion.' And then, 'I just love what I do. I love good food and wine. It's always been a part of my life. It may be a bit sad. I may be a bit extreme. But that's what I do.' Quite simply put, by deciding to invest the riches he had been left by his father into his own set of catering businesses, he had turned eating into a career. He thought for a moment. 'It may not be the most worthy profession in the world, but it's also not the most unworthy.'

I wondered if I could adopt that as a personal mission statement: I'm not as bad as some people.

Now the main courses. First, the whole Dover sole, a foot and a half long, and half that across. It was displayed to us like a painting up for auction before, in a series of neat nips and tucks, the fillets were off the bone and on a plate in front of us. As that was being served, a dish of the roast Aubrac veal – pink meat, crisp fat, a little light *jus* – arrived between us.

'We can't possibly eat all this,' I said. Most of my starters had already gone back half finished. I was appalled but at the same time intrigued to discover that there were in fact limits to my greed, and I was, right now, being introduced to them.

'Just taste,' he said. Attacking the meat. 'Isn't that great? Isn't that the best? It will go very well with the Kistler Pinot Noir from California. Have you tried it before? It's very good. And what about this sole? It's such a meaty fish.'

The monologue was constant, like the commentary on a sports game. As each dish arrived, and I ate less and less of each one, I began to feel that I was disappointing him. There was Abela, with his slender hips and narrow chest and multi-millionaire bonhomie, valiantly defeating each plateful. And there I was pushing the food around, surrendering with a whimper. Sure, he sent some food back, but I began to suspect he was doing it to make me feel better.

He insisted on cheese and grumbled when the trolley headed to another table before us.

'They're paying customers, Marlon,' I said. 'Ought they not be served first? After all, we're probably consuming the entire profits from that table.'

Abela grinned and leaned into me conspiratorially. 'We're eating the profits from a number of tables, believe me.' Now he ordered dessert: a millefeuille of earthy-tasting tonka bean parfait with praline and whisky ice cream, a plate of shiny black chocolate leaves atop a chocolate mousse with salted caramel ice cream and shards of peanuts, which he said was the kitchen's take on a Snickers bar; a black rectangle of more chocolate with praline ice cream, which he said 'the ladies love'. Each plateful was beautiful until I shattered it with my spoon, cracking off a corner here, splintering an arrangement of crisp chocolate sheets there, tasting now but not eating. Into my mind came the image of a spittoon of the sort used at a wine-tasting, only filled to the brim with masticated high-class desserts. I felt queasy.

I said, 'Doesn't the waste upset you?'

'That's why I try to eat everything.'

I nodded and, taking the hint, tried another spoonful of the re-engineered Snickers bar, but it was too much. It was a tragedy, or at least it was if you had an overly developed interest in your dinner: I had been served a great meal. I had been served a truly fabulous meal. The problem was, it had been hidden away beneath enough food to make up more than three others.

I decided to take refuge at Le Gavroche, because nothing bad could ever happen there. When it first opened in 1967, good food was literally illegal in Britain. Most of the ingredients the brothers Albert and Michel Roux needed were not available. Albert was forced to dispatch his wife to Rungis Market in Paris, where she stocked up on foie gras and truffles, goose fat and duck breasts. She stowed it in the boot of her car, drove back to the nearest Channel port, where, because of desperate British customs laws, which forbade the importation of anything that tasted nice, she risked being turned away if the contraband was found. When that happened, she simply drove down the coast to the next port until she was able to board a ferry. From such determination had been born a legend: Le Gavroche was the first restaurant in Britain to win one, then two, then three Michelin stars (though it had returned to being a two-star when Albert Roux had handed over the kitchen to his son Michel Junior in the 1990s).

There is nothing else like Le Gavroche in London, nothing quite so classical or old school. When it is 8.30 p.m. in London, it is 1967 at Le Gavroche. I would never forget my first proper meal there, notionally booked to celebrate my wife's birthday, though shamefully arranged so much more with my own interests in mind than hers. I had eaten woodcock served in the traditional style, the head bisected and impaled on the breast by its long, thin beak. I marvelled that such a grotesque and fabulous dish was still available from a London kitchen. It also tasted nice, the delicate skull crunching beneath my teeth to release the soft brains.

I had returned to Le Gavroche many times after that, and

thrilled at the work of the maître d', Silvano Giraldin, who, in a masterful piece of theatrical misdirection, would receive your order without taking a single note, leaving that to the boy positioned 10 feet away, just in earshot. I loved the soufflé Suisse with its ballast of Gruyère cheese, and the sweet indulgence of the omelette Rothschild. Mostly I loved the set-price lunch, which included half a bottle of seriously good wine per person, all of it at a smaller charge than the cost of just the food at many lesser places.

In my head there was a map of London, of *my* London, described entirely by its restaurants: Covent Garden was for Rules and Joe Allen. Over in Smithfield was St John and Comptoir Gascon. In Mayfair was the Square, in Kensington Petrus, and here, on Upper Brook Street, in a basement decorated in antiquated shades of red and green, the tables heavy with garish animal sculptures fashioned from silver cutlery, was Le Gavroche, where nothing bad ever happened.

So I came here now to eat their impeccable duck terrine and their lamb chops and their own ice creams from the ice-cream trolley, the oval scoops arranged on the plate like the petals of a flower, and regretted for a moment the loss of innocence that repetition of experiences entailed. For nothing would ever match the arrival of that woodcock at the table.

It struck me now that in the days before a visit to an apparently classy restaurant we fictionalise ourselves. We imagine ourselves at the table as the wittiest, most tasteful and, of course, happiest version of ourselves that it is possible to be. The problem was that few restaurants can ever deliver on that anticipation, and even if it could, like heroin or crack, the buzz is never as good the second or third time round.

London

It was inevitable, really. Travelling the world through its greatest restaurants, in search of the perfect meal, had made me question the very point of them. It wasn't that I was sated. It is one of the glories of the human condition that we are made to be addicted to food. If we don't get a fix at least once or twice a day, we are mad, bad and dangerous to know, and a little after that we are dead. It was more to do with the whole process of the restaurant meal. It suddenly seemed so feeble, so ephemeral when examined closely. I felt like a straight man doubting his sexuality, like a priest questioning his vocation. Was I really losing my religion?

I decided there was only one way to find out: I had to test the high-end restaurant experience to destruction, take the once in a lifetime and make it every day, make it ordinary. Only once it was stripped of all notions of specialness, I decided, could I truly understand what it was about.

It would not be a simple venture. It would demand a certain commitment, not to mention shedloads of cash, but I knew exactly how to do it. I also knew exactly where to go.

7. Paris

Day zero

It is the day before my trip to Paris and I am lying on an examination table in a consulting room at one of London's most expensive hospitals, my shirt hitched up to just below my ribs. My friend Sarah Burnett, a highly regarded doctor, is running a sensor coated in water-based jelly across my stomach and studying an image on a monitor beside me. She is managing to do this without looking appalled, which is kind.

'When we consume excess calories,' Sarah says casually, as she sweeps from one side of my rippling belly to the other, 'they are stored as fat, obviously beneath the skin but also within our organs and particularly the liver. That's how foie gras is made. The geese are overfed so their livers blow up with fat. So, now,' she says with a little too much enthusiasm, 'let's have a look at yours.' She throws me a sympathetic glance. 'Please don't take this the wrong way, but I wouldn't be surprised if it was fattier than normal in the first place, given what you do – even before the week you've got coming.'

She tells me that fat shows up white on an ultrasound and I turn to the screen expecting to see something akin to the polar ice cap emerge out of the fuzzy image.

'Well, well,' Sarah says. 'You are not particularly fatty there at all. I think we can safely say that Gordon Ramsay would reject your liver for being gritty and unpalatable.'

As I button up my shirt, I ask her if she thinks what I am about to do is madness.

She laughs. 'No, not at all. I'd do it given half the chance.'

'But then you are not as other doctors.'

'That's true. I am not as other doctors.'

We became friends because Sarah was a contestant on the pilot for a BBC television food show called *Eating with the Enemy*, in which home cooks would cook for and be judged by restaurant critics, of which I was one. She had done something very nice with chorizo, followed that with a pork-belly dish and easily trounced the opposition. As well as being a doctor, she gave cookery classes and was pursuing an interest in food writing. When I decided I would be going to Paris and that a doctor should be involved, she was the obvious choice. Sarah quickly volunteered her medical services for free, in return for a nice meal somewhere. That was fine by me. I was always good for a nice meal somewhere.

My idea was simple. I wanted to do the high-end *Super Size Me*. In the original documentary, released in 2004, film-maker Morgan Spurlock investigated the fast-food industry and its effect on American life by eating nothing but McDonald's, three times a day for thirty days. And if he was invited to 'super size' his meal – to increase the portion size for a limited increase in price – he had to do so.

The Man Who Ate The World

The high-end version would require me to eat in a Michelin-three-star restaurant in Paris every day for a week, and if I was invited to take the tasting menu I would have to say yes. Partly I wanted to see how my attitude to these 'treat' restaurants, which were meant to be enjoyed only rarely, would change if I visited them once every twenty-four hours. But I was also curious about the impact on my physical well-being. Was high-end food any better for you than McDonald's just because it cost 100 times more? As a result of the *Super Size Me* experiment, Spurlock put on 11 kilograms (24 pounds), developed symptoms of sugar addiction and depression, and turned his liver into pâté. What would happen to my body if I traipsed from three-star to three-star?

Admittedly my body would be starting in a very different place to Spurlock's. At the beginning he was a perfect physical specimen. I, too, was a specimen but only of the sort that would be found stowed away in a bottle somewhere in a laboratory to be brought out and laughed at during the Christmas party. Our experiments would also, by necessity, be different. For one, Spurlock had eaten three meals a day in McDonald's. I could only eat one of mine in a three-star, not least because it cost too bloody much to do otherwise. For the same reason, I would only be doing this for seven days, rather than thirty. At the point when I made what I regarded as the selfless decision to eat in the French capital, there were ten three-stars located there, more than in any other city in the world. Two were closed for renovation, leaving eight, and one of those – L'Ambrosie – proved impossible to visit, no matter how willing I was to degrade myself to get a booking. And anyway, a week felt neater to me.

Also, Spurlock reduced his physical activity to better match that of the average American during the process. He dropped from walking around 3 miles a day to 1.5 miles. Then again, he didn't have the responsibility of being a father of two small children and, with that in mind, I was clear that I would continue my workouts – although I believed it brought a certain consistency to the exercise. I would simply be behaving normally throughout.

I was already pleased to see that the efforts I had made over the previous few months on my elliptical cross-tracker had borne results. No one could pretend I looked like a fit man; I looked like a fit man's degenerate brother. But when my blood pressure was taken, my underlying resting rate – the diastolic – was sixty-six, considerably better than the average of eighty. My systolic, the peak pressure, was way up at 160, as against 120, but Sarah kindly ascribed that to anxiety, brought on by me having just seen my weight.

I had told Sarah I was the wrong side of 115 kilograms (18 stone and 2 pounds), which was really only a guess because I never weighed myself. I judged where I was by the fit of my clothes. Sarah now saw the scales, laughed and said, 'Oh, yes, that is on the wrong side of a hundred and fifteen kilograms.' (Don't expect me to give you the number; I may be a journalist but even I have limits when it comes to the invasion of my own privacy.) Certainly it was a disappointment. I had been working out especially hard in recent months and even dropped a trouser size. Sarah said a few soothing things about muscle mass weighing more than fat and I told myself that had to be the explanation: I wasn't actually fatter. I was just more muscular.

Yeah, right.

I also told Sarah that I had developed certain strategies to get through the week in Paris. For a start, other than the two I would eat at the weekend, I would be taking most of the meals at lunchtime because I hoped that would allow me more time to digest the food. Also, I wouldn't be drinking. I imagined that boozing for seven days straight would be a complete killer, especially as I wasn't much of a drinker.

Sarah said, 'I think that's cheating.'

'Hang on. You're a doctor, and you're telling me to drink heavily?'

'I'm just pointing out the parameters of the experiment. And it's only for a week.'

'I might have a glass or two.'

She said she would call me later that same day with the results of various blood tests, and I made an appointment to see her immediately after my return so she could have another look at my liver, to find out whether it was any more ready for Ramsay's pan.

When she telephoned that afternoon, she said she had both good news and some that was less so. The good news was that my cholesterol score was just below the average, which was probably the result of all the exercise. I also had a very positive ratio of good to bad cholesterol. On paper I should have been a cholesterol disaster; in reality I was a paragon of virtue.

The bad news concerned my blood glucose. She told me that a score of seven or above indicates type-2 diabetes, the variety brought on by a combination of genetic pre-disposition and piss-poor lifestyle. (Or what I liked to call 'my job'.) Anything over six was into the danger zone.

Mine, she said, was at 5.9.

Paris

'It has to be said if you put on any more weight you really could be at risk of tipping into type-2, and that's something you need to think about.'

I did think about it, a lot. In the days before I became a food writer, some of the stories I had covered, particularly those concerning the security services, had involved a modicum of risk, which Pat had not liked at all. I talked to strange men in shadowy places. I suspected my telephone was bugged. The usual. Eventually she asked me to stop doing those stories and, believing I had a responsibility to the woman I had married, I said I would. For the same reason, and the more so when our boys arrived, I turned down major commissions to go to Rwanda, Iraqi Kurdistan and the Laotian–Cambodian border. I could still cover tough subjects, but essentially I believed in living safely.

Yet here I was, apparently teetering on the edge of type-2 diabetes, a manageable but debilitating disease with explicit consequences for life expectancy. Did not exactly the same conditions apply as to the threat of gunshot or bomb in a war zone?

Well, yes, I told myself, but this was different. This was a chronic situation, not an acute one. And I was sure I could lessen the impact of my behaviour through exercise and by modifying my diet on my return. Of course, I was just making excuses to myself. I was convinced my journey in search of the perfect meal would not be complete unless I went to Paris, and God knows the effort, the begging, the shameless pleading it had taken me to get the consecutive bookings in seven of the world's greatest restaurants. I couldn't just cancel the trip after all that.

OK. I didn't *want* to.

And so, for the very last time, I pulled down the suitcase and began packing.

Day one

Restaurant Alain Ducasse

It was when the maître d' over-ruled my choice of first course in my very first Parisian three-star that I realised just how challenging this experiment might be. Admittedly I had tried to order a dish that was, by anybody's standards, girls' food: *légumes et fruits cuits/crus, marmelade de tomates/truffes*. In short, and in English, a plate of vegetables. But was that really such a crime?

The man in the grey suit thought so. 'Let me bring you something else,' he said with a pained expression. 'It's nice, of course, but it is just . . . vegetables.' Well, yes, that's why I ordered it. Sure, I was usually the pâté guy or the spider-crab guy, but I had a long way to go here, so I thought . . .

'I bring you this,' he said, pointing to something else on the menu. 'It is cockscomb, lobster, truffle, pasta. You'll like it.'

I couldn't deny that I did, the long-braised and gelatinous cockscombs standing proudly to attention across a plate scattered with impeccable rounds of lobster, slices of black truffle and curls of soft pasta, the whole bound by a rich, defiantly classical butter and cream sauce.

It was, I realised, the very first dish I had ever liked in a restaurant with Alain Ducasse's name on it. Usually I made a point of hating Ducasse restaurants, much as I made a point of hating evangelical Christians or people who appeared in *Hello!* magazine. It was a matter of principle. I had hated

Mix in Las Vegas so much I had considered suicide, just to spite them; in London I had hated Spoon, for its self-conscious hipness and stupid concept, involving a menu written in pidgin English that allowed the punters to put together food items that didn't deserve to be in the same restaurant let alone on the same plate. I had even hated the venerable Parisian bistro Benoit, which Ducasse had recently purchased, for its lazy, cynical service and its lazy, cynical pricing. Hating Alain Ducasse restaurants was what I did.

Still, I knew that he must have something going for him. After winning three stars at the Hôtel Louis XV in Monaco in 1990, he had opened in Paris, first at Hôtel Le Parc Sofitel Demeure, later here at the Hôtel Plaza Athénée, just off the Champs-Elysées. It's the sort of ludicrously glitzy place where you might, as I did, see a woman in a Louis Vuitton eye-patch, where just one of the cars parked outside is worth more than your own house. In 2001 Alain Ducasse at the Plaza Athénée won its third star and he became the only chef in the world to have two restaurants with the maximum rating (before becoming the only chef in the world with three such restaurants, when he added the Essex House in New York, which later he closed). He was the king of the globalised chef crew, the master of the diffusion line. I might have hated his restaurants, but a lot of other people liked them.

Now I was beginning to like one as well. I even liked the curious orange and grey interior and the exploded chandeliers that scattered the room with shards of light. True, it had some silly affectations: the pull-out shelves built into the seats so women had somewhere to put their handbags, the holders for the menus because, as one of my companions put it, 'Heaven forfend rich people should have to do anything as strenuous as hold something themselves.' But the service was relaxed and genuinely friendly. They hadn't even flinched when they saw my friend Joe in his jeans and trainers and T-shirt.

In the days before my trip I had sent out an email to those in my circle with an equally profound interest in their lunch and the willingness to spend big money on it. I couldn't afford to buy them a meal in a Paris three-star, I said, but I could give them the excuse to come and have a meal in a Paris three-star. A whole bunch of people had said yes, starting today with Maureen, a London restaurant PR who made a habit of coming to Paris to eat, and Joe, a food writer and magazine editor in his late-thirties, who was famed for dressing like a bloody teenager.

'I'm a good test of the service, actually,' he said defensively. 'If they treat me well despite what I'm wearing, it's a good place.'

'You are,' I said, 'the canary in the mineshaft.'

'Exactly.'

Soon I forgot about his garish T-shirt as we focused on the menu. As well as a few spectacular dishes involving caviar and the like, clearly priced in such a way as to appeal to deposed world leaders looking for the means by which to spend the wealth they had plundered from their former subjects, the menu listed nine dishes priced at the 85-euro mark (about £59). Although it wasn't specifically pointed out to us, we could also have three of these plus cheese and dessert for 220 euros (or £153) as a tasting menu. In the twisted, looking-glass world of the Paris three-star this is what is known as a bargain.

'Here's the question,' I said. 'Have I been offered the tasting menu?'

'It has been placed before you,' Joe said.

'But does that mean we should have it?'

They both looked at me as if I was an idiot. Of course we should have it: nine dishes, three people. Do the maths. We could eat the whole menu.

So we did, sharing every plate with each other as we went. There was the spider crab, in its shell, topped by a sweet-savoury foam that was like inhaling the taste of the sea; there was the tranche of turbot with the old-school red wine sauce that I found myself spooning from its little jug straight to my mouth; the perfectly cooked piece of sea bass with the citrus sauce; the deep-pink pigeon with the mustardy crust, the sweetbread with girolles. There was nothing startling here, nothing unusual or showy, just clean, refined neo-classicism. I decided I might be in for a rather thrilling week, the more so when the waiter fumbled a piece of lamb and sent it flying through the air in a gentle parabola.

I have always loved these moments. High-end restaurants are meant to keep the world at bay. They are meant to be a place where the real world does not intrude. And yet, every now and then it does, in all its glorious and random untidiness. At Jean-Georges in New York I once saw a waiter upend an entire shot glass of something white and creamy over a diner. Now I watched as a waiter took a spoon and fork and used them to chuck a piece of what was probably the most expensive lamb on the planet across the carpet.

But even that moment was upstaged by the arrival of my dessert, a classic rum baba, the sponge deep-glazed and laid in a gold-plated bowl so the reflection of one against the other seemed to make the baba glow. A trolley laden with bottles was brought to the table. I was invited to taste any number of the twenty different rums to find the one I wished to have poured on to my dessert. I tasted just the two before choosing something with hints of vanilla from Venezuela. A jug of light whipped cream was placed before me, the one to be introduced to the other. I did as I was told and it was, of course, delightful, the light, boozy sponge playing catch in my mouth with the chilled cream. It was the gastronomic equivalent of that moment at the end of the day when hot, tired feet touch cool, crisp linen bedsheets.

Even so, all I could think as I ate it, the only words that kept playing in my head were 'Blood glucose 5.9, blood glucose 5.9.' Even without the medical statistics, this sort of experience might be a cause for guilt, especially for a Jewish boy with a suspicion that his life had taken an unworthy turn; with the awful blood sugar reading, it was a psycho-drama on a plate or, to be more literal, in a gold-plated bowl.

Afterwards I stood outside on the ritzy Avenue Montaigne, queuing for a cab in the early autumn sunshine, and gave myself a talking-to. What was the point of doing this if I was only going to feel bad about it? How could a man whose job was the investigation of pleasure be so diffident about it, so uncertain, so unwilling to give himself to it? Or was it that sense of shame, that sense of badness, that made me enjoy it all the more? Or, to put it another way, just exactly how fucked up was I? Casually, more as a way to pass the time than anything else, I turned on my mobile phone.

There was one voicemail. It was from Sarah Burnett. The message crackled, as if she had called while on a train, but I could still make out what she was saying. There had been a mistake in the communication of some of the blood-test results. The fax had got mangled, the digits muddled.

'Your blood glucose is actually 5.2 . . . which is fine. Nothing to worry about.' She said she was looking forward to seeing me in a week's time and told me to enjoy myself in Paris. I grinned, closed my phone and decided I should do as instructed.

Day two

Guy Savoy
It is a warm Saturday night, I am half cut on champagne and I have just worked out the whole point of three-star restaurants. It is all about the peas. Not peas in general. Not just any peas. These peas, the ones in the bowl in front of me, here at Restaurant Guy Savoy by the Arc de Triomphe. They are just so . . . so . . . damn pea-ish. This dish is the very essence of the pea; it is pea incarnate, a veritable hymn to the pea.

And to think I almost didn't order it. Our waiter, Hubert, had made such a meal of selling the pea thing to us I wanted to choose something else just to spite him. After all, how good could a pea get? It didn't even have a pulse.

'Every pea in this pea salad is sliced in half,' Hubert said in a conspiratorial whisper. 'Every pea.' Pause. 'In half.'

'Gosh,' we said. In half. Fancy that.

'And do you know why they slice every pea in half?' We shook our heads, both now baffled and amazed that any man could be such an unselfconscious prick and yet still draw breath. He leaned closer into Maureen as if limbering up to put his hand down the front of her dress. Now he dropped his voice to an even more breathy whisper. 'Double the pleasure,' he hissed, and gave a long, slow nod as if to say, 'Believe me. That's some seriously hot pea action.'

And blow me if he isn't right. The all-important bisected peas lie around the outside of the bowl on top of a light, silky pea purée. Further into the bowl is a more coarse pea purée, and then something even denser as though the flavour of pea has been reduced to its very essence. In the middle is a single poached egg. Once the plate has been put before us, our waiters each take a knife, make an incision in the white and let the yolk flow out across the surrounding emerald sea.

I take one mouthful and suddenly I understand. The point of cooking at this level is to make every ingredient taste as much of itself as possible. It is to make you love the humblest of foodstuffs, even the pea. In most restaurants the cost of the ingredients of a dish should be 30 per cent of its overall menu price. In this case there is no point making such calculations. The pea salad costs 47 euros (or £33), cheap for a restaurant at this level, but an awful lot of money for a handful of peas and an egg. Still, I have no doubt it is worth the expense.

When they bring us a bowl of artichoke soup, made with no butter or cream but layered with slivers of the best Parmesan and black truffle, I decide Guy Savoy is a god, nothing more and certainly nothing less. This bowl of soup is an essay on the virtues of the artichoke, an illustrated lecture. I also believe these dishes provide an answer to the age-old question of whether cooking like this at its very highest level is an art or a craft. Encouraged by the booze, I argue that while great art should reflect on the human condition, true craftsmanship takes the natural world and presents it to us to its best advantage. By that standard Savoy is a true master craftsman. I know some people regard the label 'craftsman' as lesser than that of 'artist', but not me and not tonight. I don't want a chef trying to tell me something about myself. I want him telling me stuff about peas and artichokes, and I am delighted that this one has.

I am now terribly excited about the main course – veal roasted on the bone and served with truffled pommes purée. Sure, it's 160 euros (£111) for two, which is the price of a reasonable hotel room for the night in this town. But we have done the pea thing and the artichoke thing so we are up for it.

Which probably explains why the disappointment is so great, our mood so low, when the meat arrives and it is dull and insipid, and the mash simply weird, with a strange gaseous backtaste rather than the earthy arm-pit pungency of truffles. Even the *jus*, the business end of a dish like this, where all the fireworks should be, is nothing more than workmanlike. We plough through it all, morosely telling each other about better roast-veal dishes we have eaten at restaurants in London for a quarter of the price. In just a few minutes Restaurant Guy Savoy has gone from being a gastronomic temple to being a gastronomic scout hut.

We know who to blame for all this because we can see him. At first when we were eating his pea salad and his artichoke soup, the sight of the grey-haired and bearded Guy Savoy striding about the chambers of his restaurant, shaking hands with his guests like his life depended upon it, was reassuring. But now that the meal has taken a dark turn we are noticing things. We are noticing that he never actually seems to be anywhere *except* the dining room. He certainly doesn't seem to be in the kitchen. We are noticing that his whites are spotless, as in snowfield white. Not a sauce splatter, not a mark. He looks like he has been as close to a stove as, well, I have.

Sure, he must have a terrific brigade of cooks in that kitchen of his. They did the peas and the artichokes, but now that I am disappointed by his 160-euro veal dish I don't care about them. I care about him and the fact he doesn't appear to be cooking for me.

Later that evening, as we leave, muttering to each other about the way we have been done wrong, Guy Savoy is standing outside the restaurant on the step. I calculate that he is now literally as far as it is possible for him to be from his own kitchen while still standing on part of the property. This makes me very cross indeed.

Maureen, who has had more hot dinners in Paris three-stars than I've had hot dinners, suggests I may be over-reacting. She tells me to go back to my hotel and get some sleep. I have a big day ahead of me tomorrow, she says. I have a lot of big days ahead of me, as it happens. I do hope the chefs of Paris are aware of this.

Day three

Pierre Gagnaire
It is on the morning of the third day, a Sunday, that the scale of the sacrifice I am making hits me. I am wandering the huge outdoor market on Boulevard Richard Lenoir, just off the Bastille, admiring the charcuterie stalls with their dense pâtés and fine, knobbly *saucissons*. There are stalls here dedicated

to hot roast chickens and ducks, which are crisping up nicely in mobile rotisserie ovens and filling the air with their luscious, savoury stench, and others laid with delicate pastries and cakes. It all looks beautiful, but I know I can't eat any of it, and I can't eat any of it because I am simply not hungry.

This strikes me as a tragedy. I am in one of my favourite food cities in the world and the stuff I want to eat, the stuff I so love to eat, is not available to me. I think back to my fortieth birthday, just a year before, when I had also chosen to come to Paris, though not to eat at any of the city's three-star gastro-palaces. I had gone instead to L'Ami Louis, a legendary old-style Parisian bistro once frequented by Ernest Hemingway and Orson Welles, where I had eaten escargots followed by the best roast chicken in the world, accompanied by nothing more than a foot-high stack of thin, rustling chips and a salad. There are many who regard L'Ami Louis as a tourist trap, and it is true that it is usually full of people who aren't French, but it still does its thing beautifully. The food is exactly as it should be, even if at a fearsome price, and that was what came to mind when I thought of Paris, but I couldn't go there this time, nor to Bofinger, the *über*-Parisian brasserie, where they serve oysters on the half-shell and an impeccable choucroute.

Instead I had to comfort myself with dinner at another one of those bloody Parisian three-stars – and, in this case, one I specifically hadn't wanted to visit. I felt I had got to grips with Pierre Gagnaire's food in Tokyo, come to understand what it was all about. I didn't want to go there again and certainly not in Paris, where there was the serious risk that Gagnaire himself might be cooking and therefore might go off menu and 'create'. I knew where that could get me. There was just one problem. Gagnaire was the only three-star open in Paris on a Sunday night. If I was going to manage seven consecutive three-star meals in seven days, then I had to eat there.

So I went that night and sat alone in the beautiful dining room, with its shimmering deep-varnished wood-panelled walls and its elegant art, and admired the cooking of a restless mind, the intent of which was so far from that of Guy Savoy's simplicity. I was hugely impressed by the way he combined the flavours of oysters with a lightly acidulated beetroot purée and some beef jelly, the whole overlaid by the very thinnest slice of melted Beaufort cheese on toast. This could have been the edible equivalent of an orchestra tuning up, but it worked and allowed the oysters to sing their song. I liked salty chargrilled shrimps with a sauce flavoured with bitter grapefruit and a cooling cone of crab mousse, and another dish which paired blue lobster with ultra-chickeny chicken. I also adored the service, the way the waiters seemed to communicate with each other by the raise of an eyebrow or the arch of a back. What I needed was anticipated before I was entirely aware I needed it by the waiter in charge of my table, who had tiny feet and a tidy moustache waxed each side to a curling point.

The problem was that, despite the great act of willpower that had enabled me not to eat anything in the market, I still wasn't really hungry. Two three-star meals in two days had already blunted my appetite. I was like the short-sighted man in the cinema who has left his glasses at home, the opera buff in a muffled world because of an ear infection. I could be impressed by what Gagnaire was doing. I could marvel at the technique, but without the imperative of at least a modicum of hunger the exercise felt sterile and self-defeating.

Naturally, as the meal went on I became fuller and fuller. My response to this, like the driver who discovers they are running out of petrol and so drives faster in the hope of getting to the petrol station sooner, was to clear my plate as quickly as possible. The quicker I ate, the sooner the food went away. This led to enquiries as to whether I would like more. Dear God, no, please! No more. Not that.

Already during my stay in Paris I had done two workouts, battering away on the machine in the basement gym of my achingly hip hotel as if my life depended upon it, which, of course, it did (though not as much as I'd thought the other day). It seemed to me I needed to do more. A lot more.

Day four

Le Grand Véfour

There are just fourteen hours between the end of my dinner at Pierre Gagnaire and the beginning of my lunch at Le Grand Véfour, and the moment I awake this strikes me as appalling. I don't want lunch. I don't want breakfast. I don't want to eat at all, and I can't imagine wanting to eat again until there's at least a new digit on the end of the year.

I know that I am meant to be doing more than just eat. I have to concentrate. I have to be able to observe every plateful of food, examine every flavour profile, in an attempt to discern the chef's intention and decide whether he has achieved it. I am meant to be forensic in my dining. But I am spent, and in the taxi on my way to lunch my attention is elsewhere: on the Parisian street life passing by, the waters of the Seine shining in the noonday sunlight, the plane trees and the statuary and the thought of being able to walk among them.

I do at least feel guilty about this. My friend Val has come from London to join me and she deserves a little enthusiasm from her dining partner, but I am finding it hard to muster any. Lunch in a three-star no longer strikes me as a pleasure. To me, it seems to be a cruel and unusual punishment.

And perhaps I might have continued to feel distracted and inattentive, even while I was at the table, were it not for one thing: Le Grand Véfour was not like any of the other restaurants I had visited, which is to say a slick, professional gastro-palace, serving food of exquisite beauty, utilising the best ingredients known to humanity. Le Grand Véfour was different. Le Grand Véfour was bad, and there is nothing better calculated to catch my attention or focus my thoughts than a really, really bad restaurant.

It was not what I expected. Le Grand Véfour isn't just a restaurant. It's an institution. (Mind you, so is a secure psychiatric hospital and no one would choose to go there for lunch.) There has been a restaurant on the site of Le Grand Véfour since 1784, when it opened as the fashionable Café de Chartres, by the Palais Royal. It is situated in a colonnaded gallery that looks out over the Palais Royal Gardens. Inside it is all red velvet banquettes, antique mirrors and ornately painted ceramic panels in the grand style. No one with a hangover should ever be forced to sit in this room.

It is a child's picture-book version of a grand Parisian restaurant, a museum piece that demands a good ten-minute gawp before you can even turn to the menu, and the waiters wear this history about as lightly as a Park Avenue heiress in a $50,000 mink. Boy, are they pleased with themselves. As we were being seated, the waiter pointed out the plaques celebrating the previous custom of Balzac, Victor Hugo, Jean Cocteau and Napoleon, as if by making a booking we had joined their ranks. I understood immediately that people didn't just come here to eat. They came here to worship.

That is its problem. Le Grand Véfour is so very pleased with itself, so very self-satisfied, that it no longer cares about its basic function. If ever you wondered why French waiters have a reputation for being haughty and pompous, go book a table at Le Grand Véfour. Even a Buddhist monk who has committed himself to sparing the life of the tiniest ant would soon want to take this lot down a dark alley for a good kicking. Bread rolls were dropped on to side plates from on high as though it were target practice. Canapés were plonked on to the table without any explanation of what they might be. Glasses of wine weren't brought until after the food had arrived. We even had to ask if we might, perhaps, be allowed some water.

OK, so now you think I've turned into a princess, a prissy, demanding prima donna who can only find happiness in the subservience of others, and perhaps I have, but that's what the three-star game is all about: it is about being offered water when you sit down, about being told what the canapés are, about being given bread with a certain grace and style. What the hell else do you think people spend the equivalent of £180 a head for?

That's before I had tried any of the food. My starter was a rectangle of shellfish jelly, encasing crayfish. It was topped with a line of curious jellied balls containing a centre of a chilled seafood sauce. Those in turn were topped with dollops of caviar and gold leaf. This wasn't food to be eaten. It was food as status symbol. I could admire the technique required to create it. I just didn't like putting it in my mouth, which, where food is concerned, is not a good thing. On the tongue it became a jellied fishy mess, and I didn't like the way the jelly balls popped on the tongue. Yours for 92 euros (£64).

For my main course, I ordered one of their classics, an oxtail parmentier. I knew this dish well because I had eaten two other versions of it in the previous year. The strands of oxtail should be dark and luscious and sticky, so that you are unsure where meat ends and sauce begins. Here, it was dull and salty rather than flavoursome. The mashed potato on top should be silky and smooth and rich. Here, it was loose and watery, as if scooped from the bottom of the pan when the good stuff had gone. Both of the other versions I had eaten – the first at a one-Michelin-star restaurant in London called Chez Bruce, the second at Galvin (the place where I went with my parents for lunch), which has no stars – were better than this. Both were a quarter of the 88 euros (£61) I was charged at Le Grand Véfour.

But the real disaster was the dessert. Granted, it did look odd on the menu. You would have to think long and hard before willingly ordering a crème brûlée with artichokes and you would have to think particularly long and hard before doing so if you are me. I am firmly of the view that there is nothing you can introduce to a crème brûlée that will improve it, and certainly not a thistle from the family *Asteraceae*. You might as well put a dead hamster in it for all the difference it would make to me. But by now I was agog.

It read appallingly and I needed to know the scale of the atrocity. I wanted to eat it so you wouldn't have to.

As a result I may now require therapy. It was not simply that sweetened artichoke and the light custard of a crème brûlée are the worst partnership since Stalin decided to sign his non-aggression pact with Hitler. It was that the crème had split. Instead of a light set custard, there was sweet scrambled egg, a basic mistake in a corner bistro, truly staggering in a Michelin three-star.

I shoved the uneaten plate of food to the side of the table. In the other restaurants I had visited, this would have been noted within seconds. Here, it took ten minutes for a young waiter to amble across and ask if there was a problem. I explained. He told me I was wrong, that it was a crème Catalane.

'Then it's a split crème Catalane.'

Finally the maître d' came across, took one look, muttered about the water from the artichokes and whisked the dish away as if it were vermin that needed to be exterminated.

At least it meant I didn't have to eat it. Anything I now didn't have to eat was OK by me. We settled the bill – my share was 293 euros (£203) – and queasily I left the restaurant. To be fair, Val had eaten better than me: an interesting vegetarian starter, a solid cod dish in which the fish came roasted with a rust-coloured overcoat of paprika, but none of this excused the lacklustre meal I had suffered. There has long been the suspicion in foodie circles that certain restaurants retain high scores from Michelin because they are such landmarks that to remove their stars would actually undermine the authority of the guide itself, that the guide has to include these places as much for reasons of politics as culture. Such speculation had always seemed a little silly to me but walking away now from the tawdry Grand Véfour, I began to wonder if there might not be something to it.

Suddenly, beneath the mid-afternoon sun, the high-end *Super Size Me* notion didn't seem like such a good idea after all. Michelin-three-star restaurants? Day after day after day? How grotesque. How bloody stupid. After lunch at Le Grand Véfour, how very, very unpleasant. I disliked myself. I disliked high-end restaurants. Mostly I disliked my liver, which I was now convinced had the consistency of foie gras.

Day five

L'Astrance

And then, praise be, a truly great restaurant comes along and everything is all right again. I stop worrying about the fact that I am sleeping badly, that I think my complexion is deteriorating, that my energy levels are shot and my suit jacket feels tighter than when I arrived. I am interested only in the food on my plate, which is exactly what L'Astrance is about.

L'Astrance, I quickly realise, is not like other three-stars in Paris and it is easier to explain why that is so by describing the things it does not have than those it does. It does not have liveried doormen. It does not have walls splattered with gold leaf like King Midas has had a nosebleed. There are no brigades of waiters, nobody to fuss over your napkin if you drop it and nobody to follow you to the toilet and back again, should you choose to go. There is just a simple, rather attractive room with elegant grey-painted walls, which seats no more than twenty-five people, overseen by fewer than half a dozen nice chaps in suits. Their answer-machine doesn't take messages so people can't bombard the place with requests for reservations, which in any case can't be taken more than a month in advance. As a result many people end up going there in person to book a table (or, if they are me, call on a friend who has a friend who knows the young chef, Pascal Barbot).

Among the things there aren't is a proper menu. Instead there is just a list of tasting menus, from the 88-euro (£61) lunch choice to the 170-euro (£118) top-of-the-range option, which is still more than 70 euros (nearly £50) cheaper than those offered by most of the competition. Mostly there is the food, which is light and vibrant and shocking both in its good taste and in the way it does not rely upon cream, butter and salt to make its point.

I am there with a Parisian friend from one of the Internet discussion boards, a French food writer and translator of cookbooks called Sophie Brissaud, and I am delighted to have her here on the other side of the table. My original companion had dropped out at the last minute and Sophie had offered both her company and her credit card as an emergency replacement. The two of us are anticipating great things.

We start with a chilled, lightly acidic tomato soup topped with a cooling milk foam. Next a gateau made of thinly sliced leaves of white mushroom layered with foie gras and served with a touch of confit lemon and a puddle of hazelnut oil. There is a dish with two glorious langoustines in a clear langoustine bouillon with single leaves of fresh herbs and vivid purple flower petals, looking like a Monet watercolour, and the tiniest quenelle of a lightly spiced satay sauce, so that the dish is both about the flavours of South-East Asia and of the coast which gave us the shellfish.

We are served a perfectly seared tranche of Arctic char with caramelised new-season ceps on a Parmesan cream; a little bowl of white beans, soya beans, corn kernels and the sweetest tomatoes in a sprightly broth, which looks complicated but eats so simply; some of the best roast pigeon I have ever tasted, the skin crisp, the meat pink and gamey, the liver spread on a sliver of toast to remind you that this was an animal from the inside out.

At the end, after a succession of equally perfect desserts, there is not some cumbersome platter of lead-heavy chocolates or costume-jewellery tartlets. There are four tiny madeleines, an eggshell each full of light egg nog flavoured with orange water and a platter of fresh-cut fruit, generously sprinkled with the tiny special joy that is wild strawberries. Nothing expressed to me the self-confidence of this restaurant and its chef more than that final gesture: finish with a plate of fruit, Barbot was saying; at this point in the meal I can do nothing to improve upon that which nature has already prepared for you.

What struck me most was the way in which the quality shone through, despite the fact that it was my fifth three-star restaurant in five days. Yesterday I had become jaded and, following pretty little plateful after pretty little plateful in myriad gastro-palaces, I had concluded I would not now be able to tell the difference between one and another. There was no doubt in my mind that a lot of the effect achieved by the Parisian three-star – and by high-end restaurants in general – has little to do with the food itself and everything to do with the supplementaries. Chuck enough gold at the walls, hang enough crystal off the ceiling, employ enough pretty twenty-somethings to care for your every need and follow you to the toilet and, if it's done with the requisite professionalism, most people will regard it as a good night out before they have eaten a thing. By setting the Paris restaurants up in sequence, I had cut through all that. There was now nothing a waitress could do for me, short of administering a little light fellatio under the table without any of the other guests noticing, that would have surprised or impressed me. To my mind, it was now all about the food. On that score L'Astrance and Pascal Barbot had won hands down.

Or did I already make that clear?

Day six

Ledoyen
Oh, God. I don't know. Another Parisian three-star. Doormen in peaked caps. Claw-foot chairs. Side tables for the ladies to put their handbags on. The food was standard three-star stuff: langoustines on sticks wrapped in seawater foam, beetroot meringues, yeast ice cream decorated with silver leaf. You know the score by now.

It has all left me feeling tired and irritable, and poor. I keep looking at the bill, all the bills, and blinking. I'm going for a lie-down. Or a workout.

Probably a lie-down.

Day seven

L'Arpège

It has always been the plan that Pat should come out to Paris to meet me for the last meal, and this morning I am waiting for her when she arrives off the Eurostar at Gare du Nord. Before my week here I had joked that she didn't need to bring much, just a defibrillator and a bucket of Gaviscon. The joke doesn't feel very funny any more. I ask her how I look. I quickly realise that I am asking her to tell me I look awful. Partly this is because I really do feel sluggish and dulled by the week's events. Mostly, I quickly conclude, it's because of my gnawing guilt. If she does indeed tell me I look like crap, then I genuinely will have made some form of sacrifice and not simply been out here having a high old time of it. There is also my guilt as a parent. I have left Pat to deal with the kids by herself while I have spent what will eventually amount to more than twenty-four hours of the past week sitting in comfortable chairs at expensive tables eating ludicrous food.

Of course she tells me I look just like me, no different at all, and isn't it great to be here in Paris in the sunshine, for lunch. How naughty! What a treat! That's when the reversal strikes me. Usually I'm the one thrilled by the notion of a meal in a high-end restaurant and Pat is the one with the long-suffering look on her face. Today, I'm the one who wants to be somewhere else and Pat is the bundle of excitement and anticipation.

Then again I have chosen this last restaurant carefully to suit her tastes. L'Arpège is not one of the gold-leaf and Chinoiserie nightmares that she so hates. It is a simple room, panelled in smooth, curving wood which is even, in places, slightly down at heel. The carpet is scuffed. There are a few marks on the walls. The chairs are made from tubular aluminium. By the end of our lunch this modern but lived-in simplicity will strike me as an affectation, for there is no doubting the seriousness of this restaurant. Friends of mine have described L'Arpège and its chef, Alain Passard, as the greatest in all of Paris and therefore, by association, the world. They have venerated the simplicity of his food, the intensity of his flavours and the manner in which his cooking serves the ingredients. Mostly they have talked about his way with vegetables.

In 2001, five years after winning his third Michelin star, Passard shocked Paris by announcing that he was removing red meat from his menu. 'I believe I have come far in the areas of poultry and meat-based cuisine,' he said. 'Today I aspire to another exploration based in vegetables. I voluntarily erase, without regret, twelve signature dishes of the house. I sense a fabulous adventure.' Fish stayed on the menu, and over the years a little duck and lamb has crept on there too, but today L'Arpège is regarded as a restaurant which specialises in that which grows from the ground. In 2002 he even opened a farm, on a site 150 miles to the south-west of Paris, which supplies every single grown thing served here, all of it delivered daily.

Obviously this costs, and when we open the menu and see the price of the tasting menu we discover just how much. Pat makes a small involuntary noise and points, like someone catching sight for the first time of a meteor that is heading straight for them. I nod solemnly, having taken many tiny steps towards this moment. I observe that this is not merely the last meal of my trip to Paris, but also of my entire journey in search of the perfect meal. Yes, there might be cheaper options (though the term is only relative), but I owe it to myself to ignore them. We close the menu and declare we will have the tasting menu. It will, I realise, be the most expensive lunch I have ever eaten and I am expecting great things.

Some of them are. It is a thrill, for example, to eat the 'Arpège egg', a dish I had heard a lot about over the years, the yolk sweetened with a little maple syrup, the white foamed. There is a truly stunning gazpacho that tastes of the sunshine that has nurtured the vegetables, and in the middle a scoop of grain-mustard ice cream, the tiny seeds bursting in the mouth. At the end of the meal there is the 'Arpège tomato', a dish designed to make a point about the vitality of the fruit and vegetables served here. It is stuffed with twelve different flavourings – curls of citrus zest, spices, herbs – then cooked tableside in a bubbling, sweet-sour caramel and served with a scoop of wildflower ice cream. It is summer on a plate. It is one of the greatest dishes I have ever eaten.

Other things are less thrilling. There is a plate of lightly dressed vegetables, focusing on beetroots and turnips with a little couscous, which is again attempting to make you worship the ingredients, but turns out to be merely tiresome. We are shown a slow-grilled whole turbot, smelling marvellously of rosemary, but when it is served to us the flavour is so subtle, so understated, as to be dull. Rounds of lobster come in a cloying, gelatinous honey and mustard dressing, which obscures its beauty, and a dish of mussels in a saffron broth has some lovely seafood but tastes of saffron not at all.

The point of the restaurant is made to me by the

presentation of a dish at the next table: a huge silver platter bearing half a dozen large beetroot that have been baked under a small child's weight of gravel-like grey salt. It looks like a moonscape and when, with much ceremony, they chip away at the salt to reveal the beetroot, it doesn't look a whole lot prettier. I suddenly understand that this isn't simply a restaurant, which is to say a place serving nice stuff to eat in return for a big wedge of your cash. It is an intellectual exercise, an introduction to a particular aesthetic that takes the ingredient-led approach to its ultimate. At L'Arpège you are not merely paying the usual costs of a restaurant: ingredients, staff, overheads. You are paying to run a farm, created solely in your service. The dishes are meant to be admired even before you eat them. And if, on eating them, they do not deliver, then you have missed the point. Here, lunch is political, which can be a real pain in the arse if you just happen to be hungry and in search of something nice to eat.

After the lovely Arpège tomato and a cup of mint tea each, they bring the bill. We have not drunk much, a glass of champagne each, and a couple of other wines by the glass. Nevertheless, we are staring at a piece of paper bearing the legend '855 euros' (£594). This is because the tasting menu is 340 euros (£236) a head.

Pat is silent for a moment. 'You know, if I came to Paris for the day and sat on the banks of the Seine and ate a salade Niçoise I would be equally as happy.'

'It's an unequal comparison.'

'Why?'

'Because it's yours, not mine. You have to be interested in this sort of experience in the first place to accept the expense, and I am.'

'So you're happy with that bill?'

No, I say. I am not. I can see how some people might be. I can see how Passard, a nice-looking chap in a blue cheesecloth shirt and crisp, white ankle-length apron, could engender that sort of respect and devotion. But today his meal hasn't done it for me. My willingness to pay big money for a great restaurant experience still stands, but today hasn't justified the expense.

'At least,' Pat says, 'we can think of it as an investment.'

On this she has a point, though to pursue it we – and by 'we' I mean you the reader and I – must allow the conceit of a book like this to slip for a moment. Because obviously I would not be sitting here in this restaurant on the Left Bank of the Seine, with a bill for 855 euros in my hands, were I not writing a book about restaurants around the world. If you have bought my book, therefore, you have justified my decision to have the tasting menu and also, inevitably, helped me to pay for it. What can I say but thank you. I really do appreciate being given the chance to visit L'Arpège, regardless of my disappointment in it.

If, on the other hand, you have borrowed this book or, worse still, stolen it either from a friend's house or a bookshop – and I know it does happen – then you are of no use to me whatsoever. I'm still sitting here with this monstrous restaurant bill to which you have contributed nothing. How does that make you feel? After all, if you've read this far, presumably you've enjoyed it. Would it be too much to ask that you now go out and buy a copy, if only to give as a gift to a friend? Come on. This is big money we're talking – 855 euros. I need all the help I can get.

There is a last rhubarb macaroon sitting on the petits-fours plate. I ask Pat if she wants it, but she declines. I pick it up, pop it into my mouth and feel the sweet and sour meringue with its soft, fruity centre collapse between my teeth. I realise it is the very last thing that I will eat on this journey, and I feel no regret about this at all.

'Sweetheart,' Pat says, 'I think it's time I took you home.'

I slip my credit card from my wallet, place it on the plate next to the bill and together we sit and wait for it to burst spontaneously into flames.

Bill, Please

In the year or so that I had been travelling from Las Vegas to Moscow, from Dubai to Tokyo and beyond, Alain Ducasse closed his flagship restaurant at the Essex House in New York and announced that he would be replacing it with two others, a new venture at the St Regis Hotel and a version of the Paris brasserie Benoit in midtown Manhattan. Alan Yau, the consultant on Turandot in Moscow, announced plans for new restaurants in Kuala Lumpur and Abu Dhabi, plus a number of others in London. Nobu opened new outposts in Hong Kong and Melbourne, with others to come in Cape Town, Moscow and Dubai.

Pierre Gagnaire, encouraged by the success of his venture in Tokyo, announced restaurants in Dubai – clearly now the gastronomic capital of Asia – South Korea and in the French Alps (though only for the skiing season). Joël Robuchon continued rolling out the L'Atelier brand with further restaurants in New York, London and Hong Kong, and opened up negotiations for other ventures in the US. In autumn 2007 Gordon Ramsay embarked upon a reorganisation of his portfolio in London with the announcement that Angela Hartnett would be pulling out of the Connaught Hotel, but would be reopening elsewhere in Mayfair. Meanwhile he pushed ahead with those openings in Los Angeles, Dublin, Prague, Amsterdam and Paris, despite reports in the press that he was now spreading himself too thin and that his customers were losing faith in the brand. Despite the low-key response from local media, his restaurant in New York received two Michelin stars when its first rating was published in autumn 2007, placing it among the best nine in the city.

Many of the hardcore restaurant-goers on the Internet food forums that I spent far too much of my time on expressed regret at what was happening in the business, with the sort of death-of-civilisation hyperbole usually reserved for terrorist acts. As one of them said to me, echoing Mario Batali's comments, 'The food coming out of these kitchens looks the same wherever it happens to be in the world.' I knew what she meant. There were times on my journey, when I was sitting in a Gordon Ramsay restaurant wondering how all the other English people had got there or experiencing some young chef's peculiar take on foams and jellies in Dubai, when I really would have been hard pushed to identify exactly which city I was in. That had nothing to do with either the amount of alcohol I had consumed or the jet lag.

Still, a lot of the moaning struck me as an unattractive brand of piety in a business that was entirely unworthy of it. If there was the money to pay for these experiences, why shouldn't people elsewhere in the world get the chance to try them, without the expense of having to fly to London, New

York or Paris – even if these knock-offs weren't quite as good as the originals? By the same token, the often-heard accusation that big-name chefs were merely cashing in on their reputations struck me as unreasonable. For decades restaurant cookery, even at the highest level, was about as well paid as a life in the clergy, only with much longer hours and no promise of eternal salvation at the end. These complaints seemed all the more unreasonable as, unsurprisingly, they tended to come from the very people who were already wealthy enough to eat in the restaurants they were complaining about. It was OK, apparently, to have the money to afford dinner in these places, but not OK for the chefs themselves to make serious cash from them.

What was discussed far less was what was happening to the food on the plate. The general assumption was that high-end dining still meant French dining and, in the restaurants of Gordon Ramsay, Alain Ducasse or, over in Las Vegas, Guy Savoy, it was an argument easily made. But if my year on the road – and in the air, and at the table – had taught me anything, it was that these pure French neo-classicists were now becoming the exception, not the rule, that a new culinary Esperanto had developed which, like the language, drew on the traditions of France but was not mortgaged to them.

Not long ago I was rightly chastised by a reader of my column in the *Observer* for describing a menu in this way – as culinary Esperanto – and for implying that I meant this in a derogatory sense for a set of dishes that were rootless and lacking in coherence. As my dutiful reader pointed out, Esperanto isn't mere babble. It is a fully developed language with its own vocabulary and grammar.

So is the new cookery, as practised by the likes of Pierre

Gagnaire, Joël Robuchon and many of the lesser-known chefs whose food I tried in London, say, or Dubai and Tokyo. It is a full and proper fusion of the French and Japanese aesthetics and method, with the occasional nod to Spain and Italy. Think multi-course menus. Think miniaturism rather than grand platters. Think the use of seaweed-extract jellies, of foams stiffened with industrial emulsifiers like lecithin, of long, slow cookery under vacuum. Then apply much of that to dishes with flavour profiles that even Auguste Escoffier would recognise.

There was one school of thought that this was all smoke and mirrors, the use of all these modern – or even ancient-Japanese techniques – a mere sleight of hand. And sure, some of it is. (Literally so, in the case of the famed Fat Duck in Bray, just outside London. There, the chef, Heston Blumenthal, had employed a close-up magician to train his front-of-house team in a few tricks – turning a rose petal into an egg tableside before it is cracked into a bowl of liquid nitrogen to be whisked up into smoky-bacon ice cream – purely as a way of augmenting the experience.) But the assumption that followed from this, that it was used to disguise a lack of classical cooking knowledge and skill, seems to me entirely wrong. Chefs like Blumenthal, Gagnaire and Robuchon are not inventing cookery from scratch. They are reinventing it from a classical base.

More to the point, the whole argument seems to me redundant. If my journey round the world had taught me anything, it is that there is only one way to decide whether cooking is good or bad and it is this: does it taste nice? Some of what I ate tasted very nice indeed. Sadly, for me at least, a lot of what I ate did not.

And that perfect meal? There were moments when I felt I came close to it, and always those experiences were in the one-off restaurants of vivid personalities. My lunch at Pascal Barbot's L'Astrance was almost perfect. So too were my dinners at Yukimura and at Okei-Sushi with Mr Suzuki and his flashing blade. But the wonderful thing about perfection is that it is, of course, unobtainable. That didn't stop me searching for it. That hasn't stopped me wondering about it. All I need is the appetite. There is only one problem. I'm no longer sure I have one.

The aesthetic arguments aside, there is one aspect of the world's new high-end restaurants that is indefensible: their environmental impact. The problem is not the ingredients themselves. It is in the nature of what they do that chefs want the best, and the best can only be achieved using the most virtuous methods. There is no doubt that the meat and vegetables served in the world's great restaurants are, for the most part, produced in the most environmentally sound manner possible.

The problem is the way in which those ingredients reach those restaurants. I will never forget the moment Joël Robuchon told me that the lobster I was eating in Las Vegas had flown there from Brittany. Everything served in Las Vegas came from somewhere else; the lobster just happened to have come from a lot further away than the rest of it. In Dubai the situation was even worse. Absolutely nothing came from there. It all arrived by air, and the sight of another lobster, the glorious seventy-year-old specimen dragged from the cold waters off the New England coast to be the centrepiece of a New Year's Eve banquet – in spite of the fact that it would be terribly poor eating – depressed me greatly.

On my return from Dubai I decided to do something about it. I sent an email to Chris Hutcheson, who is Gordon Ramsay's father-in-law and the man who runs Gordon Ramsay Holdings, the parent company for his growing range of commercial ventures. I wanted to encourage him to offset the carbon emissions produced by the air-freighting of ingredients to all their restaurants about the world. I told him it made commercial sense to do so.

'As I'm sure you'll agree, all the best business decisions come with a cast-iron narrative, and this has one,' I wrote. 'Gordon is a top-flight chef and therefore loves top-quality ingredients. Those ingredients depend upon a healthy environment, therefore it is natural that he should want to do something to protect it.' I pointed out that the amount they air-freighted compared with, say, Nobu or Robuchon was relatively small, that any payments they made would be tax deductible and that they could easily introduce a £1-a-head carbon-offset levy for each customer. 'It is such a live issue that I would be genuinely staggered if any punters felt able to object,' I said.

My motives for this were not pure. Although it would make me feel a little better if I were able to encourage Gordon Ramsay Holdings to play ball, I was also thinking like a journalist. 'Gordon Goes Green' would be a fabulous story, all the more so for me if I was the one responsible for making it happen. I explained to Hutcheson that it would be a story that would run and run, and that therefore any costs they did incur could be thought of as a marketing expense. I really did feel that I had it all worked out. My intention was that, once Ramsay Holdings said yes – and I couldn't see how they would not – I would go to work on Robuchon, Nobu and Ducasse. I would single-handedly green the global high-end restaurant business.

Hutcheson said it was an interesting proposition and that he would think about it. A couple of months later, in response to a nudge from me, he said he had recently seen a television documentary that had described the thesis that global warming was a man-made phenomenon as 'a load of bunk and that I can carry on driving a big car'. I pointed out that the documentary he had watched – *The Great Global-Warming Swindle* – had been roundly discredited by vast swathes of the scientific community, but I could already tell it was no use. I was not surprised when he told me, in the summer of 2007, that carbon-offsetting was not something the company would be pursuing. Gordon Ramsay would not be going green.

I was disappointed. Clearly there was only one thing for it. I went online, found a carbon-offsetting charity – Global Cool – and paid to offset the emissions of all the flights I had taken. It was, literally, the very least I could do.

The day after my return from Paris, my forty-first birthday, I went to see Sarah Burnett again, and lay on the couch while she ran another scan of my liver.

'Well, it's certainly fattier,' she said, studying the mottled white object on the screen. I felt strangely proud. I hadn't just emasculated my credit card in the past week; I had also fattened up one of my vital organs.

'I still don't think it's ready for Ramsay's pan, though,' she added.

This was believable because, my liver aside, it turned out that the impact of my week in Paris had been negligible. Granted, I had done three workouts while I had been there, and eaten very few meals other than those in the three-stars. I had been too full to do otherwise. But I had still expected to see some result. Instead, my weight had remained exactly the same, as, bizarrely, had both my cholesterol and blood glucose levels. It looked like I had devised the most luxurious – for which read 'most expensive' – weight-maintenance diet in the history of modern nutrition. I thought that was rather impressive, even when Sarah suggested to me that I really hadn't been trying hard enough.

'You didn't drink, did you?' she said, as she wiped the water-based jelly off the ultrasound scanner.

'I had a few glasses with each meal.'

She shook her head. 'Call yourself a restaurant critic?' I was, apparently, a disgrace to my profession.

I hadn't eaten anything the evening we got back from Paris after our meal at L'Arpège. The cholesterol test also demanded that I did not eat anything that morning either. In short, by the lunchtime I had not eaten in twenty-four hours. Now I was in the centre of London with an hour or two to kill before a meeting, and yet it seemed preposterous to me that I should go and sit in yet another restaurant and get something to eat. Eventually I realised I was getting light-headed from lack of food. However absurd this seemed, it was undeniable. I went to a café and ordered a tuna sandwich. It was fine.

My questions about the pleasure of restaurants remained. It wasn't exactly that I had fallen out of love with them. It just seemed to me odd that I could somehow maintain my interest, having eaten my way through some of the greatest and certainly some of the most exclusive establishments on the planet. By that point I had been the *Observer*'s restaurant critic for over eight years and I was fully aware that there was a limit to how long one could stay in the job. I didn't want to end up like a former rival who had been a British newspaper restaurant critic for fifteen years after a long career writing about anything and everything that wasn't to do with food: by the time he stepped down nobody could remember that he used to write about other things, and nobody was particularly interested in what he had to say about those other things now. His career had withered and he had all but left journalism. It seemed a terrible waste, and not one I wanted to repeat.

I told Pat that I wasn't sure how much longer I could continue in the job.

'Don't be silly,' she said. 'You love it.'

'Maybe I *loved* it. In the past tense.'

I had a meeting coming up with the editor of the magazine supplement where my reviews appeared. Naturally, we were going to get together over lunch.

'Go to the meeting,' Pat said. 'You'll know what to do when you get there.'

So we went to lunch, the editor and I, at St John, the famed British restaurant in London's Clerkenwell, where chef Fergus Henderson serves roasted bone marrow with parsley salad, and makes a virtue of the cheap cuts of offal that too many other restaurants reject. I ate the bone marrow on sourdough toast and told my editor all about my travels. He listened politely.

Later that afternoon I went home. Pat was in the kitchen at the sink, doing the washing-up from the kids' tea. I sat down at the table and watched her, in the way spouses often watch each other.

'How did it go?'

'Fine.'

She looked at me and slowly began to smile. 'You didn't quit the column, did you?'

I looked at the floor. 'Well . . .'

'I knew it. I knew you couldn't give it up.'

'I told him I'd do it for a bit longer. Not indefinitely. Just for a while.'

'You don't have to make excuses to me.'

'I just feel I have a bit more to say.'

'Really, love. You should just do what makes you happy.'

I agreed that I would. Doing what made me happy was something I knew a lot about. It was something I had a lot of experience in. I got up and, casually, opened the fridge and looked inside. It was late in the week and as ever, at this point, the pickings were meagre.

I said, 'What do you fancy for dinner? I could do a pasta thing, the one with the peas and bacon that you like.' I hesitated. 'Or, you know . . . we could go out.'

Pat looked at me in silence for a moment. 'You really are a lost cause, aren't you?'

I looked up from the open fridge door and tried to manufacture an expression that conveyed how hurtful I found that comment, but my heart wasn't in it. Whatever I said now in mitigation, I knew the truth. I was guilty as charged.

Acknowledgements

A small element of this book started life elsewhere, albeit in a different form. The passages in defence of expensive meals, on the cult of authenticity, the pursuit of the perfect vinegar and why expensive meals are wasted on the people who can afford them all first appeared in *Arena* magazine; the section on my mother's career as a vegetarian TV chef appeared in *Gourmet*. I am grateful, respectively, to Matt Smith at *Arena*, and Ruth Reichl and Jocelyn Zuckerman at *Gourmet* for those commissions.

Obviously the entirety of this book is underpinned by knowledge and experience gained while serving as restaurant critic for the *Observer*. I would like to thank Sheryl Garrett for first giving me the gig, as well as Allan Jenkins, the current editor of the *Observer Magazine* and Nicola Jeal of *Observer Food Monthly* for their constant support and editorial wisdom – and for continuing to sign my expenses. I would also like to record my gratitude to Roger Alton, editor of the *Observer*, for allowing me to continue in the job, despite his better judgement.

The Man Who Ate The World

A year of travelling and eating like this would not have been possible were it not for the help and support of numerous people, who patiently put up with me attempting to blag the most outrageous things for free, or gave generously of their time for interviews. I owe them all my thanks.

For their help, assistance and wisdom across multiple cities: Jo Barnes and her staff at Sauce Communications; Jennifer Baum, Bullfrog and Baum Public Relations; Heston Blumenthal; Richard Bowron; Camilla Hacking, Elizabeth Crompton-Batt Public Relations; Simon Hopkinson; Kristine Keefer, Thomas Keller Restaurants; Jeremy King; Caroline Kirkman, Gordon Ramsay Holdings; Annouschka Menzies, Bacchus Public Relations; Maureen Mills, Network London; Guillaume Rochette, Eureka Executive Search.

For Las Vegas: Gamal Aziz, the MGM Grand Hotel; Mike Burdine, McCarran International Airport, Las Vegas; Eric Drache; June Fujise, Nobu; Mark Hooper, Bouchon; Melanie Jones, Cellet Public Relations; Kenneth Langdon and Greg Waldron, Caesar's Palace; Grant McPherson, Bellagio; Frank Savoy, Restaurant Guy Savoy, Las Vegas; Erika Yowell, Las Vegas Convention and Visitors' Authority.

For Moscow: Katya Dovlatov; Chrystia Freeland; Tom Parfitt of the *Guardian*; Janina and Alexander Wolkow, Sumosan; Alan Yau. I would also like to record my special gratitude to my fabulous and patient translator and co-conspirator, Yulia Ochetova.

For Dubai: Edward Barnfield, World Trade Club; Anne Bleeker, Luc Delafosse and Willi Elsner, Burj Al Arab Hotel; Simon Ings; Jason Levy; Ewe Micheels, Dubai Guild of Chefs; Rob Orchard; 'Malik'; Andy Round; Brandy Scott; Mateo Willis.

Acknowledgements

For Tokyo: Ian Buruma; Paul Charles, Virgin Atlantic; Andy Cook, Restaurant Gordon Ramsay, Tokyo; Christian Hassing, Oliver Rodriguez, Hide Yamamoto, Mandarin Oriental Hotel, Tokyo; Chie Kobayashi; David Nicholls, Mandarin Oriental Hotel, London; Jeff Ramsey; Robb Satterwhite; Yoshiki Tsuji, Tsuji Culinary Institute.

For New York: Mario Batali; the London Hotel, New York; Josh Emett, Restaurant Gordon Ramsay at the London Hotel; Gary Alan Fine; Michelle Lehmann and Danny Meyer, Union Square Hospitality Group; Ben Leventhal, eater.com; Michael Mahle, Zagat; Josh Ozersky and Adam Platt, *New York Magazine*; Jason and Rachel Perlow; Steven A. Shaw, egullet.org; Greg Williams; Tim and Nina Zagat.

For Paris: Claude Bosi; Sophie Brissaud; Sarah Burnett; Julien Dubos, Eureka Executive Search; Stephen Harris; the Kube Hotel, Paris; Angelika Kwan; Joe Warwick.

Let me also take this opportunity to pay tribute to that selfless band of eaters who, over the years, have volunteered to be my dining companions across Britain more often than is strictly necessary: Catriona Dry, Henry Harris, Angela Hartnett, Thom Hetherington, Catherine Kanter, Simon Majumdar and Robert Saunders.

My agents, Pat Kavanagh in London and Zoe Pagnamenta in New York, were endlessly supportive all the way through this project. I was also blessed with two hungry editors, Val Hudson at Headline and Sarah Knight at Henry Holt, both of whom understood this book from the very first and who helped me to make it much better than it might otherwise have been.

However, I owe my greatest debt of gratitude to my family: firstly, to my boys, Eddie and Daniel, who dealt with my absences with huge and undeserved understanding, but mostly to my wife, Pat Gordon Smith, who encouraged me all the way through the research and writing of this book, moved heaven and earth to create the space in our lives so I could keep leaving the country, read every word as I wrote it and kept me on the editorial straight and narrow. I simply could not have done it without her. Many people would show their gratitude to such a fabulous spouse by forcing them out for a special dinner in a fantastic restaurant. I will prove how much I love her specifically by not doing so.